17 DAYS *to a* MORE *POWERFUL* Vocabulary

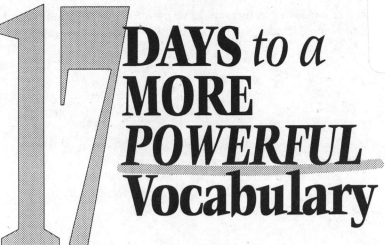

T. Rajkumar

Borough of Manhattan Community College
City University of New York

McGraw-Hill, Inc.
College Custom Series

New York St. Louis San Francisco Auckland Bogotá
Caracas Lisbon London Madrid Mexico Milan Montreal
New Delhi Paris San Juan Singapore Sydney Tokyo Toronto

17 DAYS *to a* **More POWERFUL Vocabulary**

1 2 3 4 5 6 7 8 9 0   HAM HAM   9 0 9 8 7 6

ISBN 0-07-052410-6

Editor: M. A. Hollander
Cover Design: Maggie Lytle
Printer/Binder: HAMCO Corporation

CONTENTS

THIRTEENTH DAY

FOURTEENTH DAY

FIFTEENTH DAY

SIXTEENTH DAY

SEVENTEENTH DAY

Vocabulary Translations

Below are over 1,700 words carefully selected to build your vocabulary. They are translated into Spanish, Chinese, French, and Russian for your convenience and reference. Look under the next section for partial meanings of selected words from this list.

English	Spanish	French	Russian	Chinese

PALABRAS DE REFERENCIA

A continuación aparecen más de 1,500 palabras, seleccionadas cuidadosamente, para que forme su vocabulario. Para su conveniencia y referencia, están traducidas al español, chino, francés, y ruso.

Inglés	Español	Francés	Ruso	Chino

VOCABULAIRE DE REFERENCE

Vous trouverez ci-dessous plus de 1500 mots pour vous constituer un vocabulaire. Ils sont traduits en espagnol, en chinois, en français et en russe pour vous servir et pour que vous puissiez vous y référer.

Anglais	Espagnol	Français	Russe	Chinois

БАЗОВЫЕ СЛОВА

Ниже приведены более 1500 слов, тщательно отобранных для построения Вашего словаря. Для Вашего удобства и в справочных целях эти слова переведены на испанский, китайский, французский, русский и языки.

АНГЛИЙСКИЙ	ИСПАНСКИЙ	КИТАЙСКИЙ	РУССКИЙ	ФРАНЦУЗСКИЙ

参考词语

下面是1,500个精选的词语，用以建立你的词汇量。为了方便你查阅参考，这些词语译成了西班牙语、汉语法语和俄语。

英语	西班牙语	法语	俄语	中文

English	Spanish	French	Russian	Chinese
abandon	abandonar	abandonner	оставлять	弃置
abbreviate	abreviar	abréger	сокращать	缩略
abduct	secuestrar	détourner	похищать	劫持
abhor	aborrecer	abhorrer	ненавидеть	憎恶
abnormal	anormal	anormal	необычный	反常的
abolish	abolir	abolir	отменять	废除
abrupt	repentino, na	abrupte	внезапный	突然
absent	ausente	absent	отсутствующий	缺席
absent-minded	distraído, da	distrait	рассеянный	心不在焉
abstain	abstenerse	s'abstenir	воздерживаться	克制
abstract	abstracto	abstrait	абстрактный	抽象的
absurd	absurdo, da	absurde	нелепый	荒唐的
abundant	abundante	abondant	обильный	丰富的
abuse	abusar	abuser	оскорблять	滥用
accelerate	acelerar	accélérer	ускорять	加速
accept	aceptar	accepter	принимать	接受
access	acceso	accéder	доступ	进入
accident	accidente	accident	несчастный случай	事故
acclaimed	aclamado, da	acclamé	одобренный	倍受赞扬的
accommodate	acomodar	accommoder	приспосабливать	迁就
accompany	acompañar	accompagner	сопровождать	陪同
accuse	acusar	accuser	обвинять	指控
achieve	lograr	accomplir	достигать	取得
acknowledge	reconocer	reconnaître	признавать	承认
acquaint	familiarizar	présenter	знакомить	熟悉
acquire	adquirir	acquérir	приобретать	得到
acrimonious	amargado, da	caustique	желчный	刻薄的
acupuncture	acupuntura	acuponcture	иглотерапия	针灸
acute	agudo, da	sévère	острый	激烈的
adamant	inflexible	intransigeant	непреклонный	坚定的
adequate	adecuado, da	adéquat	достаточный	足够的
adhere	adherirse	adhérer	прилипать	坚持
adjust	ajustar	ajuster	регулировать	调整
admit	admitir	admettre	допускать	同意
admonish	advertir	gronder	предостерегать	告诫
adoption	adoptar	adoption	усваивать	采取
adroit	hábil	adroit	искусный	熟练的
adversary	adversario, ria	adversaire	противник	对手
adverse	adverso, sa	adverse	неблагоприятный	险恶的
advocate	defensor, ra	défenseur	сторонник	提倡
aesthetic	estético, ca	esthétique	художественные взгляды	美观的
affection	afecto	affection	привязанность	柔情
affiliated	afiliado	affilié	присоединённый	附属
affirm	afirmar	affirmer	подтверждать	赞同
affluence	riqueza	richesse	изобилие	富有 财富
aggrandize	agrandar	agrandir	увеличивать	扩充
aggravate	agravar	irriter	ухудшать	加剧
aggressive	agresivo, va	agressif	напористый	放肆的
agile	ágil	agile	подвижный	敏捷的
agitate	agitar	agiter	волновать	挑逗
agronomy	agronomía	agronomie	агрономия	农学
ailment	padecimiento	affliction	недомогание	疾病
alias	alias	alias	прозвище	绰号
alien	ajeno, na	étranger	иностранный	外国的
allegiance	fidelidad	loyauté	верность	忠诚
allergy	alergia	allergie	аллергия	过敏
alleviate	aliviar	soulager	облегчать	减轻
allude	aludir	faire allusion	намекать	暗示
aloof	lejos	tête en l'air	в отдалении	孤傲的

English	Spanish	French	Russian	Chinese
alternative	alternativa	alternative	альтернатива	另外的方法
altruistic	desinteresado, da	altruiste	альтруистический	慷慨的
ambiguous	ambiguo, gua	ambigu	неопределенный	含胡的
ambivalent	ambivalente	ambivalent	двойственный	既爱又恨
ambulance	ambulancia	ambulance	"скорая помощь"	救护车
amoeba	amiba	amibe	амёба	变形虫
ample	amplio, ia	ample	обильный	丰富的
analyze	analizar	analyser	анализировать	分析
anemia	anemia	anémie	анемия	贫血症
anesthesia	anestesia	anesthésie	анестезия	麻醉药
angle	ángulo	angle	угол	角度
animosity	animosidad	animosité	враждебность	敌意
annihilate	aniquilar	annihiler	стереть с лица земли	消灭
annual	anual	annuel	ежегодный	每年的
anonymous	anónimo	anonyme	анонимный	匿名的
antagonize	contrariar	provoquer	противодействовать	对抗
anthropology	antropología	anthropologie	антропология	人类学
anticipate	anticipar	anticiper	ожидать	预见
antihistamine	antihistamina	antihistaminique	антигистамин	抗组胺药
apartment	apartamento	appartement	квартира	公寓
apathy	apatía	apathie	апатия	冷漠
apparent	aparente	apparent	явный	明显的
appease	calmar	apaiser	успокаивать	安抚
applaud	aplaudir	applaudir	аплодировать	赞扬
appoint	nombrar	désigner	назначать	任命
appreciate	apreciar	apprécier	ценить	欣赏
apprehensive	aprehensivo, va	réticent	опасающийся	害怕的
apprentice	aprendiz	apprenti	ученик	学徒
appropriate	apropiado, da	approprié	соответствующий	合适的
arbitrary	arbitrario, ria	arbitraire	произвольный	武断的
arbitrator	arbitrador, ra	arbitre	арбитр	仲裁人
archaeology	arqueología	archéologie	археология	考古学
aristocrat	aristócrata	aristocrate	аристократ, аристократка	贵族
arrogant	arrogante	arrogant	высокомерный	傲慢的
arsonist	incendiario	incendiaire	поджигатель	纵火犯
arteriosclerosis	arteriosclerosis	artériosclérose	артериосклероз	动脉硬化
artery	arteria	artère	артерия	血管
articulate	articulado, da	articuler	членораздельный	发音清晰
ascertain	descubrir	s'assurer	выяснять	确证
askew	desviado, da	de travers	косой; кривой	斜的
aspire	aspirar	aspirer	стремиться	渴望
assertive	asertivo	affirmatif	самоуверенный	过分自信
assiduous	aplicado, da	assidu	усердный	勤奋的
assimilate	asimilar	assimiler	поглощать	消化
assist	socorrer	aider	помогать	辅助
assume	asumir	supposer	принимать	假设
assurance	certeza	assurance	гарантия	保证
astonish	asombrar	surprendre	удивлять	使吃惊
astronomy	astronomía	astronomie	астрономия	天文学
astute	astuto, ta	brillant	сообразительный	敏锐的
attain	obtener	réussir	достигать	达到
attest	certificar	certifier	удостоверять	证明
attrition	desgaste	attrition	истирание	摩擦
audible	audible	audible	слышимый	听得清的
audit	practicar auditorías	contrôler	ревизия	审计
auspicious	favorable	propice	благоприятный	吉祥的
austere	austero, ra	austère	строгий	坚苦的
authenticate	autenticar	authentifier	удостоверять	证明是真的
available	disponible	disponible	наличный	现有的

English	Spanish	French	Russian	Chinese
awkward	torpe	gauche	неуклюжий	别扭的
bacteria +	bacteria	bactérie	бактерии	细菌
bad	perverso, sa	mauvais	плохой	坏的
baffle	desconcertar	étonner	озадачивать	使困惑
bailiff	alguacil	huissier	помощник шерифа	管家
baker	panadero, ra	boulanger	пекарь	面包师傅
balance	balance	équilibre	равновесие	平衡
ban	negar	défendre	запрещать	禁止
bankrupt	quebrar	banqueroute	обанкротившийся	破产
barometer	barómetro	baromètre	барометр	晴雨表
barren	estéril	stérile	бесплодный	荒芜的
barrier	barrera	barrière	барьер	障碍
belated	demorado, da	retardé	задержавшийся	来迟的
belief	creencia	croyance	вера	信仰
belligerent	belicoso, sa	belligérant	агрессивный	好战的
benefactor	benefactor, ra	bienfaiteur	благодетель	捐助人
beneficial	beneficioso, sa	bénéfique	благотворный	有益的
beneficiary	beneficiario, ria	bénéficiaire	бенефициарий	得益者
benevolent	benévolo, la	bénévole	благожелательный	仁慈的
benign	benigno, na	bénin	неопасный	良性的
bereft	privar	priver de	утративший	缺乏
betray	traicionar	tromper	обманывать	背叛
better	mejor	mieux	лучший	更好
bewilder	aturdir	préjudigé	сбивать с толку	使迷惑
bigot	intolerante	bigot	расист	偏执的人
bilingual	bilingüe	bilingue	говорящий на двух языках	说两种语言者
biology	biología	biologie	биология	生物学
biopsy	biopsia	biopsie	проводить биопсию	活组织检查
bitter	agrio	amère	горький	痛苦的
blame	culpa	blâmer	вина	责怪
blatant	divisable	évident	очевидный	公然的
blemish +	mancha	souiller	пятнать	斑点
boast	presumir	se vanter	хвастаться	吹牛
boisterous	ruidoso, sa	turbulent	неистовый	喧闹的
boredom	aburrimiento	ennui	скука	厌倦
borrow	prestar	emprunter	одалживать	借
boss	jefe	patron	босс	上司
botany	botánica	botanique	ботаника	植物学
bother	molestar	ennuyer	надоедать	打扰
boundary	límite	limite	граница	边界
bourgeois	burgués, sa	bourgeois	буржуа	资产阶级的
boycott	boicotear	boycotter	бойкотировать	抵制
brave	bravo	brave	храбрый	勇敢的
brawl	alboroto	querelle	скандалить	争吵
break	romper	casser	разбивать	打破
brevity	brevedad	brièveté	краткость	简练
brief	breve	bref	короткий	简短的
bright	lustroso, sa	clair	яркий	明亮的
brilliant	brillante	brillant	яркий	聪明的
brisk	activo, va	vif	живой	活泼的
browse	curiosear	bouquiner	просмотреть	流览
brutal	brutal	brutal	жестокий	残忍的
budget	presupuesto	budget	бюджет	预算
buffet	bufé	buffet	буфет	自助餐
bulbs	bulbos	ampoules	луковицы	灯泡
bundle	paquete	liasse	связывать	包裹
buoyant	boyante	flottant	плавучий	活泼的
burden	carga	fardeau	бремя	负担
bursar	tesorería	trésorier	казначей	财务主管

English	Spanish	French	Russian	Chinese
burst	estallar	éclater	взрываться	胀裂
butcher	carnicero, ra	boucher	мясник	屠夫
buy	comprar	acheter	покупать	购买
cab	taxi	taxi	такси	出租汽车
cafe	café	café	кафе	小餐馆
cafeteria	cafetería	cafétéria	кафетерий	自助餐厅
calamity	calamidad	calamité	бедствие	灾难
calculate	calcular	calculer	вычислять	计算
callous	insensible	calleux	бесчувственный	毫无痛痒的
calm	calma	calme	тихий	镇静
camouflage	camuflaje	camoufler	маскировать	伪装
cancel	cancelar	annuler	аннулировать	取消
cancer	cáncer	cancer	рак	癌症
candid	cándido, da	candide	искренний	坦率的
candidate	candidato, ta	candidat	кандидат	候选人
cantankerous	pendenciero, ra	bourru	сварливый	唱反调的
capability	aptitud	capacité	способность	能量
capacitate	capacitar	investir	делать способным	使具有能力
capacity	capacidad	capacité	способность	容量
capitalism	capitalismo	capitalisme	капитализм	资本主义
capitulate	capitular	capituler	капитулировать	投降
capricious	caprichoso, sa	capricieux	капризный	反复无常的
capsize	volcar	chavirer	опрокидывать	倾覆
capture	capturar	capturer	взять в плен	抓获
carcinoma	carcinoma	carcinome	карцинома	癌
cardiologist	cardiólogo, ga	cardiologue	кардиолог	心血管病医生
cardiovascular	cardiovascular	cardio-vasculaire	сердечно-сосудистый	心血管的
care	cuidado	soin	уход	关心
career	carrera	carrière	профессия	生涯
caress	acariciar	caresse	ласкать	爱抚
carnivore	carnívoro, ra	carnivore	плотоядное животное	食肉动物
carpenter	carpintero, ra	charpentier	плотник	木匠
casual	casual	désinvolte	случайный	非正式的
catalyst	catalizador	catalyseur	катализатор	催化剂
catastrophe	catástrofe	catastrophe	катастрофа	大灾难
categorize	agrupar	classer	распределять по категориям	使归类
cause	causa	causer	причина	原因
caution	cautela	attention	осторожность	小心
cease	cesar	cesser	останавливать	停止
celebrate	celebrar	célébrer	праздновать	庆祝
cell	celda	cellule	клетка	细胞
censure	censurar	censurer	порицать	责备
century	siglo	siècle	столетие	世纪
cerebellum	cerebelo	cervelet	мозжечок	小脑
cerebrum	cerebro	cérébrum	головной мозг	大脑
challenge	retar	défi	бросать вызов	挑战
chance	riesgo	risque	риск	机会
change	cambiar	changement	изменять	改变
chaos	caos	chaos	хаос	混乱
charisma	carisma	charisme	притягательная сила	魅力
charismatic	carismático, ca	charismatique	притягательный	有魅力的
charm	cautivar	charme	очаровывать	魅力
chastise	corregir	châtier	подвергать наказанию	责罚
cheap	económico, ca	bon marché	дешевый	廉价的
cheat	engañar	tricher	мошенничать	欺骗
check	comprobar	vérifier	проверять	支票
cherish	estimar	apprécier	лелеять	爱护
chief	primario, ria	chef	главный	首领
chilly	frío, ía	froid	холодный	寒冷的

English	Spanish	French	Russian	Chinese
cholesterol	colesterol	cholestérol	холестерин	胆固醇
chore	quehacer	corvée	подённая работа	家务
chronometer	cronómetro	chronomètre	хронометр	天文钟
chubby	gordiflón, na	potelé	круглолицый	圆胖的
circumference	circunferencia	circonférence	окружность	周长
circumvent	evadir	circonvenir	обойти	防止
cite	citar	citer	ссылаться	引用
clandestine	clandestino, na	clandestin	тайный	秘密的
clarify	clarificar	clarifier	разъяснять	澄清
classify	clasificar	classer	классифицировать	分类
claustrophobia	claustrofobia	claustrophobie	клаустрофобия	幽闭恐怖症
clean	limpio, pia	propre	чистый	干净的
coach	entrenar	entraîneur	тренировать	教练
coerce	coercer	obliger	удерживать	强迫
cognizant	informado, da	conscient	осведомлённый	认识到
coherent	coherente	cohérent	связный	有连贯性的
cohesive	cohesivo, va	cohésif	связанный	团结的
coincide	coincidir	coïncider	совпадать	巧合
cold	frígido, da	froid	холодный	寒冷
collaborate	colaborar	collaborer	сотрудничать	合作
collapsed	caído, da	effondré	обрушенный	崩溃
collide	chocar	heurter	сталкиваться	碰撞
combine	combinar	combiner	объединять	结合
comedian	comediante	comédien	комик	喜剧演员
comfort	confortar	confort	утешать	安慰
comfortable	confortable	confortable	спокойный	舒适的
commitment	compromiso	engament	обязательство	承诺
commotion	conmoción	agitation	волнение	骚动
communism	comunismo	communisme	коммунизм	共产主义
compare	comparar	comparer	сравнивать	对比
comparison	comparación	comparaison	сравнение	比较
compassion	compasión	compassion	сочувствие	感情
compatible	compatible	compatible	совместимый	可对比的
compel	compeler	obliger	заставлять	驱逐
compensate	compensar	compenser	платить	补偿
competent	competente	compétent	компетентный	能干的
complacent	complaciente	complaisant	самодовольный	自满的
complain	quejarse	plaindre	жаловаться	抱怨
complex	complejo	complexe	сложный	复杂的
complicate	complicar	compliquer	осложнять	使复杂
compliment	lisonjear	complimenter	хвалить	恭维
comply	obedecer	respecter	исполнять	服从
component	componente	composant	составная часть	组成部分
compose	componer	composer	сочинять	创作
comprehensive	comprehensivo, va	large	обширный	综合的
compulsory	obligado, da	obligatoire	обязательный	义务的
concede	conceder	concéder	допускать	承认
conceited	engreído, da	suffisant	самодовольный	自负的
concept	concepto	concept	концепция	概念
conciliate	conciliar	concilier	снискать доверие	安抚
concise	conciso, sa	concis	краткий	简明的
conclude	concluir	conclure	заканчивать	作出结论
concoct	confeccionar	préparer	состряпать	调制
concur	concurrir	être d'accord avec	соглашаться	同意
concurrent	concurrente	concomitant	согласованный	同时发生的
condemn	condenar	condamner	осуждать	谴责
condescend	condescender	condescendre	унижаться	俯就
condone	condonar	excuser	потворствовать	原谅
conductor	director de orquesta	chef d'orchestre	дирижёр	指挥

English	Spanish	French	Russian	Chinese
confess	confesar	admettre	признавать	坦白
confide	confiar	confier	доверять	吐露秘密
confidence	confianza	confiance	уверенность	信心
confirm	confirmar	confirmer	подтверждать	确认
confiscate	confiscar	confisquer	конфисковать	没收
conflagration	conflagración	conflagration	большой пожар	大火灾
conform	conformar	conformer	согласовать	遵照
confront	confrontar	s'confronter	противостоять	对峙
congenial	congenial	convivial	приятный	协调的
conscious	consciente	conscient	понимающий	有意识的
consecutive	consecutivo, va	consécutif	последовательный	连续的
consensus	consenso	consensus	согласие	意见一致
consequence	consecuencia	conséquence	следствие	后果
conservative	conservador, ra	conservateur	консервативный	保守的
considerable	considerable	considérable	значительный	相当的
consistent	continuo, nua	stable	совместимый	一贯的
conspicuous	conspicuo, cua	ostensible	видимый	显著的
conspire	conspirar	comploter	устраивать заговор	密谋
constant	constante	constant	постоянный	一贯的
consternation	consternación	consternation	оцепенение	一惊恐
constituent	elemento	composant	составная часть	选民
constitute	constituir	constituer	составлять	构成
constrain	constreñir	contraindre	принуждать	克制
constrict	apretar	étriqué	стягивать	约束
contemplate	contemplar	envisager	созерцать	周密考虑
contemporary	contemporáneo, nea	contemporain	современник	当代的
contemptible	despreciable	méprisable	презренный	可鄙的
content	contento, ta	satisfait	довольный	内容
contradict	contradecir	contredire	противоречить	使矛盾
controversy	controversia	controverse	полемика	争议
convenient	conveniente	pratique	удобный	方便的
conventional	convencional	conventionnel	обычный	常规的
converse	conversar	converser	беседовать	相反的
convert	convertir	convertir	превращать	使转换
convey	comunicar	pourvoir	передавать	输送
convince	convencer	convaincre	убеждать	使信服
cop	polizonte	flic	полицейский	警察
copious	copioso, sa	copieux	обильный	丰富的
corpse	cadáver	cadavre	труп	尸体
corridor	corredor	corridor	коридор	走廊
corroborate	corroborar	corroborer	подтверждать	合作
counselor	consejero, ra	conseiller	консультант	律师
counterfeit	falsificación	frauder	подделывать	伪造
course	curso	cours	курс (лекций, обучения)	过程
court	corte	court	суд	法庭
courteous	cortés	courtois	вежливый	有礼貌的
covert	cubierto	secret	скрытый	隐秘的
credible	creíble	crédible	правдоподобный	可相信的
credit	crédito	crédit	зачёт	荣誉
criminal	criminal	criminel	преступник	罪犯
criminology	criminología	criminologie	криминология	犯罪学
crinkle	ondulación	froisser	извиваться	起皱子
cripple	lisiado, da	estropier	калечить	跛
crisis	crisis	crise	кризис	危机
criteria	criterio	critère	критерий	标准
criticize	criticar	critiquer	критиковать	批评
crown	corona	couronne	корона	王冠
cry	llorar	pleurer	плакать	哭
cumbersome	molesto, ta	encombrant	громоздкий	累赘的

English	Spanish	French	Russian	Chinese
curtail	acortar	tronquer	сокращать	削减
damage	dañar	endommager	повреждать	损坏
dangle	bambolear	pendiller	свободно свисать	悬挂
darkness	obscuridad	obscurité	темнота	黑暗
data	datos	données	данные	数据
dean	decano, na	doyen	декан	系主任
debate	debate	débat	дискуссия	辩论
debilitate	debilitar	affaiblir	ослаблять	使衰弱
decagon	decágono, na	décagone	десятиугольник	十边形
decease	morir	décéder	скончаться	死亡
deceive	timar	tromper	обманывать	欺骗
decipher	descifrar	déchiffrer	расшифровывать	破译
decision	decisión	décision	решение	决定
decrease	decrecer	baisser	уменьшать	下降
dedicate	dedicar	dédier	посвящать	奉献
deduct	deducir	déduire	вычитать	扣除
defeat	derrotar	vaincre	наносить поражение	击败
defendant	acusado, da	défendeur	обвиняемый	被告
deficient	deficiente	déficient	недостаточный	有缺陷的
deficit	déficit	déficit	дефицит	赤字
definite	determinado, da	défini	определённый	确定的
defraud	defraudar	frauder	обманывать	骗取
defy	desafiar	défier	открыто не повиноваться	违抗
degenerate	degenerar	dégénérer	вырождаться	堕落
deliberate	premeditado, da	délibérer	преднамеренный	故意的
delicate	delicado, da	délicat	слабый	细致的
delicious	delicioso, sa	délicieux	очень вкусный	可口的
deliver	entregar	livrer	передавать	输送
demand	demanda	exiger	требовать	要求
demolish	demoler	démolir	разрушать	毁坏
demonstrate	demostrar	manifester	наглядно показывать	显示
denounce	denunciar	dénoncer	осуждать	谴责
dentist	dentista	dentiste	зубной врач	牙医
depart	partir	partir	покидать	出发
deplete	vaciar	vider	истощать	耗尽
deplore	deplorar	déplorer	сожалеть	悲叹
deposit	depositar	déposer	отдавать на хранение	押金
depreciate	depreciar	amortir	обесценивать	贬值
deprive	privar	priver	лишать	剥夺
derelict	vago, ga	abandonné	бездельник	玩忽职守
derive	ganar	dériver	извлекать	取得
dermatologist	dermatólogo, ga	dermatologue	дерматолог	皮肤病医生
dermis	dermis	derme	кожа	皮肤
derogatory	derogatorio, ria	dérogatoire	уничижающий	贬意的
describe	describir	décrire	описывать	描述
designate	designar	désigner	определять	指定
desist	desistir	désister	переставать	停止
despair	desesperación	désespérer	отчаяние	绝望
desperate	desesperado, da	désespérer	крайне необходимый	绝望的
despondent	desesperanzado, da	abattu	унылый	沮丧的
destination	destino	destination	место назначения	目的地
destroy	destruir	détruire	разрушать	摧毁
detail	detalle	détailler	подробность	细节
detain	detener	détenir	задерживать	拘留
detect	detectar	détecter	обнаруживать	侦查
deter	desanimar	repousser	удерживать	制止
deteriorate	deteriorar	se dégrader	ухудшать	恶化
determine	determinar	déterminer	определять	决定
detest	detestar	détester	ненавидеть	厌恶

English	Spanish	French	Russian	Chinese
detract	detractar	dénigrer	отвлекать	诋毁
detrimental	dañoso, sa	préjudiciable	вредный	有害的
devastate	devastar	dévaster	опустошать	破坏
deviate	desviar	dévier	отклоняться	偏离
devise	inventar	élaborer	разрабатывать	装置
dexterous	diestro, tra	adroit	ловкий	灵巧的
dictator	dictador, ra	dictateur	диктатор	独裁
different	diferente	différent	несходный	不同的
difficult	difícil	difficile	трудный	困难的
digress	divagar	faire une digression	отклоняться	离题
dilapidate	dilapidar	dilapider	приходить в упадок	失修
dilemma	dilema	dilemme	дилемма	困境
diligent	diligente	diligent	прилежный	勤奋的
dilute	diluir	diluer	разбавлять	稀释
diminish	disminuir	diminuer	преуменьшать	减少
diplomacy	diplomacia	diplomatie	дипломатичность	外交
diplomat	diplomático, ca	diplomate	дипломат	外交家
dirty	sucio, cia	sale	грязный	脏的
disagreeable	desconvenir	désagréable	расходиться во мнениях	可不同意的
disappear	desaparecer	disparaître	исчезать	消失
discard	descartar	jeter	отвергать	抛弃
discipline	disciplinar	discipline	наказывать	纪律
discount	descuento	escompter	скидка	折价
discreet	discreto, ta	discret	осторожный	谨慎的
discriminate	discriminar	discriminer	различать	歧视的
disenchanted	desilusionado, da	désenchanté	разочарованный	醒悟的
disengage	soltar	relâcher	освобождать	使脱离
disgrace	vergüenza	disgrâce	позорить	丢脸
disillusion	desilusión	désillusion	разочарование	醒悟
dislocate	dislocar	détacher	вывихнуть	改变位置
disloyal	desleal	déloyal	неверный	不忠实
dismantle	desarmar	démonter	разбирать	拆除
disparity	disparidad	disparité	различие	差异
disperse	dirpersar	disperser	рассеивать	分散
dispose	disponer	jeter	удалять	处理
dispute	disputar	querelle	дискуссия	争执
dissatisfied	descontento, ta	mécontent	недовольный	不满意的
dissent	disentir	désaccord	расходиться во мнениях	不同意
dissident	disidente	dissident	диссидент	持不同政见者
dissipate	disipar	dissiper	рассеивать	挥霍
dissuade	disuadir	dissuader	отговаривать	说服
distinct	distinto, ta	distinct	определённый	不同的
distinction	distinción	distinction	различие	区别
distinguish	distinguir	distinguer	отличать	区分
distress	apuro	détresse	тревожить	痛苦
disturb	disturbar	déranger	беспокоить	扰乱
diurnal	diurno, na	diurne	дневной	白天的
diverge	divergir	s'écarter de	отлоняться	分叉
diversity	diversidad	diversité	разнообразие	差异
docile	dócil	docile	послушный	温顺的
doldrums	calmas ecuatoriales	arrêt passager	депрессия	忧郁
domain	dominio	domaine	владение	领域
dominate	dominar	dominer	господствовать	统治
donate	donar	faire don de	передавать в дар	捐献
donor	donador, ra	donneur	даритель	捐献人
dormancy	quietud	léthargie	состояние бездействия	休眠状态
draft	dibujo	esquisse	делать эскиз	草案
drastic	drástico, ca	draconien	радикальный	激烈的
drip	gotear	goutter	капать	滴下

English	Spanish	French	Russian	Chinese
dubious	dudoso, sa	à double sens	сомнительный	胡含的
dwindle	menguar	diminuer	сокращать	缩小
dynamic	dinámico, ca	dynamique	энергичный	有活力的
eager	ansioso, sa	avide	нетерпеливый	渴望的
earn	percibir	gagner	добывать	挣得
easy	fácil	facile	лёгкий	容易
eccentric	excéntrico, ca	excentrique	чудак	怪僻的人
ecology	ecología	écologie	экология	生态学
economical	económico, ca	économique	экономичный	经济的
ecstasy	éxtasis	extase	экстаз	狂喜
egocentric	egocéntrico, ca	égocentrique	эгоцентрический	自我为中心的
eject	expulsar	éjecter	выбрасывать	喷出
elaborate	elaborado, da	élaborer	тщательно разработанный	细说
elated	exaltado, da	ravi	ликующий	兴奋的
elder	mayor	aîné	старший по возрасту	长者
elective	electivo, va	au choix	факультативный	选举产生的
electrician	electricista	électricien	электромонтёр	电工
elicit	atraer	montrer	вызвать	引出
eligible	elegible	être habilité à	подходящий	合格的
eliminate	eliminar	éliminer	устранять	淘汰
elite	elite	élite	элита	上等阶层
eloquent	elocuente	éloquent	красноречивый	雄辩的
embarrass	apenar	embarrasser	смущать	使难堪
embezzle	desfalcar	détourner	присваивать	贪污
emerge	emerger	émerger	появляться	涌现
eminent	eminente	éminent	выдающийся	著名的
emit	emitir	émettre	испускать	射出
emotional	emocional	émotionnel	эмоциональный	情绪激动的
empathy	empatía	compassion	сочувствие	移情
emphasize	enfatizar	souligner	подчёркивать	强调
employ	emplear	employer	нанимать	雇佣
empower	comisionar	habiliter	уполномочивать	授权
encounter	topar	rencontrer	неожиданно встретить	遭遇
encourage	alentar	encourager	поддерживать	鼓励
endeavor	intentar	s'efforcer	стараться	努力
endorse	endosar	approuverson	расписываться	赞同
endow	dotar	doter	одарять	资助
endure	soportar	endurer	переносить	忍受
enemy	enemigo, ga	ennemi	враг	敌人
enhance	mejorar	rehausser	увеличивать	加强
enigmatic	enigmático, ca	énigmatique	загадочный	费解的
enlarge	amplificar	agrandir	увеличивать	扩大
enlighten	instruir	éclairer	просвещать	启发
enmity	enemistad	rivalité	ненависть	故意
enormous	enorme	énorme	громадный	巨大的
enough	bastante	assez	достаточный	足够的
entertain	entretener	divertir	развлекать	娱乐
entire	entero	entier	целый	整体
envy	envidia	envier	зависть	羡慕
enzyme	enzima	enzyme	фермент	酶
epidermis	epidermis	épiderme	эпидерма	表皮
epitome	epítome	représentant	олицетворение	梗概
equate	igualar	égaler	считать равным	使等于
equip	equipar	équiper	оборудовать	装备
equivocal	equívoco	équivoque	двусмысленный	含胡的
eradicate	erradicar	anéantir	искоренять	根除
erase	borrar	effacer	стирать	擦掉
errand	mandado	course	задание	任务
erratic	errático, ca	irrégulier	изменчивый	不规则的

English	Spanish	French	Russian	Chinese
erupt	explotar	entrer en éruption	прорываться	喷发
escalate	escalar	monter	расти	战争升级
esoteric	esotérico, ca	ésotérique	понятный лишь немногим	奥秘的
espionage	espionaje	espionnage	шпионаж	间谍
essay	ensayo	essai	очерк	散文
establish	establecer	établir	учреждать	建立
esteem	estima	estime	уважать	荣誉
estrange	apartar	s'éloigner de	разойтись	使疏远
eternal	eternal	éternel	вечный	永恒的
evacuate	evacuar	évacuer	эвакуировать	撤离
evasive	evasivo, va	évasif	уклончивый	含胡的
evident	evidente	évident	очевидный	明显的
exacerbate	exacerbar	exacerber	усиливать	使恶化
exaggerate	exagerar	exagérer	преувеличивать	夸张
excel	sobresalir	exceller	превосходить	超越
exceptional	excepcional	exceptionnel	незаурядный	例外的
excess	exceso	excès	избыток	过量
excessive	excesivo, va	excessif	избыточный	过度的
excitement	excitación	excitation	возбуждение	激动
exclude	excluir	exclure	исключить	排斥
exemplify	ejemplificar	montrer	приводить пример	举例证明
exempt	exento, ta	exempter	освобождать	免除
exhaust	agotar	extraire	истощать	耗尽
exhilarate	regocijar	amuser	веселить	使高兴
exonerate	exonerar	exonérer	признать невиновным	使免受指控
exorbitant	exorbitante	exorbitant	чрезмерный	价格过高
expedite	apresurar	accélérer	ускорять	加速行动
expel	expeler	évincer	исключать	驱逐
experiment	experimento	expérimenter	эксперимент	试验
explain	explicar	expliquer	объяснять	解释
explicit	explícito, ta	explicite	определенный	明白的
extensive	extensivo, va	à grande échelle	обширный	广泛的
exterior	exterior	extérieur	внешний	外部
external	externo,na	externe	наружный	外部的
extra-terrestrial	extraterrestre	extra terrestre	внеземной	外星际的
extraordinary	extraordinario, ria	extraordinaire	необычный	非凡的
extravagant	extravagante	extravagant	экстравагантный	奢侈的
extricate	desembrollar	dégager	выпутываться	使脱离
extrinsic	extrínseco, ca	extrinsèque	внешний	外在的
extrovert	extrovertido, da	extraverti	экстроверт	外向的
exuberant	exuberante	exubérant	жизнерадостный	茂盛的
fabulous	fabuloso, sa	fabuleux	невероятный	惊人的
facade	fachada	façade	видимость	门面
facetious	gracioso, sa	en plaisantant	игривый	滑稽的
facilitate	facilitar	permettre	способствовать	促进
fade	descolorarse	délaverpasser	блекнуть	退色
fail	fallar	manquer	терпеть неудачуj	失败
faith	fe	foi	вера	信仰
fake	impostura	faux	подделка	假的
fallacy	falacia	mensonge	ошибка	谬论
fallible	falible	faillible	ошибочный	容易出错的
false	falso	faux	ложный	错误的
falter	balbucear	hésiter	колебаться	蹒跚
fame	fama	célébrité	слава	声誉
familiar	familiar	familier	хорошо знакомый (с чем-либо)	熟悉的
famine	hambruna	famine	голод	饥荒
famish	hambrear	faim	голодать	使挨饿
famous	famoso, sa	célèbre	знаменитый	著名的
fantastic	fantástico, ca	fantastique	эстравагантный	非常的

English	Spanish	French	Russian	Chinese
fantasy	fantasía	fantaisie	воображение	幻想
farewell	despedida	départ	прощание	告別
fascinate	fascinar	fasciner	пленять	使着迷
fashion	moda	mode	мода	时髦
fast	veloz	rapide	быстрый	迅速的
fasten	sujetar	attacher	скреплять	扣住
fastidious	quisquilloso, sa	fastidieux	привередливый	爱挑剔的
fatal	fatal	mortel	губительный	致命的
fatigue	fatiga	fatigue	усталость	疲劳
fatuous	fatuo, tua	simple d'esprit	глупый	愚昧的
fault	imperfección	faute	ошибка	缺点
faulty	defectuoso, sa	défectueux	ошибочный	有缺点的
favor	favorecer	faveur	содействовать	恩惠
favorite	favorito, ta	favori	любимый	宠物
feasible	factible	faisable	осуществимый	可行的
fee	honorarios	honoraires	плата за услуги	费用
feeble	enclenque	faible	слабый	虚弱的
feminine	femenino, na	féminin	женский	女性的
ferocious	feroz	féroce	свирепый	凶恶的
fervent	ferviente	fervent	пылкий	热烈的
fervor	fervor	ferveur	рвение	热烈
festive	festivo, va	faste	праздничный	节日的
fetch	traer	aller chercher	сходить и принести	拿来
feud	contienda	querelle	вражда	世仇
fever	fiebre	fièvre	жар	发烧
fiction	ficción	fiction	вымысел	小说
fictitious	ficticio, cia	factice	вымышленный	虚构的
fidelity	fidelidad	fidélité	верность	忠诚
fiduciary	fiduciario, ria	fiduciaire	доверенный	信托的
final	final	final	окончательный	最终的
finish	terminar	arrivé	кончать	结束
fireman	bombero	pompier	пожарный	消防员
fisherman	pescador, ra	pêcheur	рыбак	渔夫
fit	apto, ta	aller	подходящий	匹配
flagrant	flagrante	flagrant	ужасный	公然的
flamboyant	llamativo, va	flamboyant	вычурный	灿烂的
flame	llama	flamme	пылать	火焰
flatter	adular	flatter	льстить	奉承
flaunt	lucir	exhiber	рисоватся	夸耀
flaw	defecto	faille	порок	缺点
flippant	impertinente	impertinent	дерзкий	轻率的
flourish	florecer	fleurir	процветать	茂盛
fluctuate	fluctuar	fluctuer	колебаться	上下浮动
fluent	fluido, da	de façon courante	свободно говорящий	流利的
fluster	aturdir	faire rougir	волновать	使慌张
foe	antagonista	ennemi	враг	敌人
fond	cariñoso, sa	aimant	любящий	喜爱的
foot	pie	pied	ступня	脚
forecast	pronóstico	prévision	прогноз	预报
foremost	primero, ra	avant-tout	основной	首要的
forever	siempre	à jamais	навсегда	永远
forfeit	confiscación	renoncer	поплатиться	丧失
forgive	absolver	pardonner	прощать	原谅
formal	formal	solennel	формальный	正式的
formidable	formidable	formidable	очень трудный	可怕的
formulate	formular	formuler	подготовить	构想
forsake	desamparar	abandonner	покидать	抛弃
fortitude	fortaleza	force	стойкость	刚毅
forward	adelante	en avant	продвигать вперёд	向前

English	Spanish	French	Russian	Chinese
founder	fundador, ra	fondateur	основатель	崩塌
fraction	fracción	fraction	часть	碎片
fragile	frágil	fragile	хрупкий	易碎的
fragrant	fragante	parfumé	ароматный	芳香的
frail	endeble	fragile	хрупкий	脆弱的
frank	franco, ca	franc	откровенный	坦率的
frantic	frenético, ca	frénétique	неистовый	狂热的
fraternity	fraternidad	fraternité	братство	友爱
fraud	fraude	escroc	обман	欺骗
frequent	frecuente	fréquent	обычный	频繁的
frigid	frígido, da	glacé	холодность	寒冷的
frivolous	frívolo, la	frivole	легкомысленный	轻薄的
frolic	alegre	sauter joyeusement	веселье	嬉闹
frugal	frugal	frugal	бережливый	节省的
frustrated	frustrado, da	frustré	разочарованный	烦恼的
fun	divertido, da	plaisir	веселье	乐趣
fungi	hongos	fongide	грибок	真菌
fury	furia	furie	ярость	狂怒
futile	fútil	futile	бесполезность	无效的
gait	andadura	démarche	походка	步态
gallant	galante	brave	доблестный	勇敢的
gamut	escala	gamme	диапазон	整个范围
gang	pandilla	gang	бригада	一帮
garrulous	gárrulo, la	loquace	болтливый	饶舌的
gather	reunir	rassembler	собирать	集合
gaudy	charro, rra	voyant	кричащий	艳丽的
general	general	général	широкий	将军
generate	generar	générer	производить	产生
generous	generoso, sa	généreux	великодушный	慷慨的
genesis	génesis	genèse	генезис	起源
gentle	gentil	doux	мягкий	温和的
geography	geografía	géographie	география	地理
geology	geología	géologie	геология	地质
ghastly	terrible	horrible	страшный	恐怖的
gigantic	gigantesco, ca	gigantesque	гигантский	巨大的
glamorous	encantador, ra	charmant	пленительный	富有魅力的
glimpse	vistazo	aperçu	взглянуть мельком	一瞥
gloom	tristeza	tristesse	уныние	黑暗
glucose	glucosa	glucose	глюкоза	葡萄糖
goal	meta	but	цель	目标
goodwill	benevolencia	bonne volonté	доброжелательность	友好
gossip	chisme	bavard	слухи	闲聊
gradual	gradual	progressif	постепенный	逐步的
graphic	gráfico,ca	graphique	изобразительный	图片
gratitude	gratitud	gratitude	благодарность	感激
gratuitous	gratuito, ta	gratuit	бесплатный	免费的
gregarious	gregario, ria	grégaire	общительный	合群的
grieve	afligir	attrister	горевать	感到悲痛
grotesque	grotesco, ca	grotesque	причудливый	可怕的
guest	invitado, da	hôte	гость	客人
guide	guiar	guide	направлять	向导
guilty	culpable	coupable	виновный	有罪
gullible	crédulo, la	crédule	доверчивый	易上当的
gush	brotar	jaillir	литься потоком	涌流
gynecologist	ginecólogo, ga	gynécologue	гинеколог	妇科医生
habit	costumbre	habitude	привычка	习惯
hallucinate	alucinar	halluciner	страдать галлюцинациями	使生幻觉
halt	parar	arrêt	останавливать	停止
hamper	estorbar	ralentir	мешать	妨碍

English	Spanish	French	Russian	Chinese
handsome	guapo	attirant	красивый	英俊的
handy	útil	pratique	удобный	方便的
haphazard	casualidad	au hasard	случайность	随意的
harass	acosar	importuner	беспокоить	骚扰
hardship	aflicción	épreuve	невзгоды	困苦
harm	lastimar	blesser	вредить	伤害
harmonious	armonioso, sa	harmonieux	гармоничный	和谐的
harmony	armonía	harmonie	гармония	和谐
harsh	áspero, ra	dur	жестокий	粗糙的
hasty	precipitado, da	en hâte	поспешный	匆忙的
havoc	estrago	destruction	опустошение	大灾难
hazardous	riesgoso, sa	dangereux	опасный	有危险的
heart	corazón	coeur	сердце	心脏
heinous	atroz	haineux	отвратительный	十恶不赦的
help	ayuda	aide	помощь	帮助
hemoglobin	hemoglobina	hémoglobine	гемоглобин	血红蛋白
hepatitis	hepatitis	hépatite	гепатит	肝炎
heptagon	heptágono, na	heptagone	семиугольник	七边形
herbivores	herbívoros	herbivore	травоядный	食草动物
hesitate	titubear	hésiter	сомневаться	犹豫
heterogenous	heterogéneo, nea	hétérogène	неоднородный	各种各样的
hexagon	hexágono, na	hexagone	шестиугольник	六边形
hide	ocultar	cacher	скрывать	藏
hilarious	bullicioso	très amusant	смешной	欢闹的
hinder	obstaculizar	empêcher	мешать	妨碍
hire	contratar	engager	нанимать	雇佣
histology	histología	histologie	гистология	组织学
history	historia	histoire	история	历史
hit	pegar	frapper	ударять	打击
hoax	engaño	mauvaise plaisanterie	обман	骗局
hobby	pasatiempo	passe-temps	хобби	爱好
hockey	hockey	hockey	хоккей	冰球
homage	homenaje	hommage	почтение	尊敬
homicide	homicidio	homicide	убийство	杀人
homogenous	homogéneo, nea	homogène	однородный	同种类的
horrible	horrible	horrible	ужасный	可怕的
hostile	hostil	hostile	враждебный	敌对的
hot	caliente	chaud	горячий	热
humane	humano, na	humain	гуманный	仁爱的
humble	humilde	humble	скромный	卑贱的
humiliate	humillar	humilier	унижать	使蒙耻
hurry	apurarse	se presser	спешить	匆忙
hurt	lastimar	blesser	причинять вред	伤害
hypersensitive	hipersensible	hypersensible	сверхчувствительносты	过敏的
hypertension	hipertensión	hypertension	гипертония	高血压
hyperthermia	hipertermia	hyperthermie	гипотермия	情感增盛
hyperthyroidism	hipertiroidismo	hyperthyroïdie	гипертиреоз	甲状腺功能亢进
hypocalcemia	hipocalcemia	hypocalcémie	гипокальцемия	高血钙症
hypocrite	hipócrita	hypocrite	лицемер	伪君子
hypoglycemia	hipoglucemia	hypoglycémie	гипергликемия	低血糖
hysterical	histérico, ca	hystérique	истеричный	歇斯底里的
idea	idea	idée	идея	想法
ideal	ideal	idéal	идеальный	理想
identical	identico, ca	identique	одинаковый	相同的
identify	identificar	identifier	отождествлять	辨认
idiot	idiota	idiot	идиот	白痴
idle	ocioso, sa	inactif	неработающий	空闲
ignoble	innoble	ignoble	подлый	可耻的
ignorant	ignorante	ignorant	невежественный	无知的

English	Spanish	French	Russian	Chinese
ignore	ignorar	ignorer	не замечать	不理
illegal	ilegal	illégal	незаконный	非法的
illegible	ilegible	illisible	неразборчивый	字迹不清的
illicit	ilícito, ta	illicite	запрещенный	非法的
illiterate	analfabeto, ta	illettré	безграмотный	文盲
illogical	ilógico, ca	illogique	нелогичный	不合逻辑的
illuminate	iluminar	illuminer	освещать	点亮
illustrate	ilustrar	illustrer	пояснять	演示
illustrious	ilustrativo, va	illustre	известный	杰出的
imbecile	imbécil	imbécile	слабоумный	弱智者
imitate	imitar	imiter	копировать	模仿
immaculate	inmaculado, da	immaculé	безукоризненный	纯洁的
immature	inmaduro, ra	manquant de maturité	незрелый	不成熟的
immeasurable	inmensurable	inestimable	неизмеримый	无法衡量的
immense	inmenso, sa	immense	огромный	巨大的
immerse	sumergir	immerger	погружать что-то в жидкость	使浸没
immigrate	inmigrar	immigrer	иммигрировать	移民
imminent	inminente	imminent	надвигающийся	即将发生的
immoral	inmoral	amoral	аморальный	不道德的
immune	inmune	résistant	не восприимчивый	免除的
impact	impacto	impact	столкновение	影响
impair	empeorar	affaiblir	ослаблять	削弱
impartial	imparcial	impartial	беспристрастный	公正的
impatient	impaciente	impatient	нетерпеливый	不耐心的
impeach	desacreditar	destituer	обвинять	弹劾
impeccable	impecable	impeccable	непогрешимый	无可挑剔的
impede	impedir	ralentir	препятствовать	妨碍
imperceptible	imperceptible	imperceptible	незаметный	感觉不到的
imperfect	imperfecto, ta	imparfait	несовершенный	不完美的
impetuous	impetuoso, sa	impétueux	поспешный	急躁的
implausible	inverosímil	incroyable	невероятный	难以致信的
implement	implementar	mettre en oeuvre	выполнять	执行
implicit	implícito, ta	implicite	безусловный	含蓄的
imploro	implorar	implorer	умолять	乞求
imply	implicar	entraîner	подразумевать	暗示
impolite	descortés	impoli	невежливый	不礼貌的
import	importar	importer	ввозить	进口
important	importante	important	важный	重要的
impostor	impostor, ra	imposteur	самозванец	骗子
impractical	impracticable	non réaliste	непрактичный	不切实际的
impression	impresión	impression	ощущение	印象
impromptu	impromptu	impromptu	импровизированный	即兴地
improper	impropio, pia	inadéquat	неправильный	不合适的
improve	perfeccionar	améliorer	совершенствовать	改进
imprudent	imprudente	imprudent	опрометчивый	轻率的
impure	impuro, ra	impur	нечистый	不纯洁的
inaccessible	inaccesible	inaccessible	недосягаемый	达不到的
inaccurate	incorrecto, ta	inexact	неточный	不准确的
inactive	inactivo, va	inactif	бездействующий	不活跃的
inadequate	inadecuado, da	inadéquat	неадекватный	不充分的
inadvertent	inadvertido, da	par inadvertance	непреднамеренный	漫不经心的
inanimate	inanimado, da	inanimé	неодушевлённый	无生命的
inappropriate	impropio, pia	non approprié	нецелесообразный	不合适的
incarcerate	encarcelar	incarcérer	заключать в тюрьму	监禁
incentive	incentivo	incitation	стимул	刺激
incessant	incesante	incessant	непрерывный	不停的
inclement	inclemente	sévère	суровый	严寒的
include	incluir	inclure	содержать	包括
incoherent	incoherente	incohérent	несвязный	不连贯的

English	Spanish	French	Russian	Chinese
incompetent	incompetente	incompétent	некомпетентный	无能的
incomplete	incompleto, ta	incomplet	незавершённый	不完全的
incomprehensible	incomprehensible	incompréhensible	непонятный	不可理解的
inconsiderate	desconsiderado, da	sans égards	необдуманный	考虑不周全的
inconsistent	discorde	décousu	не соответствующий	不一致的
inconspicuous	común	modeste	незаметный	不明显的
incorporate	incorporar	incorporer	включать в состав	吸收
incredible	increíble	incroyable	неправдоподобный	不可相信的
inculcate	inculcar	inculquer	внедрять	反复灌输
incurable	incurable	incurable	неизлечимый	不可救药的
indelible	indeleble	indélébile	нестираемый	擦不掉的
indicate	indicar	indiquer	указывать	指示
indifferent	indiferente	indifférent	безразличный	麻木的
indiscriminate	indiscriminadamente	au hasard	беспорядочный	一视同仁的
indispensable	indispensable	indispensable	необходимый	不可缺少的
inedible	incomestible	non comestible	несъедобный	不可食用的
inept	inepto, ta	inepte	неспособный	不合适的
inert	inerte	inerte	инертный	无生命的
inevitable	inevitable	inévitable	неизбежный	必然的
inexorable	inexorable	inexorable	неумолимый	不容变更的
inexpensive	barato, ta	bon marché	недорогой	廉价的
infallible	infalible	infaillible	непогрешимый	不会犯错误的
infamous	malvado, da	infâme	отвратительный	臭名昭著的
infer	inferir	sous-entendre	делать вывод	推断
inferior	inferior	inférieur	низкий по значению	低等的
infidelity	infidelidad	infidélité	вероломство	不忠诚
inflame	inflamar	enflammer	возбуждать	使燃烧
inflate	inflar	gonfler	надувать	使充气
influence	influencia	influence	влияние	影响
influenza	influenza	grippe	грипп	流感
inform	informar	informer	сообщать	通知
ingenious	ingenioso, sa	ingénieux	остроумный	灵巧的
ingredient	ingrediente	ingrédient	ингредиент	成分
inhabitant	habitante	habitant	житель	居民
inherent	inherente	inhérent	врождённый	内在的
inhibit	inhibir	inhiber	препятствовать	禁止
inhospitable	inhospitalario, ria	non hospitalier	негостеприимный	不好客的
inhuman	inhumano, na	inhumain	бесчеловечный	不人道的
initiate	iniciar	initier	начинать	发起
inmate	residente	codétenu	обитатель (например; тюрьмы)	居住人
innate	innato, ta	inné	врождённый	天生的
innocent	inocente	innocent	невинный	天真的
innocuous	inocuo, cua	bénin	безвредный	无害的
innuendo	indirecta	insinuation	косвенный намёк	含沙射影
inoculate	inocular	inoculer	делать прививку	给接种
inquisitive	inquisitivo, va	curieux	пытливый	好奇的
insane	insano, na	fou	безумный	疯狂的
insatiable	insaciable	insatiable	ненасытный	不可满足的
insidious	insidioso, sa	insidieux	вероломный	阴险的
insignificant	insignificante	insignifiant	несущественный	微不足道的
insolent	insolente	insolent	наглый	傲慢的
inspect	inspeccionar	inspecter	осматривать	检查
inspire	inspirar	inspirer	вдохновлять	鼓励
installment	plazo	traite	частичный регулярный платёж	分期付款
instigate	instigar	instiguer	подстрекать	怂恿
insulin	insulina	insuline	инсулин	胰岛素
integrity	integridad	intégrité	честность	完整性
intense	intenso, sa	intense	сильный	激烈的
intentional	intencional	intentionnel	преднамеренный	故意的

English	Spanish	French	Russian	Chinese
interminable	interminable	interminable	беконечный	无休止的
intermission	intermisión	entracte	перерыв	间歇
intermittent	intermitente	intermittent	прерывающийся	间歇的
internal	interno, na	interne	внутренний	内在的
interpret	interpretar	interprète	интерпретировать	翻译
interrogate	interrogar	interroger	задавать вопросы	盘问
intervene	intervenir	intervenir	посредничать	干预
intimate	íntimo, ma	intime	сокровенный	亲密的
intimidate	intimidar	intimider	пугать	恐吓
intoxicate	intoxicar	intoxiquer	опьянять	使喝醉
intravenous	intravenoso, sa	intraveineux	внутривенный	静脉内的
intricate	intrincado, da	compliqué	запутанный	错综复杂的
intrinsic	intrínseco, ca	intrinsèque	свойственный	内在的
introvert	introvertido, da	introverti	интроверт	内向的
intuition	intuición	intuition	интуиция	直觉
inundate	inundar	inonder	наводнять	淹没
invalid	inválido	invalide	недействительный	无效的
invert	invertir	renverser	опрокидывать	使反向
investigate	investigar	enquêter	расследовать	调查
invincible	invencible	invincible	непобедимый	不可战胜的
invite	invitar	inviter	приглашать	邀请
involve	envolver	impliquer	содержать	使参与
irate	airado, da	furieux	гневный	愤怒的
irrelevant	irrelevante	sans rapport	несоответствующий	不相干的
irreparable	irreparable	irréparable	непоправимый	不可弥补的
irresistible	irresistible	irrésistible	непреодолимый	不可抗拒的
irrevocable	irrevocable	irrévocable	необратимый	不可逆转的
irritate	irritar	irriter	раздражать	激怒
isolate	aislar	isoler	отделять	使隔离
jail	cárcel	prison	тюрьма	监狱
jailbird	presidiario, ria	prisonnier	рецидивист	囚犯
jailbreak	escape	évasion de prison	побег из тюрьмы	越狱
jealous	celoso, sa	jaloux	завистливый	妒忌
jeopardize	arriesgar	menacer	рисковать	损害
jerk	tirón	tirer avec force	рывок	颠簸
jest	bromear	plaisanter	шутить	笑话
job	trabajo	travail	задание	工作
join	unir	adhérer	соединять	加入
journal	diario	journal	дневник	杂志
journey	viaje	voyage	поездка	旅行
jovial	jovial	jovial	весёлый	愉快的
joy	alegría	joie	радость	欢乐
judge	juzgar	juge	судить	判断
judicious	juicioso, sa	judicieux	здравомыслящий	有见识的
jumble	mezcla	emmêler	смесь	使杂乱
junior	menor	junior	младший	少年
juror	jurado	juré	присяжный заседатель	陪审员
just	justo	juste	справедливый	正义
juvenile	juvenil	juvénile	юный	少年的
keen	aguzado, da	adroit	острый	锐利的
keep	conservar	garder	держать	保留
kidney	riñón	rein	почка	肾赃
kilogram	kilogramo	kilogramme	киллограмм	公斤
kilometer	kilómetro	kilomètre	километр	公里
kin	parentesco	parent	родня	亲属
kindle	encender	allumer	зажигать	点燃
kit	equipo	kit	комплект	成套工具
kleptomaniac	cleptomaníaco, ca	kleptomane	клепотоман	偷窃狂者
knock	golpear	frapper	стучать	敲

18

English	Spanish	French	Russian	Chinese
label	etiqueta	étiquette	этикетка	标签
labor	forcejar	main d'oeuvre	прилагать усилия	劳动
laboratory	laboratorio	laboratoire	лаборатория	实验室
lacerate	lacerado, da	lacérer	рваный	撕裂
lack	carecer	manquer	нуждаться	缺乏
landlord	propietario, ria	propriétaire	владелец недвижимости	房东
languid	lánguido, da	exténué	слабый	没精打采的
lapse	caída	s'écouler	отклонение	失误
large	grande	grand	большой	大的
laryngitis	laringitis	laryngite	ларингит	喉炎
last	último	dernier	последний	最终的
latent	latente	latent	скрытый	潜在的
lateral	lateral	latéral	боковой	横向的
laugh	reír	rire	смеяться	笑
lavish	pródigo, ga	luxueux	щедрый	浪费的
lawyer	abogado,da	avocat	юрист	律师
lax	laxo, xa	insouciant	небрежный	松弛的
lazy	flojo, ja	paresseux	ленивый	懒惰的
lead	dirigir	mener	руководить	领导
learn	aprender	apprendre	усваивать	学习
leave	marchar	quitter	покидать	离开
lecture	instrucción	leçon	лекция	讲演
legal	legal	légal	законный	合法的
legible	legible	lisible	чёткий	字迹清楚的
legitimate	legítimo, ma	justifié	законный	合法的
leisure	comodidad	loisir	досуг	悠闲
lenient	indulgente	facile	кроткий	宽容的
lethal	letal	mortel	летальный	致命的
lethargy	letargia	léthargie	вялость	懒散
leukemia	leucemia	leucémie	лейкоз	白血病
liable	sujeto, ta	responsable	ответственный	有义务的
liberal	liberal	libéral	щедрый	自由的
lien	gravamen	titre	право удержания имущества	留置权
light	liviano, na	léger	лёгкий	光
limp	flojo, ja	boiter	нежесткий	软的
linger	subsistir	traîner	задерживаться	留恋徘徊
literate	literato, ta	lettré	образованный	有文化的
litigation	litigación	procès	судебный процесс	诉讼
liver	hígado	foi	печень	肝脏
load	cargar	charger	нагружать	负荷
locate	localizar	situer	определять	设置在
logical	lógico, ca	logique	логичный	合乎逻辑的
loiter	holgazanear	traîner	мешкать	游荡
loud	ruidoso, sa	bruyant	громкий	响
lucid	lúcido, da	lucide	понятный	明晰的
lucrative	lucrativo, va	lucratif	прибыльный	有利可图的
ludicrous	absurdo, da	risible	смехотворный	荒唐可笑的
luminous	luminoso, sa	lumineux	светящийся	发光的
lunar	lunar	lunaire	лунный	月球的
lung	pulmón	poumon	лёгкое	肺
lure	tentar	attirance	привлекать	诱惑力
luscious	sabroso, sa	délicieux	сочный и сладкий	美味的
lustrous	lustroso, sa	luisant	блестящий	发亮的
luxury	lujo	luxe	роскошь	奢侈
macronutrients	macronutrientes	macroéléments	питательные микроэлементы	大量营养素
mad	loco, ca	fou	сумасшедший	疯的
magnanimous	magnánimo, ma	magnanime	великодушный	宽宏大量的
magnificent	magnífico, ca	magnifique	великолепный	宏伟的
magnify	magrificar	agrandir	увеличенный	放大

English	Spanish	French	Russian	Chinese
magnitude	magnitud	magnitude	величина	巨大
main	fundamental	principal	главный	主要的
maintain	mantener	maintenir	поддерживать	维护
majestic	majestuoso, sa	majestueux	величественный	雄伟的
malady	enfermedad	maladie	болезнь	疾病
malice	malicia	malice	злоба	恶意
malicious	malicioso, sa	malicieux	злобный	恶意的
malignant	maligno, na	maligne	зловредный	恶性的
mammal	mamífero	mammifère	млекопитающее	哺乳动物
mammoth	inmenso, sa	mammouth	громадный	猛犸
mandate	mandar	exiger	поручать	委任
mandatory	obligatorio, ria	obligatoire	обязательный	强制性的
mania	manía	manie	мания	狂热
manipulate	manipular	manipuler	обрабатывать (кого-либо)	操纵
manometer	manómetro	manomètre	манометр	压力表
manslaughter	matar	homicide	совершать убийство	杀人
manual	manual	manuel	с ручным управлением	手工的
masculine	masculino, na	masculin	мужской	男性的
massacre	masacre	massacre	резня	大屠杀
massage	masaje	massage	делать массаж	按摩
maternal	maternal	maternel	материнский	母系的
mathematics	matemáticas	mathématiques	математика	数学
matrimony	matrimonio	matrimonial	супружество	婚姻关系
mature	maduro, ra	mûrir vieillir	зрелый	成熟
maximum	máximo	maximum	максимальный	最大的
meander	meandro	serpenter	изгиб	漫步
mechanic	mecánico, ca	mécanicien	механик	机械的
mediocre	mediocre	médiocre	заурядный	平庸的
meiosis	meiosis	méiose	мейоз	瞳孔缩小
melancholy	melancolía	mélancolie	меланхолия	忧郁
menace	amenaza	menace	угрожать	威胁
merchandise	mercancía	marchandise	товары	货物
merge	juntar	fusionner	сливаться	合并
mesmerizo	hipnotizar	ébahlr	зачаровывать	迷住
message	mensaje	message	сообщение	信息
metamorphosis	metamorfosis	métamorphose	метаморфоза	变形
meteorology	meteorología	métrés	метеорология	气象学
meticulous	meticuloso, sa	méticuleux	педантичный	谨慎的
micronutrient	micronutriente	microélément	микроэлемент	微量营养素
microscope	microscopio	microscope	микроскоп	显微镜
militant	militante	militant	борец	军事的
miniature	miniatura	miniature	миниатюра	漫画
minimum	mínimo, ma	minimum	минимум	最小的
minute	diminuto, ta	minute	мелкий	分钟
miscellaneous	misceláneo, nea	divers	смешанный	各种其它的
mischievous	malévolo, la	espiègle	озорной	淘气的
misery	miseria	misère	горе	悲伤
misfortune	desgracia	infortune	несчастье	不幸
mishap	contratiempo	accident	казус	小灾难
mistake	error	faire erreur	ошибка	错误
mistletoe	muérdago	houx	омела белая	寄生属植物
mistreat	maltratar	maltraiter	плохо обращаться	亏待
mitigate	mitigar	alléger	смягчать	使缓和
mitosis	mitosis	mitose	митоз	有丝分裂
mobile	móvil	mobile	подвижной, ый	移动式的
moderate	moderado, da	modérer	умеренный	温和的
modest	modesto, ta	modeste	застенчивый	谦虚的
modify	modificar	modifier	видоизменять	修改
molecule	molécula	molécule	молекула	分子

English	Spanish	French	Russian	Chinese
monotonous	monótono, na	monotone	монотонный	单调的
monumental	monumental	monumental	колоссальный	纪念性的
moral	ético, ca	moral	(высоко)нравственный	道德的
morale	moral	morale	моральное состояние	士气
morbid	mórbido, da	morbide	ужасный	致病的
more	más	plus	дополнительный	更多的
motivate	motivar	motiver	побуждать	鼓励
motive	motivo	motif	мотив	动机
mourn	lamentar	pleurer	оплакивать	感到遗憾
multiple	múltiple	multiple	многочисленный	多种的
multiply	multiplicar	multiplier	умножать	相乘
murmur	murmurar	murmurer	шептать	小声咕哝
mutual	mutuo, tua	mutuel	взаимный	相互的
nag	sermonear	gronder	изводить	唠叨
naive	ingenuo, nua	naïf	наивный	天真的
naked	desnudo, da	nu	голый	赤裸的
nap	dormitar	sieste	вздремнуть	午睡
narcotics	narcóticos	narcotiques	наркотики	药品
nausea	náusea	nausée	отвращение	恶心
nebulous	nebuloso, sa	nébuleux	неясный	模糊不清的
necessary	necesario, ria	nécessaire	необходимый	必要的
need	necesitar	besoin	нуждаться	需要
negative	negativo, va	négatif	пессимистический	否定的
neglect	descuidar	négliger	не обращать внимания	忽视
negligent	negligente	négligeant	беспечный	疏忽
negotiate	negociar	négocier	вести переговоры	谈判
nervous	nervioso, sa	nerveux	нервный	紧张的
nest	nido	nid	гнездо	鸟巢
neurologist	neurólogo, ga	neurologue	невропатолог	神经病学家
neurosis	neurosis	névrose	невроз	神经机能病
neutral	neutral	neutre	беспристрастный	中性的
niche	nicho	niche	ниша	合适的职务
nocturnal	nocturno, na	nocturne	ночной	夜间的
nod	asentir	hocher la tête	кивать головой	点头
nominal	nominal	nominal	ничтожный	名义上的
nonagon	nonágono, na	ennéagone	девятиугольник	九边形
nonchalant	indolente	nonchalant	беззаботный	冷淡的
normal	normal	normal	нормальный	正常的
nostalgia	nostalgia	nostalgie	ностальгия	怀乡病
notify	notificar	prévenir	уведомлять	通知
notorious	notorio, ria	notoire	пресловутый	臭名昭著的
novice	novato, ta	novice	новичок	新手
noxious	nocivo, va	nocif	вредный	有害的
nuisance	molestia	nuisance	досада	讨厌的东西
nullify	anular	annuler	делать недействительным	使无效
numerous	numeroso, sa	nombreux	многочисленный	无数的
nurse	enfermero, ra	infirmier (ère)	сиделка	护士
nurture	criar	nourrir	воспитывать	抚育
nutritious	nutritivo, va	nourrissant	питательный	有营养的
obey	obedecer	obéir	слушать	服从
objective	objetivo, va	objectif	непредубеждённый	客观的
obligate	obligar	obliger	обязать	强使
oblivious	olvidadizo, za	indifférent	не помнящий	健忘的
oblong	oblongo, ga	oblong	продолговатый	长椭圆形的
obnoxious	ofensivo, va	embêtant	оскорбительный	可憎的
obscene	obsceno, na	obscène	омерзительный	下流的
obscure	obscuro, ra	obscur	невразумительный	费解的
obsequious	obsequioso, sa	soumis	подобострастный	巴结的
observe	observar	observer	замечать	观察

English	Spanish	French	Russian	Chinese
obsess	obsesionar	obséder	завладеть умом	使着迷
obsolete	obsoleto, ta	obsolète	устарелый	过时的
obstacle	obstáculo	obstacle	препятствие	障碍
obstinate	obstinado, da	obstiné	настойчивый	顽固的
obstruct	obstruir	boucher	препятствовать	阻碍
obtain	obtener	obtenir	получать	获得
obvious	obvio, via	évident	явный	明显的
occasionally	ocasionalmente	occasionnellement	изредка	偶尔的
occurred	ocurrido	arrivé	имевший место	已发生的
octagon	octágono, na	octogone	восьмиугольник	八边形
odd	raro	impair	странный	古怪的
odor	olor	odeur	запах	气味
offend	ofender	offenser	оскорблять	得罪
often	frecuentemente	souvent	часто	经常
old	viejo, ja	vieux	старинный	老的
ominous	abominable	désespéré	зловещий	不吉利的
omit	omitir	omettre	не включать	省去
omnipotent	omnipotente	omnipotent	всемогущий	无处不在的
omnivorous	omnívoro, ra	omnivore	всеядный	杂食动物的
onset	principio	début	начало	开端
opaque	opaco	opaque	непрозрачный	不透明的
ophthalmologist	oftalmólogo, ga	ophtalmologiste	офтальмолог	眼科医生
opponent	oponente	adversaire	соперник	对手
oppose	oponerse	se battre contre	противостоять	反对
optimistic	optimista	optimiste	оптимистичный	乐观
optimum	óptimo, ma	optimum	оптимум	最佳效果
optional	opcional	en option	факультативный	随意选择的
oral	oral	oral	устный	口头的
ordeal	odisea	épreuve	тяжёлое испытание	苦难经历
ordinary	ordinario, ria	ordinaire	обычный	普通的
organ	órgano	orgue	орган	器官
organize	organizar	organiser	приводить в порядок	组织
orientation	orientación	orientation	курс	方向
originate	orlglnar	avoir pour origine	брать начало	来源
orthopedics	ortopedia	orthopédie	ортопедия	整形外科
oscillate	oscilar	osciller	качаться	摆动
ostensible	ostensible	ostensiblo	очевидный	表面的
ostentatious	ostentoso, sa	prétentieux	показной	卖弄的
ostracize	desterrar	frapper d'ostracisme	подвергать остракизму	放逐
outcome	resultado	résultat	результат	结果
outrageous	ultrajoso, sa	scandaleux	возмутительный	惊人的
ovary	ovario	ovaire	завязь	卵巢
overt	abiertamente	ouvert	открытый	公开的
overwhelm	agobiar	envahir	преодолевать	制服
owe	deber	devoir	быть обязанным	欠
own	tener	posséder	владеть	拥有
oxygen	oxígeno	oxygène	кислород	氧气
pace	paso	rythme	темп	步子
pacify	pacificar	calmer	умиротворять	使平静
pain	dolor	douleur	боль	疼痛
palpitate	palpitar	palpiter	пульсировать	心跳加快
panacea	panacea	panacée	панацея	灵丹妙药
pandemonium	pandemónium	émoi	смятение	大混乱
panic	pánico	panique	паника	惊恐
panorama	panorama	vue	панорама	全景画
parade	desfile	défilé	процессия	游行
parallel	paralelo, la	parallèle	аналогичный	平行
paralyze	paralizar	paralyser	парализовать	麻痹
paramount	supremo, ma	proéminent	первостепенный	至高无上的

English	Spanish	French	Russian	Chinese
pardon	perdonar	pardonner	прощать	原谅
partial	parcial	intéressé	частичный	偏袒的
particular	particular	particulier	особенный	特别的
passion	pasión	passion	проявлять чувства	激情
passive	pasivo, va	passif	пассивный	消极的
pathetic	patético, ca	pathétique	трогательный	可悲的
patience	paciencia	patience	терпение	耐心
patron	cliente	client	клиент	资助人
pedestrian	caminante	piéton	пешеход	行人
penalize	penalizar	pénaliser	штрафовать	惩罚
penalty	penalidad	pénalité	штраф	处罚
penicillin	penicilina	pénicilline	пенициллин	青霉素
pensive	pensativo, va	pensif	задумчивый	忧虑的
pentagon	pentágono, na	pentagone	пятиугольник	五角大楼
per diem	por día	par jour	за день	每日地
percentage	porcentaje	pourcentage	процентное содержание	百分比
perceptive	perceptivo, va	perceptif	вопринимающий	感觉的
perch	perca	percher	окунь	栖息处
perennials	perenne	permanent	многолетние растения	多年生的植物
permanent	permanente	permanent	постоянный	永久的
pernicious	pernicioso, sa	pernicieux	пагубный	有害的
perpetual	perpetuo, tua	perpétuel	вечный	永久的
perplexed	perplejo, ja	perplexe	недоумевающий	迷惑的
persevere	perseverar	persévérer	упорно продолжать	坚持不懈
persist	persistir	persister	упорствовать	坚持不懈
perspicacious	perspicaz	perspicace	проницательный	敏锐的
persuade	persuadir	persuader	убеждать	说服
pertain	pertenecer	appartenir	иметь отношение	归属
perturb	perturbar	perturber	беспокоить	使烦恼
petite	pequeño, ña	petite	изящная (о женщине)	娇小的
pharmacist	farmacéutico, ca	pharmacien	фармацевт	药学家
phloem	floema	vaisseauxxx	флоэма	韧皮
phobia	fobia	phobie	фобия	恐怖症
photosynthesis	fotosíntesis	photosynthèse	фотосинтез	光合作用
pilfer	hurtar	voler	воровать	小偷小摸
pilot	piloto	pilote	лётчик	飞行员
pious	piadoso, sa	pieux	набожный	虔诚的
pity	lástima	pitié	жалеть	可惜
placid	plácido, da	placide	безмятежный	宁静的
plagiarize	plagiar	copier	заниматься плагиатом	剽窃
plague	plaga	peste	чума	瘟疫
plasma	plasma	plasma	плазма	血浆
plausible	realizable	plausible	правдоподобный	貌似有理的
pleasant	agradable	plaisant	приятный	愉快的
pledge	juramento	promettre	обет	誓言
plentiful	cuantioso, sa	en abondance	обильный	丰富的
plumber	plomero, ra	plombier	водопроводчик	管子工
pneumonia	pulmonía	pneumonie	пневмония	肺炎
podiatrist	podiatra	pédicure	врач-ортопед	足病医生
poignant	conmovedor	poignant	трогательный	辛酸的
poisonous	venenoso, sa	vénéneux	ядовитый	有毒的
policeman	policía	policier	полицейский	警官
polite	educado, da	poli	вежливый	礼貌的
pompous	pomposo, sa	pompeux	напыщенный	自负的
ponder	reflexionar	réfléchir	размышлять	考虑
positive	positivo, va	positif	определённый	正面的
possess	poseer	posséder	владеть	拥有
possible	posible	possible	возможный	有可能的
postman	cartero	facteur	почтальон	邮递员

English	Spanish	French	Russian	Chinese
postpone	posponer	remettre	откладывать	推迟
posture	postura	posture	поза	姿态
potent	potente	fort	сильный	强有力的
potpourri	popurrí	pot-pourri	сухие духи	杂烩
practice	practicar	entraînement	тренироваться	实践
prank	broma	farce	выходка	恶作剧
precedent	precedente	antécédent	прецедент	先例
precious	preciado, da	précieux	дорогой	宝贵的
preclude	evitar	exclure d'emblée	предотвращать	排除
predict	predecir	prédire	предсказывать	预测
predominant	predominante	prédominant	преобладающий	占主导地位的
prefer	preferir	préférer	предпочитать	更喜爱
prejudice	prejuicio	préjudice	предубеждать	偏见
prelude	preludio	prélude	вступление	前奏
premature	prematuro, ra	prématuré	преждевременный	早熟的
preposterous	descabellado, da	absurde	нелепый	荒谬的
prerequisite	requisito	préalable	требуемый	先决条件
preserve	preservar	conserver	сохранять	保护
pretend	aparentar	simuler	притворяться	假装
prevail	prevalecer	prévaloir	преобладать	流行
prevalent	reinante	dominant	широко распространённый	流行的
prevent	prevenir	empêcher	предотвращать	防止
previous	previo, via	précédent	предыдущий	以前的
priest	sacerdote	prêtre	священник	神父
principal	principal	principal	глава	校长
probation	prueba	épreuve	испытательный срок	试用期
procedure	proceso	procédure	процедура	程序
procrastinate	procrastinar	différer	медлить	推出
profanity	profanidad	juron	богохульство	下流行为
proficient	proficiente	capable	умелый	效率高的
profit	ganancia	profit	извлекать пользу	利润
profound	profundo, da	profond	глубокии	深刻的
prognosis	prognosis	pronostique	прогноз	预测
prohibit	prohlblr	interdire	мешать	禁止
prolong	prolongar	prolonger	продлевать	延长
prominent	prominente	proéminent	известный	著名的
promiscuous	promiscuo, cua	dévergondé	беспорядочный	杂乱的
prompt	expedito, ta	inciter	исполнительный	迅速的
prone	inclinado, da	enclin	склонный	有某种倾向的
proponent	proponedor, ra	présentateur	лицо, вносящее предложение	支持者
proposal	proposición	proposition	предложение	提议
prosperous	próspero, ra	prospère	успешный	繁荣的
protest	protestar	protester	протестовать	抗议
proud	orgulloso, sa	fier	горделивый	自豪的
proverb	proverbio	proverbe	пословица	谚语
provocative	provocativo, va	provocant	раздражающий	挑衅性的
provoke	provocar	provoquer	раздражать	挑衅
prowess	proeza	prouesse	отвага	勇猛
prudent	prudente	prudent	осторожный	谨慎的
pseudopodia	pseudopodia	prothèse	псевдоподия	假足
psychic	psíquico, ca	voyant	экстрасенс	精神的
psychology	psicología	psychologie	психология	心理学
punctual	puntual	ponctuel	пунктуальный	准时的
punish	castigar	punir	наказывать	惩罚
pupil	pupila	élève	зрачок	学生
purchase	comprar	acheter	покупать	购买
purpose	propósito	objet	намереваться	目的
purposeful	intensionado, da	utile	преднамеренный	有目的的
pursue	perseguir	poursuivre	преследовать	追求

English	Spanish	French	Russian	Chinese
puzzle	confundir	intriguer	озадачивать	难题
quadrangle	cuadrángulo, la	quadrangle	четырёхугольник	四方院
quadruple	cuádruple	quadruple	четырёхкратный	四倍的
quagmire	atolladero	fondrière	затруднительное положение	沼泽地
qualm	duda	doute	сомнение	担忧
quandary	incertidumbre	embarras	недоумение	困境
quantity	cantidad	quantité	количество	数量
quarrelsome	peleón, na	querelleur	сварливый	爱争吵的
queer	extraño	étrange	странный	古怪的
quell	tranquilizar	réprimer	успокаивать	压制
query	interrogar	question	спрашивать	查询
question	preguntar	question	спрашивать	问题
questionable	cuestionable	douteux	сомнительный	有问题的
quick	pronto	rapide	быстрый	迅速的
quiet	callado, da	calme	тихий	平静的
quirk	desviación	tique	каламбур	怪僻
quit	dejar	quitter	прекращать	放弃
quite	completamente	assez	действительно	非常
quiver	temblar	trembler	дрожать	颤抖
quiz	examen	test	контрольный опрос в классе	测验
quota	proporción	quota	доля	配额
radiant	radiante	rayonnant	сияющий	灿烂的
radius	radio	rayon	радиус	半径
rage	rabia	rage	быть в гневе	狂怒
rancor	rencor	rancoeur	озлобление	积冤
rank	posición	rang	должность	队伍
rapacious	rapaz	rapace	захватнический	贪婪的
rapid	rápido	rapide	быстрый	迅速的
ratify	ratificar	ratifier	утверждать	批准
rational	racional	rationnel	рациональный	合理的
ravage	destrucción	ravage	портить	毁坏
ready	listo	prêt	подготовленный	准备好的
real	real	réel	действительный	真实的
rebuke	reprochar	rejeter	укорять	指责
recall	rememorar	rappeler	вспоминать	回忆
recede	retroceder	se retirer	отступать	后退
receive	recibir	recevoir	получать	接受
recess	vacación	retrait	перерыв в работе	休息
recession	recesión	récession	спад	衰退
recipe	receta	recette	рецепт	食谱
reciprocate	corresponder	revaloir	отплачивать	相互作用
recite	recitar	réciter	декламировать	背诵
reckless	descuidado, da	imprudent	беспечный	毫无顾虑
recognize	reconocer	reconnaître	опознавать	承认
recollect	acordarse	se rappeler	вспоминать	回顾
recommend	recomendar	recommander	рекомендовать	推荐
reconciliation	reconciliación	réconciliation	примирение	和好
record	registrar	enregistrer	регистрировать	记录
recover	reponer	récupérer	получать обратно	收复
recruit	recluta	recruter	новичок	招工
rectify	rectificar	rectifier	исправлять	改正
recur	recurrir	se reproduire	повторяться	重新发生
reduce	reducir	réduire	уменьшать	减少
redundant	redundante	superflu	многословный	多余的
refrain	refrenar	se retenir	воздерживаться	忍住
refuge	refugio	refuge	убежище	避难
refund	restitución	rembourser	возмещение	退款
refuse	rehusar	refuser	отвергать	废物
refute	refutar	réfuter	опровергать	驳斥

English	Spanish	French	Russian	Chinese
register	inscribir	enregistrer	записаться	登记
registrar	registrador, ra	greffier	секретарь учебного заведения	登记员
regret	arrepentimiento	regret	сожаление	后悔
regular	regular	régulier	обычный	普通的
regulate	regular (verbo)	réglementer	регулировать	调整
rehearse	ensayar	répéter	репетировать	排练
reinforce	reforzar	renforcer	усиливать	加强
reject	rechazar	rejeter	отвергать	拒绝
relapse	recaer	rechuter	браться за старое	回复
relax	relajar	détendu	отдыхать	放松
release	soltar	lâcher	освобождать	释放
relentless	implacable	sans répit	упорный	毫不留情
relevant	relevante	lié	уместный	有关的
reliable	confiable	fiable	надёжный	可靠的
relinquish	ceder	renoncer	оставлять	放弃
relish	disfrutar	déguster	получать удовольствие	品味
reluctant	renuente	réticent	делающий с неохотой	犹豫的
rely	atenerse	compter	полагаться	依靠
remain	permanecer	rester	оставаться	保持
remarkable	notable	remarquable	замечательный	出色的
remedial	remediador, ra	curatif	исправительный	弥补的
remedy	remedio	remède	лекарство	医治
remember	recordar	se souvenir	вспоминать	记住
remorse	remordimiento	remords	раскаяние	后悔
remote	remoto, ta	éloigné	отдалённый	遥远的
removed	apartado, da	retiré	смещённый с должности	远离的
render	rendir	interpréter	отдавать	给予
rent	renta	loyer	арендная плата	出租
repair	reparar	réparer	ремонтировать	修理
repeat	repetir	répéter	повторять	重复
replenish	rellenar	remplir	пополнять	补充
replete	repleto, ta	plein	наполненный	充满的
replicate	réplicar	copier	копировать	复制
reply	contestar	répondre	отвечать	回答
reprehend	reprender	réprimander	критиковать	理解
representative	representante	représentant	представитель	代表
reprimand	regañar	réprimander	делать выговор	指责
roptile	reptil	reptile	рептилия	爬行动物
repudiate	repudiar	répudier	отвергать	驳斥
repugnant	repugnante	répugnant	отвратительный	令人厌恶的
reputation	reputación	réputation	репутация	声誉
request	pedir	requête	просить	请求
require	requerir	demander	требовать	请求
rescue	rescatar	sauver	спасать	抢救
research	explorar	recherche	исследовать	研究
resentment	resentimiento	ressentiment	возмущение	怨恨
reserve	reservar	réserve	бронировать	保留
reside	residir	résider	проживать	居住
resign	renunciar	démissionner	слагать с себя обязанности	辞职
resilient	elástico, ca	flexible	упругий	有弹性的
resist	resistir	résister	сопротивляться	抵抗
resourceful	ingenioso, sa	habile	находчивый	资源充足的
respond	responder	répondre	отвечать	回答
responsible	responsable	responsable	надёжный	负责任的
restrain	limitar	se limiter	сдерживать	抑制
restrict	restringir	restreindre	ограничивать	限制
resume	reasumir	reprendre	возобновлять	继续
retain	retener	retenir	удержвить	保留
retaliate	desquitarse	se venger	отплачивать тем же	报复

English	Spanish	French	Russian	Chinese
reticent	reticente	réticent	молчаливый	沉默的
retreat	retirar	se retrancher	отходить	后退
retrospect	retrospección	rétrospective	обращение к прошлому	回顾
reveal	revelar	révéler	обнаруживать	暴露
revert	revertir	recours	возвращаться	回返
revise	revisar	revoir	проверять	修改
revoke	derogar	révoquer	отменять	吊销
rhizomes	rizomas	rhizomes	ризома	根茎
ridiculous	ridículo, la	ridicule	нелепый	可笑的
rigid	rígido, da	rigide	жёсткий	僵硬的
rigorous	riguroso, sa	rigoureux	строгий	严格的
rough	tosco, ca	rugueux	неровный	毛糙的
rupture	ruptura	rupture	разрыв	破裂
rural	rural	rural	сельский	乡村的
sabotage	sabotaje	sabotage	саботаж	破坏
salient	saliente	saillant	выдающийся	特征的
salute	saludar	salut	приветствовать	敬礼
sane	sano, na	sain	разумный	清醒的
sarcastic	sarcástico, ca	sarcastique	саркастический	讽刺的
satisfy	satisfacer	satisfaire	удовлетворять	满足
saturate	saturar	saturer	наполнять	饱和
scandal	escándalo	scandale	позорный факт	丑闻
scatter	esparcir	éparpiller	разбрасывать	分散
scrupulous	escrupuloso, sa	scrupuleux	скрупулёзный	有顾忌的
scrutinize	escudriñar	scruter	внимательно рассматривать	仔细打量
scurrilous	grosero, ra	grossier	непристойный	恶言诽谤的
seal	sellar	cachet	плотно закрывать	印记
sedative	sedativo, va	sédatif	успокаивающее средство	镇静剂
seduce	seducir	séduire	соблазнять	引诱
seldom	raramente	rarement	редко	难得
select	seleccionar	choisir	отбирать	选择
sensible	sensible	sensé	разумный	敏感的
sensuous	sensitivo, va	sensuel	чувственный	敏感的
sentimental	sentimental	sentimental	сентиментальный	多愁的
separate	separar	séparé	отделять	分离
serene	sereno, na	serein	тихий	宁静的
serious	serio, ria	sérieux	важный	认真的
serum	suero	sérum	сыворотка (крови)	血清
severe	severo, ra	sévère	серьёзный	严重的
shortage	escasez	déficit	нехватка	短缺
shrewd	sagaz	rusé	проницательный	狡猾的
significant	significante	significatif	важный	重大的
sinister	siniestro, tra	sinistre	зловещий	恶毒的
site	sitio	site	местоположение	场地
skeptic	escéptico, ca	sceptique	скептик	怀疑的
smile	sonreír	sourire	улыбаться	微笑
sociology	sociología	sociologie	социология	社会学
solace	solaz	soulagement	утешать	安慰
solar	solar	solaire	солнечный	太阳的
solitude	solitud	solitude	уединение	孤单
spacious	espacioso, sa	spacieux	просторный	宽敞的
spank	zurrar	fesser	шлёпать	拍打
speculate	especular	spéculer	строить предположения	思考
speedometer	velocímetro	tachymètre	спидометр	计程表
spendthrift	malgastador, ra	dépensier	расточительный	挥霍者
sphygmomanometer	esfigmomanómetro	tensiomètre	сфигмоманометр	脉搏计
spirogyra	espirogira	spyrogirus	спирогира	水绵
spontaneous	espontáneo, nea	spontané	спонтанный	自觉的
sporadic	esporádico, ca	sporadique	случайный	零星的

English	Spanish	French	Russian	Chinese
squander	derrochar	gaspiller	растрачивать	挥霍
square	cuadro	carré	квадрат	方的
standstill	detención	arrêt	остановка	停滞
stationary	estacionario	stationnaire	стационарный	静止的
stationery	papelería	papier à entête	канцелярские принадлежности	文具
steal	robar	voler	воровать	偷
stereotype	estereotipo	stéréotype	стереотип	老生常谈
sterilize	esterilizar	stériliser	стерилизовать	消毒
stethoscope	estetoscopio	stéthoscope	стетоскоп	听诊器
stimulate	estimular	stimuler	стимулировать	刺激
stingy	tacaño, ña	frugal	скудный	小气的
stomach	estómago	estomac	желудок	胃
strenuous	esforzado, da	éprouvant	напряжённый	坚苦的
stress	tensión	stress	стресс	压力
stroke	infarto	hémorragie cérébrale	паралич	打击
stubborn	necio, cia	têtu	упрямый	顽固的
sturdy	fuerte	solide	сильный	稳固的
subjective	subjetivo, va	subjectif	субъективный	主观的
subjugate	subyugar	subjuguer	покорять	征服
submit	someter	soumettre	представлять на рассмотрение	呈交
subsequent	subsecuente	suivant	последующий	后来的
subservient	subordinado, da	soumis	подчинённый	屈从的
subside	hundirse	retirer	падать	平息
subsidy	subsidio	subvention	субсидия	补贴
substitute	substituir	de remplacement de	заменять	代替
subtle	sutil	subtile	едва различимый	微妙的
successful	exitoso, sa	prospère	успешный	成功的
succinct	sucinto, ta	succinct	краткий	简明的
succulent	suculento, ta	succulent	сочный	多汁的
succumb	sucumbir	succomber	уступить	屈服
sufficient	suficiente	suffisant	достаточный	充足的
suitable	adecuado, da	adapté	подходящий	合适的
sullen	deprimente	morose	угрюмый	沉闷的
summarize	resumir	résumer	резюмировать	总结
summon	convocar	convoquer	вызывать	召唤
sumptuous	suntuoso, sa	somptueux	дорогостоящий	豪华的
superb	espléndido, da	superbe	великолепный	出类拔萃的
supercilious	soberbio, bia	hautain	высокомерный	第一流的
superficial	superficial	superficiel	поверхностный	肤浅的
superfluous	superfluo, flua	superflus	излишний	过剩的
superior	superior	supérieur	высший	优越的
superstition	superstición	superstition	суеверие	迷信
supplement	suplemento	supplément	дополнение	增补
surpass	sobrepasar	surpasser	превосходить	超过
surplus	demasía	surplus	излишек	剩余
surrender	rendirse	se rendre	сдаваться	投降
surreptitious	subrepticio, cia	clandestin	тайный	鬼鬼祟祟的
susceptible	susceptible	susceptible	чувствительный	过于敏感的
suspend	suspender	suspendre	приостанавливать	停止
suspension	suspensión	suspension	приостановка	中止
suspicious	sospechoso	suspect	подозрительный	怀疑的
sustain	sostener	soutenir	поддерживать	承受
symbiosis	simbiosis	symbiose	симбиоз	共生现象
symbolize	simbolizar	symboliser	символизировать	象征
synchronize	sincronizar	synchroniser	синхронизировать	同步
synthesize	sintetizar	synthétiser	синтезировать	合成
tailor	sastre	tailleur	портной	裁缝
talent	talento	talent	талант	才能
tangible	tangible	tangible	ощутимый	显著的

English	Spanish	French	Russian	Chinese
tantalize	provocar	tourmenter	мучить	诱惑
tantrum	berrinche	accès de colère	вспышка раздражения	发脾气
task	faena	tâche	задание	任务
taste	gusto	goût	вкус	味道
teacher	maestro, tra	enseignant	учитель	教师
tear	desgarrar	déchirer	разрывать	撕
tedious	tedioso, sa	ennuyeux	скучный	乏味的
telescope	telescopio	télescope	телескоп	望远镜
tell	notificar	raconter	говорить	告诉
temperamental	temperamental	capricieux	темпераментный	气质的
temporary	temporal	provisoire	временный	临时的
tenacious	tenaz	tenace	упорный	顽强的
tenant	inquilino, na	locataire	арендатор	房客
tense	tenso, sa	tendu	напряжённый	紧张
tentative	tentativo, va	tentative	временный	试探性的
tenuous	tenue	mince	скудный	任期的
terminal	terminal	terminal	смертельный	终端
terminate	terminar	achever	заканчивать	中止
therapeutic	terapéutico, ca	thérapeutique	терапевтический	治疗性的
thermometer	termómetro	thermomètre	термометр	晴雨表
thermostat	termostato	thermostat	термостат	调温计
thorough	completo, ta	complet	тщательный	彻底的
threaten	amenazar	menacer	угрожать	威胁
thrive	prosperar	prospérer	процветать	旺盛
timid	tímido, da	timide	застенчивый	胆小的
tolerate	tolerar	tolérer	терпеть	容忍
ton	tonelada	ton	тонна	吨
topic	tema	sujet	тема	题目
toxic	tóxico, ca	toxique	ядовитый	有毒的
traditional	tradicional	traditionnel	традиционный	传统的
tragic	trágico, ca	tragique	трагический	悲剧的
trait	cualidad	trait	характерная черта	踪迹
tranquil	tranquilo, la	tranquille	спокойный	安宁的
transfer	transferir	transférer	переносить	转移
transform	transformar	transformer	преобразовывать	改造
transgress	transgredir	transgresser	нарушать границы	违反
transient	transitorio	de passage	преходящий	短暂的
translucent	translúcido, da	translucide	просвечивающий	半透明的
transparent	transparente	transparent	прозрачный	透明的
transpire	transpirar	fuir	случаться	发生
trauma	trauma	traumatisme	травма	创伤
treacherous	traicionero, ra	dangereux	вероломный	奸诈的
treason	traición	trahison	государственная измена	叛国
tremendous	tremendo, da	grand	огромный	巨大的
tremor	tremor	secousse	дрожь	震动
trepidation	trepidación	trépidation	беспокойство	惊恐
trespass	traspasar	violer	переходить границы чего-либо	侵犯
triangle	triángulo	triangle	треугольник	三角形
triumph	triunfo	triomphe	триумф	胜利
trivial	trivial	insignifiant	незначительный	微小的
trophy	trofeo	trophée	приз	纪念品
trouble	turbar	trouble	тревожить	麻烦
tumult	tumulto	tumulte	шум	骚动
turbulent	turbulento, ta	turbulent	бурный	混乱的
turmoil	alboroto	émoi	смятение	动乱
ubiquitous	ubicuo, cua	omniprésent	вездесущий	无所不在的
ulcer	úlcera	ulcère	язва	溃疡
ultimate	último, ma	ultime	окончательный	最终的
unable	inhábil	incapable	неспособный	无能力的

English	Spanish	French	Russian	Chinese
unanimous	unánime	unanime	единодушный	一致的
unbelievable	sorprendente	incroyable	невероятный	不可相信的
uncanny	misterioso, sa	étrange	жуткий	奇怪的
uncertain	incierto, ta	incertain	сомнительный	不确定的
uncomfortable	incómodo, da	inconfortable	неудбный	不舒服的
unconscious	inconsciente	inconscient	бессознательный	失去知觉的
under	debajo	sous	ниже	在下面
undercover	secreto, ta	privé	тайный	秘密的
undermine	desmejorar	miner	подтачивать	破坏
underrate	menospreciar	sous-estimer	недооценивать	过低评价
understand	entender	comprendre	понимать	懂得
unfair	injusto, ta	injuste	несправедливый	不公平
unfit	incapaz	impropre	неподходящий	不合适
unforgettable	inolvidable	inoubliable	незабываемый	不可忘却的
unique	singular	unique	уникальный	与众不同的
universal	universal	universel	универсальный	普遍的
university	universidad	université	университет	大学
unreal	imaginario, ria	irréel	нереальный	不真实的
unrest	inquietud	remous	беспокойство	动乱
unscrupulous	inescrupuloso, sa	sans scrupules	беспринципный	毫无顾忌的
unskilled	inexperto, ta	inexpérimenté	неквалифицированный	不熟练的
unstable	inestable	instable	непостоянный	不稳固的
untidy	desordenado, da	désordonné	неопрятный	不整洁的
uproar	perturbación	émoi	шум	骚乱
urban	urbano, na	urbain	городской	城市的
urge	instar	presser	побуждать	催促
urgent	urgente	urgent	срочный	紧急的
urologist	urólogo, ga	urologue	уролог	泌尿科医师
usual	usual	usuel	обычный	通常的
utilize	utilizar	utiliser	использовать	利用
vacant	vacante	vacant	не занятый	空着的
vacation	vacaciones	vacance	отдых	假期
vacillate	vacilar	vaciller	качаться	动摇
vague	vago, ga	vague	смутный	含胡的
valiant	valiente	vaillant	храбрый	勇敢的
valid	válido, da	valable	действительный	有效的
validate	validar	valider	признавать действительным	确证
vanish	desaparecer	s'évanouir	исчезать	消失
variety	variedad	variété	разнообразие	多样化
various	varios	divers	всевозможный	各种各样
vary	variar	varier	менять	不同
vast	vasto, ta	vaste	обширный	广阔的
vehement	vehemente	véhément	сильный	热烈的
velocity	velocidad	vélocité	скорость	速度
vengeance	venganza	vengeance	возмездие	报复
vent	ventosa	évent	отверстие	通风口
verbal	verbal	verbal	словесный	文字上的
verdict	veredicto	verdict	решение	判决
verify	verificar	vérifier	проверять	证明
versatile	versátil	versatile	универсальный	多才多艺的
vertical	vertical	vertical	вертикальный	垂直的
veto	veto	veto	вето	否决
viable	viable	viable	жизнеспособный	可望成功的
vicarious	vicario, ria	par délégation	замещающий	取代的
vicinity	vecindad	voisinage	соседство	临近地区
vicious	vicioso, sa	vicieux	злой	恶毒的
victim	víctima	victime	жертва	受害者
vigilant	vigilante	vigilant	бдительный	警戒的
vigorous	vigoroso, sa	vigoureux	энергичный	精力充沛的

English	Spanish	French	Russian	Chinese
vile	vil	vil	мерзкий	卑鄙
vindicate	vindicar	venger	реабилитировать	证明正确
vindictive	vindicativo, va	vindicatif	мстительный	证明正确的
virtue	virtud	vertu	добродетель	美德
virus	virus	virus	вирус	病毒
visible	visible	visible	видимый	看得见的
vital	vital	vital	жизненный	致命的
vivacious	vivaz	vivace	живой	活泼的
vivid	vívido, da	vivide	яркий	生动的
vociferous	vocinglero, ra	bruyant	громкий	喧嚷的
void	vacío, ía	nul	пустой	空白
voluntary	voluntario, ria	volontaire	добровольный	自愿的
voracious	voraz	vorace	прожорливый	贪婪的
vulgar	vulgar	vulgaire	вульгарный	庸俗
vulnerable	vulnerable	vulnérable	уязвимый	虚弱的
wander	vagar	s'égarer	бродить	漫游
warn	advertir	prévenir	предостерегать	警告
warp	deformar	se déformer se	коробиться	使弯曲
wash	lavar	laver	мыть	洗涤
week	semana	semaine	неделя	星期
weep	sollozar	pleurer	плакать	哭泣
weird	insólito, ta	bizarre	таинственный	怪诞的
welcome	acoger	bienvenue	радушно принимать	欢迎
whine	gemir	pleumicher	плакаться	发哀叫声
whisper	susurrar	chuchoter	шептать	耳语
withdraw	aislarse	retirer	отводить	撤退
wrinkle	arruga	froisser	морщина	皱纹
xylem	xilema	xylème	ксилема	木质部
yard	yarda	cour	ярд	码
yearn	anhelar	soupirer	тосковать	渴望
yell	gritar	crier	кричать	叫喊
yield	devolver	céder	приносить доход	出产
youth	joven	jeunesse	юноша	青年
zeal	entusiasmo	zèle	рвение	热情
zest	deleite	zeste	страстность	兴趣
zoology	zoología	zoologie	зоология	动物学

Dictionary of Words

Study the partial meanings of the following words before you work the exercises. Note that the meanings selected were based on the context in which the words were used in this book.

Word	Meaning	Word	Meaning
abandon	vacant	advocate	supporter
abbreviate	shorten	aesthetic	exquisite taste
abduct	seize	affection	love
abhor	hate	affiliated	associated
abnormal	strange	affirm	confirm
abolish	cancel	affluence	wealth
abrupt	sudden	aggrandize	make greater or powerful
absent	away	aggravate	irritate
absent-minded	forgetful	aggressive	pushy
abstain	refrain	agile	fast
abstract	theoretical	agitate	disturb
absurd	foolish	ailment	disease
abundant	plentiful	alias	nickname
abuse	violate	alien	foreign
accelerate	speed-up	allegiance	support; loyalty
accept	approve	alleviate	lessen; relieve
access	entry	allude	indirect reference
accident	misfortune or disaster	aloof	distant
acclaim	praise; honor	alternative	option
accommodate	adjust	altruistic	generous
accompany	to go with	ambiguous	vague; unclear
accuse	blame	ambivalent	doubtful, conflicting feeling
achieve	accomplish	ample	plenty
acknowledge	admit	analyze	examine
acquaint	familiarize	animosity	hatred
acquire	gain	annihilate	wipe-out or destroy completely
acrimonious	bitter in speech and manner	annual	yearly
acute	sharp or severe	anonymous	unidentified
adamant	inflexible	antagonize	provoke
adept	skillful	anticipate	expect
adequate	enough	antihistamine	synthetic drug
adhere	cling	apathy	lack of emotion, feeling or interest
adjust	regulate		
admit	consent	apparent	clear
admonish	warn	appease	calm
adopt	to choose and follow something	applaud	praise; cheer
adroit	cleverly skillful	appoint	designate
adversary	enemy	appreciate	like
adverse	unfavorable	apprehensive	fearful
		apprentice	a learner or beginner

Word	Meaning	Word	Meaning
appropriate	suitable	better	superior
arbitrary	left to one's judgment or choice	bewilder	puzzle
arbitrator	one who judges a dispute	bias	prejudice
aristocrat	upper-class	bigot	intolerant of a race that is not his/her own
arrogant	haughty		
arsonist	malicious burning of property by someone	bilingual	capable of using two languages
		bitter	distasteful
articulate	well-spoken	blame	fault
ascertain	solve	blatant	conspicuous; obvious
askew	to one side	blemish	spot or stain
aspire	desire	boast	show off
assertive	bossy	boisterous	noisy
assiduous	showing care and effort	boredom	repetition
assist	help	borrow	take
assume	accept	boss	supervisor
assurance	guarantee	bother	disturb
astonish	amaze	boundary	border
astute	smart; clever	bourgeois	middle-class
attain	obtain; accomplish	boycott	ban
attest	verify	brave	courageous
attrition	decrease	brawl	fight
audible	clear	brevity	concise
audit	examination of financial records for correctness	brief	short
		bright	shining
auspicious	favorable	brilliant	bright
austere	harsh	brisk	vigorous
authenticate	verify as represented	browse	skim
available	ready	brutal	cruel
awkward	clumsy	budget	amount of money needed for specific use
bad	evil		
baffle	puzzle	bundle	package
balance	stability	buoyant	floating
ban	disallow	burden	hardship
bankrupt	deplete	bursar	office where you can pay fees in college
barren	infertile		
barrier	obstacle	burst	broken
belated	late	buy	purchase
belief	trust	cab	taxi
belligerent	ready to fight or quarrel	calamity	disaster
benefactor	supporter	calculate	figure
beneficial	helpful	callous	insensitive
beneficiary	inheritor	calm	quiet
benevolent	kind	camouflage	disguise
benign	harmless	cancel	terminate
bereft	deprive of	candid	frank
betray	trick	candidate	applicant
		cantankerous	quarrelsome

Word	Meaning	Word	Meaning
capability	ability	cold	frigid
capacitate	fit; to prepare	collaborate	cooperate
capacity	capability	collapsed	fell
capitulate	to give up or surrender	collide	crash
capricious	changeable	combine	mix
capsize	overturn	comedian	joker; jester
capture	arrest	comfort	support; console
care	protection	comfortable	relaxed
career	a profession or occupation	commitment	promise
caress	fondle	commotion	disturbance
casual	not planned	compare	match
catalyst	speeds up reaction	comparison	likeness
catastrophe	tragedy	compassion	sympathy
categorize	arrange	compatible	work well together
cause	reason	compel	force
caution	care; advise	compensate	pay
cease	stop	competent	efficient
celebrate	observe; honor	complacent	self-satisfied
censure	criticize	complain	protest
challenge	confront	complement	something added to complete a whole
chance	risk		
change	convert	complex	complicated
chaos	confusion	complicate	confuse
charisma	charm	compliment	praise
charismatic	appealing; leadership quality	comply	follow
charm	please	component	segment
chastise	punish	compose	create
cheap	inexpensive	comprehensive	extensive
cheat	rob	compulsory	necessary
check	verify	concede	admit
cherish	treasure	conceited	self-important
chief	primary	concept	an idea or thought
chilly	cool	conciliate	make friendly
chore	task	concise	brief
chubby	stocky	conclude	end
circumvent	avoid	concoct	create
cite	indicate	concur	agree
clandestine	done secretly	concurrent	agreeing
clarify	explain	condemn	disapprove of strongly; criticize
classify	categorize	condescend	beneath one's dignity
claustrophobia	abnormal fear of being in an enclosed area	condone	disregard; to forgive
		confess	admit
clean	pure	confide	trust
coach	instruct; teach	confidence	certainty
coerce	force	confirm	verify
cognizant	fully aware	confiscate	seize
coherent	consistent	conform	agree
cohesive	connect	confront	challenge
coincide	correspond	congenial	pleasant

Word	Meaning	Word	Meaning
conscious	awake	debilitate	weaken
consecutive	continuous	decagon	ten-sided figure
consensus	understanding	decease	die
consequence	result	deceive	betray
conservative	traditional	decipher	interpret; find the meaning of
considerable	sizable	decision	conclusion
consistent	steady	decrease	lessen
conspicuous ✓	easily seen or noticed	dedicate	devote
conspire	act together secretly	deduct	subtract;discount
constant	steady	defeat	overcome
consternation	great fear that makes one feel helpless	defendant	an accused person
		deficient	inadequate
constituent	component	deficit	shortage
constitute	comprise	definite	certain
constrain	force or compel	defraud	cheat
constrict	reduce	defy	disobey; oppose
contemplate	meditate	degenerate	deteriorate
contemporary	modern	deliberate ✓	intentional
contemptible	worthless; despicable	delicate	weak
content	satisfied	delicious	appetizing
contingency	emergency	deliver	handover
contradict	dispute	demand	command
controversy	conflict; opinions clash	demolish	destroy
convenient	suitable	demonstrate	explain
conventional	customary	denounce	condemn
converse	chat	depart	leave
convert	change	deplete	drain
convey	transmit	deplore	condemn
convince	persuade or encourage	deposit	store
cop	police	depreciate	reduce in value or price
copious	plentiful	deprive	withhold; rob
corroborate	give support	derelict	bum
counterfeit	fake	derive	gain
courteous	polite	derogatory	negative
covert	secret	describe	explain
credible	believable	designate	appoint
crinkle	crease	desist	stop
cripple	paralyze	despair ✓	hopelessness
crisis	emergency	desperate	urgent
criteria	measure	despondent	discouraged
cry	sob	destination	end
cumbersome	difficult to handle or deal with	destroy	ruin
curtail	shorten	detain	delay
damage	destroy	detect	notice
dangle	hang swinging loosely	deter ✓	discourage
darkness	absence of light	deteriorate	decay
data	facts	determine	calculate
dean	administrative officer in a college or school	detest ✓	hate
		detract	distract
debate	argument	detrimental	harmful

Word	Meaning	Word	Meaning
devastate	destroy	donor	supporter
deviate	depart from	dormancy	inactivity
devise	formulate	draft	sketch
dexterous	clever; skillful with hands	drastic	severe; extreme
different	unlike	drip	fall
difficult	hard	dubious	undecided; uncertainty
digress	stray	dwindle	lessen
dilapidate	decay	dynamic	powerful; spirited
dilemma	disagreement	eager	anxious
diligent	hard working	earn	obtain
dilute	weaken	easy	simple
diminish	decrease	eccentric	odd person
diplomacy	tact	economical	thrifty; frugal
dirty	unclean	ecstasy	joy
disagree	differ in opinion	egocentric	self-centered
disappear	vanish	eject	expel
discard	reject	elaborate	detail
discipline	punish	elated	happy
discount	reduction	elder	older
discreet	careful	elective	optional; not required
discriminate	separate	elicit	evoke
disenchanted	disillusioned	eligible	suitable
disengage	set loose	eliminate	remove; omit
disgrace	shame	elite	most distinguished or powerful
disillusion	disappointment	eloquent	express persuasively
dislocate	disconnect	embarrass	disgrace
disloyal	untrue	embezzle	steal
dismantle	to take apart	emerge	appear
disparity	dissimilarity	eminent	famous
disperse	scatter	emit	discharge
dispose	get rid of	emotional	excitable
dispute	argue	empathy	sharing another person's feeling
disreputable	having a bad reputation	emphasize	stress
dissatisfied	unhappy	employ	hire
dissent	differ in opinion or belief	empower	give power to
dissident	rebel	encounter	face
dissipate	disperse	encourage	support
dissuade	advise against	endeavor	attempt
distinct	clear	endorse	sponsor
distinction	excellence	endow	bestow
distinguish	to tell apart	endure	undergo
distress	trouble	enemy	foe
disturb	irritate	enhance	improve or strengthen
diurnal	happening in the day time	enigmatic	baffling person
diverge	stray	enlarge	increase
diversity	variety	enlighten	educate; inform
docile	obedient	enmity	hatred
domain	territory	enormous	large
dominate	control	enough	sufficient
donate	give	entertain	amuse

Word	Meaning	Word	Meaning
entire	complete	facade	pretense
envy	jealousy	facetious	funny; frivolously amusing
equate	equal	facilitate	assist
equip	provide	fade	pale
equivocal	vague	fail	unsuccessful
eradicate	eliminate	faith	hope
erase	delete	fake	false
errand	task	fallacy	false idea or opinion
erratic	uncertain; irregular	fallible	imperfect
erupt	explode	false	not true
escalate	increase	falter	waver
espionage	spying	fame	renown
essay	a composition	familiar	well-known
establish	organize	famine	starvation
esteem	respect	famish	hunger
estrange	separate	famous	well-known
eternal	forever	fantastic	unusual
evacuate	leave	fantasy	dream
evasive	dishonest	farewell	leaving
evident	clear	fascinate	interest
exacerbate	to aggravate; make more intense	fashion	style
exaggerate	over-state	fast	quick
excel	surpass	fasten	attach
exceptional	outstanding	fastidious	hard to please; quick to find fault
excess	extra	fatal	serious
excessive	too much	fatigue	tiredness
excitement	thrill	fatuous	silly; foolish
exclude	keep out	fault	mistake
exemplify	show	faulty	imperfect
exempt	exclude	favor	taking side
exhaust	deplete	favorite	preferred
exhilarate	enliven	feasible	possible
exonerate	declare blameless	fee	charge
exorbitant	over-priced	feeble	weak
expedite	speed up	feminine	related to females
expel	dismiss	ferocious	fierce
explain	clarify	fervent	showing great intensity of feeling
explicit	clear; definite	fervor	enthusiasm
exploit	take advantage of	festive	merry
extensive	broad	fetch	bring
exterior	outside	feud	quarrel
external	outer	fever	abnormally high temperature
extra-terrestrial	beyond earth	fiction	fantasy
extraordinary	special	fictitious	imaginary; unreal
extravagant	excessive	fidelity	faithfulness
extricate	set free from a difficulty	fiduciary	involving confidence and trust
extrinsic	outside	final	last
extrovert	person who is expressive	finish	complete; end
exuberant	extremely joyful	fit	suitable
fabulous	fantastic	flagrant	conspicuously bad; notorious

Word	Meaning	Word	Meaning
flamboyant	too showy	gather	collect; come together
flame	fire	gaudy	lacking in good taste
flatter	compliment	general	broad
flaunt	display	generate	produce
flaw	defect	generous	unselfish
flippant	rude	genesis	beginning
flourish	prosper	gentle	soft
fluctuate	change	ghastly	dreadful
fluent	well-versed	gigantic	huge
fluster	disturb	glamorous	attractive
foe	enemy	glimpse	glance
fond	loving	gloom	sadness
foolproof	assured	glucose	blood sugar
forecast	prediction	goal	aim
foremost	principal	gossip	hearsay
forever	always	gradual	slow
forfeit	lose	graphic	colorful
forgive	excuse	gratitude	appreciation; thankfulness
formal	business-like	gratuitous	provided without charge
formidable	difficult	gregarious	sociable; like company of others
formulate	prepare	grieve	mourn
forsake	abandon	grotesque	weird
fortitude	courage	guest	visitor
forward	advance onward	guide	direct
founder	discoverer	guilty	charged
fraction	portion of something	gullible	easily deceived
fragile	easily broken	gush	sudden flow
fragrant	sweet-smelling	habit	practice
frail	weak	hallucinate	to hear or see something that does not exist
frank	outspoken		
frantic	excited	halt	stop
fraternity	organization for males	hamper	hinder
fraud	trickery	handsome	attractive
frequent	regular	handy	convenient
frigid	cold	haphazard	random
frivolous	insignificant; of little value	harass	molest
frolic	fun	hardship	difficulty
frugal	not wasteful	harm	hurt
frustrated	discouraged	harmonious	agreeing
fugitive	one fleeing from justice	harmony	agreement
fulfilling	pleasing	harsh	cruel
fun	pleasure	hasty	swift
fury	anger	hazardous	dangerous
futile	useless	heinous	hateful; wicked
gait	way of walking	help	assistance
gallant	brave and noble	hesitate	pause
gamut	range	heterogenous	dissimilar
gang	group	hide	conceal
garrulous	talking too much about unimportant things	hilarious	comical
		hinder	stop

Word	Meaning	Word	Meaning
hire	employ	immense	enormous
histology	study of cells	immerse	submerge
hit	strike	immigrate	enter
hoax	fraud; trick; deception	imminent	approaching
hobby	favorite pastime	immoral	wrong
homage	respect	immune	resistant to something
homicide	murder; manslaughter	impact	effect
homogenous	similar	impair	damage; weaken
horrible	terrible	impartial	fair
hostile	unfriendly	impatient	restless
hot	heated	impeach	charge; discredit one's reputation
humane	kindness	impeccable	faultless; without flaw
humble	simple	impede	hinder
humiliate	embarrass	imperceptible	negligible
hurry	rush	imperfect	faulty
hurt	harm	impetuous	act with little thought
hypersensitive	over-sensitive	implausible	unbelievable
hypertension	high blood pressure	implement	carry out; start
hyperthermia	higher than normal body temperature	implicit	definite
		implore	appeal
hyperthyroidism	excessive activity of thyroid gland	imply	hint or suggest
hypocrite	one who pretends to be what he/she is not	impolite	rude
		import	bring in
hypoglycemia	abnormally low blood sugar	important	valuable
hysterical	emotionally uncontrolled	impostor	pretender
idea	thought	impractical	unworkable
ideal	perfect	impression	feeling
identical	alike	impromptu	unrehearsed
identify	recognize	improper	incorrect
idiot	fool	improve	develop
idle	inactive	imprudent	without thought of consequences
ignoble	disgraceful	impure	unclean
ignorant	foolish	inaccessible	unreachable
ignore	avoid	inaccurate	incorrect
illegal	unlawful	inactive	idle
illegible	unreadable	inadequate	insufficient
illicit	forbidden	inadvertent	unintentional; not attentive
illiterate	unable to read or write	inanimate	lifeless
illogical	senseless	inappropriate	unsuitable
illuminate	brighten	incarcerate	imprison
illustrate	explain	incentive	encouragement
illustrious	famous	incessant	continuous
imbecile	fool	inclement	stormy
imitate	copy	include	involve
immaculate	faultless; clean	incoherent	inconsistent
immature	underdeveloped	incompetent	unfit
immeasurable	cannot measure	incomplete	unfinished

Word	Meaning	Word	Meaning
incomprehensible	cannot be understood	inspire	encourage
inconsiderate	thoughtless	installment	payments in parts at regular intervals
inconsistent	disagreeing		
inconspicuous	low-profile	instigate	start
incorporate	include	integrity	honor
incredible	unbelievable	intense	strong
inculcate	impress by persistent urging	intentional	deliberate
incurable	not curable	interminable	endless
indelible	unremovable	intermission	break
indicate	show	intermittent	periodic
indifferent	unconcerned	internal	inside
indiscriminate	unsystematic	interpret	understand
indispensable	essential	interrogate	question
inedible	uneatable	intervene	step in
inept	incompetent	intimate	innermost
inert	inactive	intimidate	frighten
inevitable	unavoidable	intoxicate	drunk
inexorable	cannot be influenced	intravenous	taken through the vein
inexpensive	cheap	intricate	complex
infallible	incapable of error; faultless	intrinsic	not dependent on external circumstances
infamous	wicked		
infer	conclude	introvert	withdrawn
inferior	low grade	intuition	instinct
infidelity	unfaithful; disloyal	inundate	overwhelm with a great amount
inflame	increase intensity of	invalid	ineffective
inflate	swell	invert	capsize
influence	control	investigate	inquire
inform	tell	invincible	unbeatable
ingenious	clever	invite	request
ingredient	component	involve	include
inhabitant	occupant	irate	frighten; angry
inherent	inborn	irrelevant	unrelated; unconnected
inhibit	prevent; hold back	irreparable	ruined
inhospitable	not offering protection or shelter	irresistible	compelling
inhuman	heartless	irrevocable	cannot be recalled
initiate	start	irritate	annoy
inmate	person living in prison	isolate	separate
innate	inborn	jail	place for prisoners
innocent	blameless	jailbreak	break out of jail
innocuous	not likely to cause harm	jealous	envious
innuendo	suggestion; hint or sly remark	jeopardize	risk
inquisitive	curious	jerk	pull
insane	mad; crazy	jest	joke
insatiable	incapable of being satisfied	job	duty
insidious	more dangerous than seem evident	join	connect
insignificant	unimportant	journal	record of daily happening
insinuate	suggest	journey	trip
insolent	rude	jovial	joyful
inspect	examine	joy	happiness

Word	Meaning	Word	Meaning
judge	mediate	literate	educated
judicious	having or showing sound judgment	litigation	act of carrying out a lawsuit
jumble	mix	load	pack
junior	younger	locate	find
just	fair	logical	sensible
juvenile	young	loiter	idle
keen	sharp	loud	noisy
keep	hold	lucid	clear
kidnap	steal	lucrative	profitable
kin	relative	ludicrous	laughable
kindle	light	luminous	glows in the dark
kit	equipment	lunar	related to the moon
kleptomaniac	irresistible impulse to steal	lure	attract
knock	hit	luscious	sweet and pleasant to taste
label	mark	lustrous	shiny
labor	struggle	luxury	prosperity
lacerate	deeply distressed	mad	crazy
lack	need	magnanimous	having or showing generosity
landlord	owner of real estate	magnificent	splendid
languid	weak	magnify	enlarge
lapse	decline	magnitude	greatness
large	big	main	chief
last	end	maintain	keep or support
latent	hidden	majestic	dignified
lateral	side	major	main subject of study
laugh	chuckle	malady	sickness
lavish	plentiful; extravagant	malicious	spiteful
lawyer	person schooled in law	malignant	harmful or dangerous
lax	careless	mammoth	gigantic
lazy	inactive	mandate	command
lead	guide	mandatory	compulsory
learn	grasp	mania	fixation
leave	depart	manipulate	control
lecture	period of instruction	manslaughter	killing
legal	allowed	manual	hand-operated
legible	clear	masculine	related to males
legitimate	legal	massacre	slaughter
leisure	spare time	massage	stroke
lenient	lax; easy	maternal	motherly
lethal	fatal	matrimony	wedding
lethargy	lack of energy	mature	develop
liable	accountable	maximum	greatest
liberal	generous; tolerant	meander	twist
lien	claim	mediocre	inferior
light	weightless	melancholy	sadness
limp	drooping	menace	threat
linger	remain	merchandise	goods

Word	Meaning	Word	Meaning
merge	combine	neglect	ignore
mesmerize	fascinate; hypnotize	negligent	careless
message	communication	negotiate	bargain
metamorphosis	change	nervous	restless
meticulous	careful	neurosis	nervous disorder
militant	activist	neutral	impartial
miniature	small	niche	place
minimum	least	nocturnal	nightly
minute	tiny	nod	motion
miscellaneous	mixed	nominal	small
mischievous	disobedient	nonchalant	easygoing
misery	sorrow	normal	usual
misfortune	tragedy	nostalgia	longing for something of the past
mishap	unfortunate accident	notify	inform
misinterpret	interpret incorrectly	notorious	widely known in an unfavorable manner
misplace	lose		
mistake	error	novice	beginner; inexperienced person
mistreat	abuse	noxious	harmful
mitigate	to make less severe or painful	nuisance	annoyance
mobile	movable	nullify	void
moderate	average	numerous	many
modest	shy; bashful	nurture	care for
modify	change	nutritious	nourishing
monotonous	having no variety	obey	listen to
monumental	massive; very great	objective	unbiased; unprejudiced
moral	respectable	obligate	require
morale	spirit	oblivious	unaware
morbid	ghastly	oblong	elongated
more	extra	obnoxious	highly offensive
motivate	encourage	obscene	disgusting
motive	purpose	obscure	unclear
mourn	grieve	obsequious	too willing to serve or obey
multiple	many	observe	note
multiply	increase in number	obsess	preoccupy
murmur	whisper	obsolete	outdated
mutual	common	obstacle	barrier
nag	annoy	obstinate	stubborn
naive	innocent	obstruct	block
naked	undressed	obtain	acquire
nap	rest	obvious	understandable
narcotics	drugs	occasionally	sometimes
nausea	disgust	occur	happen
nebulous	unclear	octagon	eight-sided figure
necessary	required	odd	strange
need	want	odor	scent
negative	discouraging	offend	displease; insult

Word	Meaning	Word	Meaning
often	frequently	passive	inactive; lifeless
old	antique	pathetic	pitiful
ominous	threatening	patience	tolerance
omit	leave out; exclude	patron	customer
omnipotent	supreme	pedestrian	walker
omnivorous	eat plants and animals	penalize	punish
onset	beginning	penalty	fine
opaque	unclear	pensive	thoughtful
opponent	enemy	per diem	by the day; daily
oppose	resist	percentage	portion of 100
optimistic	hopeful	perceptive	observant
optimum	best	perennials	plants live year after year
optional	voluntary	permanent	lasting
oral	verbal	pernicious	damaging
ordeal	burden	perpetual ✓	lasting forever
ordinary	usual	perplex	confuse
organize	arrange	persevere	endure
orientation	introduction	persist	persevere; endure
originate	begin	perspicacious	keen judgment
orthopedics	related to bone and spine	persuade	convince
oscillate	swing to and fro	pertain	relate
ostensible	clearly evident; apparent	perturb	disturb
ostentatious	pretentious	petite	small
ostracize	to banish or exclude	phobia	persistent fear of
outcome	result		something or situation
outrageous	shocking	pilfer	steal
outstanding	excellent	pious	religious
overt	openly	pity	compassion
overwhelm	overpower	placid	calm; untroubled
owe	liable	plagiarize	take an idea and pass
own	possess		off as one's own
pace	rate	plague	contagious epidemic that's deadly
pacify	calm	plausible	believable; possible
pain	ache	pleasant	pleasing
palpitate	vibrate	pledge	oath
panacea	remedy	plentiful	abundant
pandemonium	confusion; noisy	podiatrist	foot doctor
panic	scare	poignant	emotionally touching or moving
panorama	wide view in all directions	poisonous	toxic
parade	procession	polite	courteous
paralyze	disable	pompous	self-important
paramount	ranking higher than any other	ponder	reflect
pardon	forgive	positive	confident; certain
partial	incomplete	possess	own
particular	special	possible	likely
passion	love	postpone	delay

Word	Meaning	Word	Meaning
posture	stance	punish	scold
potent	strong	purchase	buy
potpourri	mixture of fragrances	purpose	aim
practice	prepare	purposeful	intentional
prank	trick	pursue	chase
precedent	example serving as a future rule	puzzle	perplex
precious	valuable	quadruple	fourfold
preclude	keep out or prevent	quagmire	in a difficult position
predict	foretell	qualm	doubt
predominant	principal	quandary	puzzle
prefer	favor	quantity	amount
prejudice	discrimination	quarrelsome	bad-tempered
prelude	opening	queer	strange
premature	early	quell	calm
preposterous	foolish; laughable	query	question
prerequisite	required	question	ask
preserve	maintain; keep	questionable	open to doubt
pretend	feign	quick	fast
prevail	abound	quiet	still
prevalent	widespread	quirk	a strange trait or mannerism
prevent	obstruct	quit	discontinue
previous	earlier	quite	truly
principal	chief	quiver	tremble
probation	period of testing or trial	quiz	short examination
procedure	sequence of steps	quota	proportion
procrastinate	delay	radiant	shining
profanity	cursing	rage	anger
proficient	capable	rancor	feeling of bitterness or spitefulness
profit	gain		
profound	deeply felt	rank	position
prohibit	prevent	rapacious	taking by force
prolong	continue	rapid	quick
prominent	well-known	ratify	confirm; approve
promiscuous	sex with many partners	rational	sensible; logical
prompt	punctual	ravage	damage
prone	likely	ready	prepared
proponent	one who makes a proposal	real	true
proposal	offer	rebuke	scold
prosperous	successful	recall	remember
protest	complain	recede	withdraw
proud	boastful	receive	get
proverb	saying	recess	short period of break
provocative	irritating	recession	slump
provoke	irritate	recipe	formula
prowess	courage	reciprocate	return
prudent	careful; cautious	recite	repeat
pseudopodia	false feet	reckless	careless
psychic	fortuneteller	recognize	identify
punctual	prompt	recollect	remember

Word	Meaning	Word	Meaning
recommend	suggest	reprimand	rebuke severely
reconciliation	harmony	repudiate	forsake; abandon
record	register	repugnant	disgusting
recover	get back	reputation	fame
recruit	newcomer	request	ask
rectify	correct	require	need
recur	repeat	rescue	save
reduce	lessen or decrease	research	investigate
redundant	using more words than	resentment	hatred
	necessary	reserve	keep
refrain	avoid	reside	live
refuge	shelter	resign	quit
refund	repayment	resilient	flexible
refuse	reject	resist	oppose
refute	disprove	resourceful	clever
register	sign-up for	respond	reply
regress	going back	responsible	reliable
regret	sorrow	restrain	control
regular	usual	restrict	control
regulate	adjust	resume	continue
rehearse	practice	retain	maintain
reinforce	strengthen	retaliate	fight back
reject	refuse	reticent	quiet; saying little
relapse	slip back	retreat	withdraw
relax	rest	retrospect	thinking of the past
release	free	reveal	disclose
relentless	persistent	revert	return to
relevant	suitable	revise	improve
reliable	trustworthy	revoke	cancel
relinquish	to surrender or give up	ridiculous	foolish
relish	enjoy	rigid	fixed
reluctant	unwilling	rigorous	difficult
rely	depend on	rough	unsmooth
remain	stay	rupture	break
remarkable	special	rural	country
remedial	developmental	sabotage	undermine
remedy	cure	salient	noticeable; important
remember	recall	salute	honor
remorse	sorrowful repentance	sane	sensible
remote	distant	sarcastic	mocking
remove	expel	satisfy	content; please
render	give	saturate	fill
repair	fix	scandal	disgrace
repeat	restate	scatter	disperse
replenish	renew	scrupulous	careful
replete	plentifully supplied	scrutinize	examine closely
replicate	copy	scurrilous	using vulgar or indecent language
reply	answer	seal	close
reprehend	to find fault; to criticize	sedative	to soothe or quiet; lessen
representative	spokesperson		excitement or irritability

Word	Meaning	Word	Meaning
seduce	tempt	subtle	indirect
seldom	rarely	successful	prosperous
select	choose	succinct	concise
sensible	wise	succulent	juicy
sensuous	pleasing	succumb	surrender
sentimental	emotional	sufficient	enough
separate	isolate	suitable	fitting
serene	peaceful	sullen	depressing
serious	important	summarize	brief
severe	serious	sumptuous	costly; great expense
shortage	insufficient amount	superb	splendid
shrewd	smart	supercilious	characterized by pride or scorn
significant	important	superficial	shallow
sinister	evil	superfluous	excessive; unnecessary
site	location	superior	high quality
skeptic	doubtful person	superstition	belief based on ignorance
smile	grin	supplement	addition
solace	comfort	surpass	exceed
solar	related to sun	surplus	excess
solitude	isolation	surrender	submit
sorority	organisation for females in college	surreptitious	acting in a secret manner
		susceptible	helpless
spacious	roomy	suspend	postpone
spank	beat	suspension	temporary barring or stoppage
speculate	guess	suspicious	distrustful
spendthrift	extravagant	sustain	support
spontaneous	unprepared	symbiosis	mutual benefit
sporadic	irregular	symbolize	represent
squander	misuse	synchronize	match
standstill	motionless	synthesize	combine; bring together in a whole
stationary	permanent		
stationery	materials	talent	ability
steal	pilfer	tangible	concrete; touchable
stereotype	categorize	tantalize	tease
sterilize	disinfect	tantrum	outburst
stimulate	arouse	task	chore
stingy	cheap	taste	experience
strenuous	hard	teacher	one who instructs
stress	mental or physical tension	tear	rip
stubborn	obstinate	tedious	tiresome; weary
sturdy	strong	tell	notify
subjective	biased	temperamental	moody
subjugate	defeat or conquer	temporary	short-lived
submit	present	tenacious	stubborn
subsequent	following	tenant	renter
subservient	submissive	tense	anxious
subside	sink	tentative	temporary
substitute	replace	tenuous	having little substance; weak

Word	Meaning	Word	Meaning
tenure	permanent position as in academia	under	below
		undercover	private
terminal	deadly	undermine	weaken
terminate	discontinue	underrate	belittle
thorough	complete	understand	grasp
threaten	intimidate	unfair	unjust
thrive	prosper	unfit	unsuitable
timid	shy	unforgettable	lasting
tolerate	put up with; permit	unique	different
topic	subject	universal	worldwide
toxic	noxious	university	institution of higher learning
traditional	old-fashioned	unreal	imaginary
tragic	devastating	unrest	uneasiness; dissension
trait	quality	unscrupulous	without principles
tranquil	peaceful	unskilled	inexperienced
transfer	move across	unstable	unsteady; erratic
transform	convert; change	untidy	messy
transgress	go over a boundary; trespass	uproar	chaos
transient	passing	urban	city
translucent	shining through	urge	longing
transparent	clear	urgent	immediate action
transpire	occur	usual	common
trauma	shock	utilize	spend
treacherous	dangerous	vacant	empty
treason	betrayal of one's country	vacation	holiday
tremendous	vast	vacillate	to sway to and fro
tremor	vibration	vague	unclear
trepidation	fearful; apprehensive	valiant	brave
trespass	intrude	valid	genuine
triumph	success	validate	authorize
trivial	insignificant; small	vanish	disappear
trophy	prize	variety	assortment
trouble	disturb	various	many
tumult	uproar	vary	change
turbulent	violent; stormy	vast	immense
turmoil	disturbance	vehement	forceful
ubiquitous	seeming to be everywhere	velocity	speed
ultimate	final	vengeance	retaliation
unable	incapable	vent	opening
unanimous	showing complete agreement; unified	verbal	spoken
		verdict	decision
unbelievable	incredible	verify	support
uncanny	strange; mysterious	versatile	flexible
uncertain	unsure	vertical	erect
uncomfortable	uneasy	veto	reject
unconscious	unaware	viable	able to live or survive

Word	Meaning
vicarious	substitute; taking the place of another person or thing
vicinity	surrounding
vicious	cruel; corrupt
victim	sufferer
vigilant	alert
vigorous	energetic
vile	impure
vindicate	clear of accusation
vindictive	spiteful
virtue	goodness
visible	noticeable
vital	important
vivacious	lively
vivid	graphic
vociferous	loud; noisy
void	empty
voluntary	done on one's free will
voracious	greedy in eating or some desire
vulgar	obscene
vulnerable	unprotected
wander	stray
warn	caution
warp	deform
weak	feeble
weed	undesirable plant
weep	sob
weird	strange
welcome	receive
whine	complain
whisper	murmur
withdraw	retreat
wrinkle	crease
yearn	crave
yell	shout
yield	return
youth	youngster
zeal	enthusiasm
zest	passion
zoology	study of animals

Terms

A **prefix** is a letter or a group of letters with a special meaning that comes at the beginning of a word. Examples of words with common prefixes include: **semi**circle, **un**believable, **pre**trial, **post**date, and **circum**navigate.

A **suffix** is a letter or a group of letters with a special meaning that comes at the end of a word. Examples of words with common suffixes include : perish**able**, access**ible**, cool**ant**, oppos**ite**, and attract**ive**.

A **root** is the main or central portion of a word. Examples of words with common roots include: **aqu**atic, **aud**ible, in**cred**ible, **culp**able, **loc**ale, and **frag**ment.

A **synonym** is a word with the same or almost same meaning as another word.

A word opposite in meaning to another word is called an **antonym.**

Exercise 1:   Prefix

Match each prefix with its meaning.

____ 1. ab-   a. to, in, without

____ 2. ad-   b. toward, against

____ 3. anti-   c. opposite, against

____ 4. a-   d. toward, to

____ 5. ob-   e. away, from

Exercise 2:   Suffix

Match each suffix with its meaning.

____ 1. -ist   a. doer, believer

____ 2. -ant   b. state, process

____ 3. -ism   c. one that does

____ 4. -less   d. lacking

____ 5. -ard   e. agent, condition

Exercise 3:   Root

Match each root with its meaning.

____ 1. -aqu-   a. water

____ 2. -culp-   b. love

____ 3. -frag-   c. break

____ 4. -cred-   d. belief

____ 5. -amic-   e. blame

Exercise 4: Brain Teasers

Make a new word from each word below.

#	Word	Answer	#	Word	Answer
1.	play	*lap*	25.	boxer	*rob*
2.	that	hat, at.	26.	wrestler	rest
3.	runner	RUN	27.	player	layer
4.	swimmer	swim	28.	mayor	may, OK
5.	wall	All	29.	assembly	MESS, less, by
6.	hammer	ham, MAN, men	30.	together	got, tore
7.	clock	Lock	31.	forever	ever
8.	frock	Rock	32.	whenever	when, even
9.	sit	it	33.	plow	low
10.	rage	age	34.	will	ill
11.	man	AN	35.	piper	pipe
12.	son	on	36.	fragile	agile
13.	woman	man	37.	tray	Try
14.	husband	and, band	38.	sailor	sail
15.	father	the, FAR	39.	anteater	tea, ant, tear
16.	mother	more, moth	40.	farmer	far, farm
17.	perfume	fume	41.	grower	grow, owe, row
18.	chair	air, hair	42.	mower	more
19.	king	in	43.	sower	sore
20.	claw	law	44.	garland	Land
21.	wink	ink	45.	garage	age
22.	flap	lap	46.	gentle	get
23.	grip	Rip	47.	silly	ill
24.	blouse	bus	48.	tool	too

50

Exercise 5: Brain Teasers (Cont'd)

Make three words from each word below.

1.	**about**	out	but	At
2.	**abridge**	Ridge	bird	long
3.	**celebrate**	KATIE	RAT	GATE
4.	**lacerate**	ATE	LACE	RAT
5.	**paramount**	PART	MAN	Amount
6.	**legitimate**	leg	MATE	LATE
7.	**cripple**	Rip	pipe	
8.	**distinguished**	Sting	guide	guess
9.	**elaborate**	LAB	bore	RATE
10.	**encourage**	AGE	RANGE	CURE
11.	**abstain**	Stain	ANT	BAT
12.	**charm**	ARM	harm	CAR
13.	**questionable**	ABLE	TENSION	Table
14.	**dismantle**	MAN	MENTAL	TILE
15.	**apartment**	MEAN	TENT	ART
16.	**repudiate**	diet	READ	RATE
17.	**doldrums**	drums	old	Rum
18.	**abuse**	USE	base	US
19.	**resentment**	SENT	RENT	MEN
20.	**covert**	OVER	COVER	COVE

51

Exercise 6:   Brain   Teasers (Cont'd)

Make three words from each word below.

1.	**adoption**	OPTION	ON	POT
2.	**consternation**	NATION	CORNER	STERN
3.	**distress**	STRESS	dRESS	TREE
4.	**inhospitable**	TABlE	host	spit
5.	**intermittent**	TERM	iN	mitTEN
6.	**boisterous**	US	oUS	is
7.	**extravagant**	EXTRA	RAg	VAN
8.	**affluence**	FENCE	FAN	UNClE
9.	**constrain**	TRAIN	RAIN	CONTAIN
10.	**domain**	do	AIM	iN
11.	**buoyant**	boy	ANT	Toy
12.	**spendthrift**	thirst	spend	theiF
13.	**mathematics**	tics	the	ham
14.	**conflagration**	NATION	Flag	NAg
15.	**establishment**	hint	tablE	TAmE
16.	**ingredient**	diEt	gRINd	diRt
17.	**appoint**	poiNt	pot	piNt
18.	**contemptible**	TiTlE	pEtite	pET
19.	**dwindle**	WIN	widE	did
20.	**corroborate**	RAt	CAR	boTE

Exercise 7: Brain Teasers (Cont'd)

Make three words from each word below.

1. **applaud**

2. **copious**

3. **deliver**

4. **incomprehensible**

5. **scandalous**

6. **abbreviate**

7. **eradicate**

8. **accommodate**

9. **bewilder**

10. **astonish**

11. **corridor**

12. **detail**

13. **infallible**

14. **standstill**

15. **accelerate**

16. **exceptional**

17. **exorbitant**

18. **ingredient**

19. **askew**

20. **crinkle**

Exercise 8: Brain Teasers (Cont'd)

Make three words from each word below.

1. acclaimed _____ _____ _____

2. comfort _____ _____ _____

3. defraud _____ _____ _____

4. immeasurable _____ _____ _____

5. belligerent _____ _____ _____

6. camouflage _____ _____ _____

7. defeat _____ _____ _____

8. accident _____ _____ _____

9. collide _____ _____ _____

10. disagreeable _____ _____ _____

11. imperceptible _____ _____ _____

12. cantankerous _____ _____ _____

13. diplomat _____ _____ _____

14. experiment _____ _____ _____

15. catastrophe _____ _____ _____

16. combine _____ _____ _____

17. definite _____ _____ _____

18. imprudent _____ _____ _____

19. cherish _____ _____ _____

20. acute _____ _____ _____

Exercise 9: Brain Teasers (Cont'd)

Make three words from each word below.

1. abnormal   _____   _____   _____

2. abashed   _____   _____   _____

3. damage   _____   _____   _____

4. dangle   _____   _____   _____

5. darkness   _____   _____   _____

6. decrease   _____   _____   _____

7. capacity   _____   _____   _____

8. censure   _____   _____   _____

9. monumental   _____   _____   _____

10. essay   _____   _____   _____

11. enlighten   _____   _____   _____

12. allegiance   _____   _____   _____

13. farmer   _____   _____   _____

14. conventional   _____   _____   _____

15. chubby   _____   _____   _____

16. forward   _____   _____   _____

17. illiterate   _____   _____   _____

18. cafeteria   _____   _____   _____

19. crown   _____   _____   _____

20. balance   _____   _____   _____

Exercise 1: Prefix

Match each prefix with its meaning.

_____ 1. trans-

_____ 2. ex-

_____ 3. hyper-

_____ 4. pre-

_____ 5. sub-

a. excessive, beyond

b. below, under

c. in front of, before

d. across, through

e. outside, out of

Exercise 2: Suffix

Match each suffix with its meaning.

_____ 1. -ment

_____ 2. -ness

_____ 3. -ence

_____ 4. -ible

_____ 5. -some

a. fact, act

b. condition, showing

c. action, result

d. quality

e. fit, likely

Exercise 3: Root

Match each root with its meaning.

_____ 1. -fin-

_____ 2. -cycl-

_____ 3. -cog-

_____ 4. -auto-

_____ 5. -bio-

a. life

b. self

c. circle

d. end

e. know

Exercise 4:   Nouns

Indicate whether the following sentences are true or false.

_____ 1.   Common nouns provide a general name for a person, place or thing.

_____ 2.   Proper nouns do not identify a specific person, place or thing.

_____ 3.   Proper nouns must always be capitalized.

Exercise 5:   Nouns (Cont'd)

Underline the nouns in the following sentences.

1.   The athlete runs daily.

2.   General Price is very brave.

3.   We swam across the river.

4.   They came close to Kaieteur Falls.

5.   The wheel raced away.

Exercise 6:   Nouns (Cont'd)

Indicate whether the following sentences are true or false.

_____ 1.   Concrete nouns name tangible things, places or people.

_____ 2.   Abstract nouns name intangible qualities, ideals or ideas.

Exercise 7: Pronouns

Indicate whether the following sentences are true or false.

_____ 1.   Pronouns do not take the place of nouns.

_____ 2.   There are several types of pronouns.

Exercise 8: Pronouns (Cont'd)

List examples of the following types of pronouns.

1. Personal

    ____ ____ ____ ____ ____ ____

    ____ ____ ____ ____ ____ ____

    ____ ____ ____ ____ ____ ____

2. Relative

    ____ ____ ____ ____

    ____ ____ ____ ____

3. Indefinite

    ____ ____ ____ ____

    ____ ____ ____ ____

    ____ ____ ____ ____

4. Demonstrative

    ____ ____ ____ ____

5. Interrogative

    ____ ____ ____ ____

6. Reflexive

    ____ ____ ____ ____

    ____ ____ ____

Exercise 9: Verbs

Indicate whether the following sentences are true or false.

_____ 1. Verbs do not describe action or existence.

_____ 2. Verbs that show action are called action verbs.

_____ 3. Linking verbs join the subject to something that is said about the subject.

_____ 4. Four principal parts of verbs are: the present, the past, the past participle, and the present participle.

_____ 5. There are only regular verbs.

_____ 6. The present participle can be formed by adding **ing** to the present form.

_____ 7. The past tense and past participles of regular verbs can be formed by adding **d** or **ed** to their present form.

Exercise 10: Adjectives

Indicate whether the following sentences are true or false.

_____ 1. Adjectives describe nouns.

_____ 2. Adjectives describe shape, size, color, amount or mood.

_____ 3. Adjectives may come before the word they describe or after a linking verb.

_____ 4. When you are comparing things, you can add **-er** or **-est** to an adjective.

_____ 5. Adjectives do not have irregular forms.

Exercise 11: Prepositions

A preposition shows the relationship between a noun or a pronoun and another word in a sentence. List examples of common prepositions.

_____   _____   _____   _____   _____

_____   _____   _____   _____   _____

_____   _____   _____   _____   _____

_____   _____   _____   _____   _____

_____   _____   _____   _____   _____

Exercise 12: Adverbs

Indicate whether the following sentences are true or false.

_____ 1. Adverbs do not describe verbs and adjectives.

_____ 2. Adverbs tell how, when, where, and to what degree.

_____ 3. Most adverbs end in the letters **ly**.

Exercise 13: Conjunctions and Interjections

Indicate whether the following sentences are true or false.

_____ 1. Conjunctions join words or groups of words.

_____ 2. Coordinate, subordinate and adverbial are not three categories of conjunctions.

_____ 3. Coordinate conjunctions do not join sentences.

_____ 4. Subordinate conjunctions join a dependent and an independent clause.

_____ 5. Conjunctions that are used with a semi-colon to join two or more independent clauses to form a compound sentence are called adverbial conjunctions.

_____ 6. Words that are used to express strong emotions are called interjections.

_____ 7. An exclamation point usually comes after the interjection.

Exercise 14: Conjunctions

List examples of the following types of conjunctions.

1. coordinate   _____ _____ _____ _____ _____ _____

2. subordinate   _____ _____ _____ _____ _____ _____

                  _____ _____ _____ _____ _____ _____

3. adverbial   _____ _____ _____ _____ _____ _____

Exercise 15: Grammar Rules

Indicate whether the following sentences are true or false.

_____ 1. The first letter of a sentence or a direct quotation is never capitalized.

_____ 2. The names of races, languages, places and people are seldom capitalized.

_____ 3. Product names and specific school courses are always capitalized.

_____ 4. Days and months and the pronoun "I" are always capitalized.

_____ 5. Religions, nationalities, companies, clubs and organizations are always capitalized.

_____ 6. A period (.) can be used at the end of a statement.

_____ 7. A question mark (?) is never used after a question.

_____ 8. An exclamation mark (!) is used after a statement of excitement or another strong feeling.

_____ 9. A colon (:) introduces a list, a long quotation or a final fact or explanation.

_____ 10. A semi-colon (;) does not join two complete thoughts or statements.

_____ 11. A hyphen (-) joins two or more words together to describe a noun.

_____ 12. A dash (—) is not used to make a pause.

_____ 13. Parentheses, ( ), indicate that the information inside them are very important.

_____ 14. A sentence has a subject and a predicate.

_____ 15. A simple sentence does not have a subject and verb.

_____ 16. Sentences joined by connecting words are called complex sentences.

_____ 17. Sentences joined by a comma and a conjunction are called compound sentences.

Exercise 16: Prefix

Match each prefix with its meaning.

_____ 1. bi-   a. around

_____ 2. extra-   b. back

_____ 3. circum-   c. against

_____ 4. retro-   d. double, two

_____ 5. contra-   e. outside

Exercise 17: Root

Match each root with its meaning.

_____ 1. -loq-   a. many

_____ 2. -omni-   b. mind

_____ 3. -poly-   c. speech

_____ 4. -psych-   d. bad

_____ 5. -mal-   e. all

Exercise 18: Spelling Practice

Circle the words that are spelled incorrectly. Then write the correct spelling of each word.

1. singer   dancer   inklude   ilustrate   _include_   _illustrate_

2. jurney   lighter   owe   mugnett   _journey_   _magnet_

3. nieghor   posess   father   son   _neighbor_   _possess_

4. mother   daughter   repare   reduse   _repair_   _reduce_

5. qulify   persue   pillow   blanket   _qualify_   _+ pursue_

Exercise 19: Synonyms - Fill-in

Fill in the blank(s) to complete the word that is similar in meaning to the boldfaced word.

1. **pace**   ra__e

2. **palpitate**   vi__ __ate

3. **patience**   __oler__ __ce

4. **persevere**   e__ __u__e

5. **victim**   suf__ __r__r

6. **prone**   lik__ __y

7. **utilize**   __pe__d

8. **prevail**   ab__ __nd

9. **posture**   __t__n__e

10. **provocative** irri__ __ __ __ __g

11. **parade**   pro__ __ __s__ __n

12. **penalize**   __un__ __h

13. **pertain**   r__ __at__

14. **pilfer**   s__ __a__

15. **pity**   com__ __ __ion

16. **poisonous**   __ox__ __ __

17. **pledge**   o__ __h

18. **possess**   __wn

19. **practice**   pr__ __ __re

20. **prank**   tr__ __k

21. **topic**   s__ __j__ __t

22. **toxic**   no__ __ __us

23. **treacherous** da__ __ __r__us

24. **trophy**   p__ __ze

Exercise 20: Synonyms - Antonyms

Write the synonym and antonym of each boldfaced word.

			syn.	ant.			
1.	**acquire**		_____	_____	(a) gain	(b) joy	(c) lose
2.	**admit**		_____	_____	(a) consent	(b) done	(c) deny
3.	**affection**		_____	_____	(a) love	(b) sit	(c) dislike
4.	**agile**		_____	_____	(a) fast	(b) jump	(c) slow
5.	**acknowledge**		_____	_____	(a) tell	(b) admit	(c) dissent
6.	**achieve**		_____	_____	(a) sing	(b) accomplish	(c) fail
7.	**accuse**		_____	_____	(a) blame	(b) forgive	(c) rush
8.	**accept**		_____	_____	(a) approve	(b) deny	(c) run
9.	**abstract**		_____	_____	(a) concrete	(b) theoretical	(c) laughter
10.	**abolish**		_____	_____	(a) cancel	(b) like	(c) retain
11.	**abhor**		_____	_____	(a) listen	(b) hate	(c) love
12.	**aloof**		_____	_____	(a) upside	(b) distant	(c) friendly
13.	**antagonize**		_____	_____	(a) provoke	(b) affect	(c) soothe
14.	**appease**		_____	_____	(a) calm	(b) irritate	(c) fast
15.	**affirm**		_____	_____	(a) confirm	(b) deny	(c) fasten
16.	**adept**		_____	_____	(a) skillful	(b) likely	(c) unskillful
17.	**aggravate**		_____	_____	(a) soon	(b) annoy	(c) pacify
18.	**ample**		_____	_____	(a) taste	(b) plenty	(c) insufficient
19.	**awkward**		_____	_____	(a) clumsy	(b) happen	(c) graceful
20.	**absurd**		_____	_____	(a) foolish	(b) mighty	(c) sensible
21.	**arrogant**		_____	_____	(a) haughty	(b) petty	(c) humble
22.	**audible**		_____	_____	(a) clear	(b) unclear	(c) pause
23.	**auspicious**		_____	_____	(a) favorable	(b) untimely	(c) listless
24.	**austere**		_____	_____	(a) petite	(b) harsh	(c) soft

	syn.	*ant.*			
25. **available**	_____	_____	(a) sustain	(b) ready	(c) unavailable
26. **altruistic**	_____	_____	(a) generous	(b) simple	(c) selfish
27. **attest**	_____	_____	(a) verify	(b) refute	(c) tough
28. **adjust**	_____	_____	(a) regulate	(b) belittle	(c) maintain
29. **adhere**	_____	_____	(a) abhor	(b) cling	(c) detach
30. **absent**	_____	_____	(a) detest	(b) away	(c) present
31. **abrupt**	_____	_____	(a) sudden	(b) gradual	(c) yell
32. **adverse**	_____	_____	(a) unfavorable	(b) favorable	(c) youthful
33. **aspire**	_____	_____	(a) desire	(b) vacant	(c) repudiate
34. **admonish**	_____	_____	(a) warn	(b) visit	(c) praise
35. **attain**	_____	_____	(a) weird	(b) obtain	(c) lose
36. **astute**	_____	_____	(a) smart	(b) calm	(c) stupid
37. **apprehensive**	_____	_____	(a) fearful	(b) happen	(c) brave
38. **assimilate**	_____	_____	(a) integrate	(b) isolate	(c) weird
39. **attrition**	_____	_____	(a) witty	(b) decrease	(c) increase
40. **bad**	_____	_____	(a) salute	(b) evil	(c) good
41. **barren**	_____	_____	(a) unfertile	(b) speed	(c) productive
42. **belated**	_____	_____	(a) late	(b) belittle	(c) early
43. **belief**	_____	_____	(a) adhere	(b) trust	(c) doubt
44. **beneficial**	_____	_____	(a) helpful	(b) dark	(c) harmful
45. **better**	_____	_____	(a) superior	(b) full	(c) worse
46. **bitter**	_____	_____	(a) failure	(b) distasteful	(c) pleasant
47. **borrow**	_____	_____	(a) fair	(b) take	(c) lend
48. **brave**	_____	_____	(a) courageous	(b) retard	(c) cowardly
49. **break**	_____	_____	(a) crack	(b) mend	(c) fair
50. **brief**	_____	_____	(a) short	(b) long	(c) strange

64

	syn.	ant.			
51. **bright**	_____	_____	(a) shining	(b) sing	(c) dull
52. **buy**	_____	_____	(a) reject	(b) purchase	(c) sell
53. **baffle**	_____	_____	(a) honor	(b) puzzle	(c) enlighten
54. **benefactor**	_____	_____	(a) supporter	(b) city	(c) critic
55. **barrier**	_____	_____	(a) obstacle	(b) aid	(c) quiet
56. **boss**	_____	_____	(a) black	(b) supervisor	(c) employee
57. **bother**	_____	_____	(a) court	(b) disturb	(c) pacify
58. **boycott**	_____	_____	(a) ban	(b) success	(c) acceptance
59. **brilliant**	_____	_____	(a) bright	(b) dull	(c) scold
60. **burst**	_____	_____	(a) broken	(b) receive	(c) implode
61. **convert**	_____	_____	(a) change	(b) maintain	(c) confide
62. **concurrent**	_____	_____	(a) agreeing	(b) lose	(c) differing
63. **confiscate**	_____	_____	(a) seize	(b) saint	(c) donate
64. **congenial**	_____	_____	(a) scold	(b) pleasant	(c) unpleasant
65. **consensus**	_____	_____	(a) understanding	(b) disagreement	(c) distant
66. **constrict**	_____	_____	(a) reduce	(b) still	(c) enlarge
67. **contemporary**	_____	_____	(a) modern	(b) decision	(c) old-fashioned
68. **circumvent**	_____	_____	(a) avoid	(b) stick	(c) confront
69. **cause**	_____	_____	(a) reason	(b) clamor	(c) result
70. **concise**	_____	_____	(a) try	(b) brief	(c) lengthy
71. **complain**	_____	_____	(a) rim	(b) protest	(c) approve
72. **chief**	_____	_____	(a) confirm	(b) primary	(c) secondary
73. **chance**	_____	_____	(a) lose	(b) risk	(c) secure
74. **caution**	_____	_____	(a) care	(b) constant	(c) recklessness
75. **cancel**	_____	_____	(a) terminate	(b) continue	(c) confess

Exercise 21:   Synonyms in Context

Circle the letter of the word or phrase that is similar, or almost similar, in meaning to the boldfaced word.

1. to **betray** means to	(a) deceive	(b) take	(c) silent	(d) try
2. **deliberate** move	(a) intentional	(b) reality	(c) deliver	(d) distant
3. **bankrupt** means	(a) abundant	(b) plenty	(c) tired	(d) depleted
4. **demonstrate** a procedure	(a) tell	(b) show	(c) trace	(d) talk
5. **burden** means	(a) hardship	(b) battle	(c) birth	(d) beside
6. **deprive** means	(a) withhold	(b) detain	(c) give	(d) assist
7. **deviate** means	(a) stand	(b) depart from	(c) return	(d) resist
8. **brutal** enemy	(a) kind	(b) friendly	(c) loyal	(d) cruel
9. **detect** a movement	(a) notice	(b) neglect	(c) pursue	(d) follow
10. he took the **blame**	(a) praise	(b) worth	(c) fault	(d) popularity
11. **desperate** plea	(a) awful	(b) urgent	(c) bad	(d) silly
12. **boredom** means	(a) ennui	(b) unhappiness	(c) silence	(d) death
13. **bourgeois** means	(a) famous	(b) middle-class	(c) rich	(d) barely
14. **benign** means	(a) fatal	(b) dangerous	(c) harmless	(d) nightly
15. a **brisk** walk	(a) short	(b) brief	(c) lazy	(d) vigorous
16. **buoyant** means	(a) sinking	(b) heavy	(c) under	(d) floating
17. **categorize** the books	(a) arrange	(b) destroy	(c) tear	(d) throw away
18. **cease** means	(a) begin	(b) stop	(c) quiet	(d) fancy
19. **conscious** during surgery	(a) sleepy	(b) drowsy	(c) awake	(d) lifeless
20. **considerable** amount	(a) tiny	(b) little	(c) small	(d) sizable
21. **comparison** means	(a) likeness	(b) familiar	(c) dissimilar	(d) unlike
22. a **convincing** liar	(a) honest	(b) persuading	(c) truthful	(d) tough
23. a major **catastrophe**	(a) victory	(b) triumph	(c) tragedy	(d) trial
24. **conceited** millionaire	(a) self-important	(b) famous	(c) risky	(d) ignorant
25. **conclusion** means	(a) part	(b) end	(c) compose	(d) consist
26. **compulsory** means	(a) trifle	(b) betray	(c) necessary	(d) unnecessary
27. boost his **confidence**	(a) certainty	(b) religion	(c) concern	(d) care
28. a **credible** witness	(a) disloyal	(b) dishonest	(c) disturb	(d) believable
29. patient **collapsed**	(a) stood	(b) fell	(c) fought	(d) slept
30. earned a **compliment**	(a) scold	(b) ignore	(c) praise	(d) score
31. a **candid** remark	(a) frank	(b) silly	(c) dirty	(d) sweet
32. **dirty** room	(a) unclean	(b) neat	(c) small	(d) huge

Exercise 22: Words in Context

Fill in the blank with the correct word or another form of the word below.

boredom	bankrupt	detect	brutal
demonstrate	blame	deprive	betray
desperate	burden	deviate	deliberate

1. I will tell you a secret if you promise not to _____ my confidence.

2. After _____ for five hours, the jury found the defendant innocent.

3. In the end his high risk ventures _____ the company.

4. It is preferable to have someone _____ a technique than to read an instruction manual.

5. Having a handicapped child is a difficult _____ for most families to bear.

6. By _____ herself of desserts for a month she was able to lose ten pounds.

7. The rules at the school were strict, and anyone who _____ from them was expelled immediately.

8. Because the murder was so _____ the commissioner assigned 20 policemen to the case.

9. If you _____ any odor of gas in your apartment, call the utility company immediately.

10. Despite my protests that I was not even at work the day the accident happened, I was _____.

11. Because he was so _____ to buy drugs, he didn't think twice when he stole the money from his mother's wallet.

12. _____ is often a factor when children drop out of school.

Exercise 23: Words in Context (Cont'd)

Fill in the blank with the correct word or another form of the word below.

considerable	cease	catastrophe	benign
candid	buoyant	bourgeois	conscious
compliment	brisk	categorize	compulsory

1. Theresa found his _____ lifestyle so irritating that she was forced to end their relationship.

2. To everyone's relief the tumor was diagnosed as _____ .

3. As part of my exercise program I take a _____ walk for 30 minutes every day.

4. His mood was _____ when he went to work in the morning, but his spirits sank when he discovered that someone else had been recommended for the promotion.

5. Linnaeus was the first to systematically _____ the members of the plant and animal kingdom.

6. When the noise of the road repair finally _____ , the neighborhood returned again to tranquility.

7. Despite a severe blow to the head, the accident victim was still _____ .

8. A _____ number of people in the United States never exercise their right to vote.

9. Please give me your _____ opinion of this proposal.

10. Although many people found her fawning, all of her _____ were meant to be sincere.

11. Physical education is a _____ subject in most American high schools.

12. The earthquake was the greatest _____ the country had ever experienced.

All correct

THIRD DAY

Exercise 1: Matching Meanings

Match each word with its definition or best meaning.

_____ g _____ 1. university   a. a treasurer

_____ n _____ 2. tenure   b. all the teachers of a college or school

_____ f _____ 3. dean   c. a unit or course of study

_____ b _____ 4. faculty   d. counsels and advises students

_____ j _____ 5. registrar   e. profession or occupation

_____ a _____ 6. bursar   f. an administrative officer of a school, college or university

_____ d _____ 7. counselor   g. educational institution of the highest level

_____ i _____ 8. coach   h. on trial because of low grades

_____ c _____ 9. credit   i. a trainer

_____ o _____ 10. course   j. registers students; maintains records

_____ t _____ 11. major   k. a college organization for men

_____ e _____ 12. career   l. a college organization for women

_____ p _____ 13. elective   m. a room for experimentation or research

_____ m _____ 14. laboratory   n. holding one's position on a permanent basis

_____ q _____ 15. cafe   o. a unit of instruction in a subject

_____ h _____ 16. probation   p. an optional course

_____ s _____ 17. suspension   q. a small restaurant

_____ k _____ 18. fraternity   r. a person on a trial period before initiation into a fraternity or sorority

_____ l _____ 19. sorority   s. temporary barring from school

_____ r _____ 20. pledge   t. a field of study in which a student specializes and earns a degree

Exercise 2:   Synonyms Fill-in

Fill in the blank(s) to complete the word that is similar in meaning to the boldfaced word.

1.	**alternative**	op_ _ _on	13.	**concise**	b _ _ ef
2.	**acquaint**	fam_ _ _i_ _ ize	14.	**compensate**	p _ y
3.	**accompany**	e_co_t	15.	**classify**	cate _ _ _ _ _ze
4.	**access**	_ntr_	16.	**confide**	_ rus _
5.	**analyze**	ex_ _ _ne	17.	**chubby**	st _ _ ky
6.	**alien**	_orei_ _	18.	**chore**	t _ sk
7.	**ascertain**	l_ _rn	19.	**cherish**	tr _ _ _ ure
8.	**astute**	_lev_r	20.	**change**	_ onv _ rt
9.	**attain**	acco_ _ _ _ _sh	21.	**predict**	for _ _ _ l
10.	**boundary**	bo_ _er	22.	**pretend**	as _ _ me
11.	**browse**	sk_ _	23.	**profanity**	cur _ _ ng
12.	**bundle**	pac_ _ge	24.	**pursue**	_ has _

Exercise 3:   Synonyms Multiple Choice

Circle the letter of the word that is similar, or almost similar, in meaning to the boldfaced word.

1. **abundant**	(a) little	(b) less	(c) some	(d) plentiful
2. **calm**	(a) rowdy	(b) noisy	(c) angry	(d) quiet
3. **adequate**	(a) at	(b) enough	(c) last	(d) far
4. **annual**	(a) yearly	(b) weekly	(c) everyday	(d) yesterday
5. **beneficiary**	(a) cousin	(b) inheritor	(c) uncle	(d) aunt
6. **boast**	(a) show-off	(b) sick	(c) lie	(d) sleep
7. **eager**	(a) anxious	(b) first	(c) seldom	(d) settle
8. **chilly**	(a) cool	(b) hot	(c) humid	(d) calm
9. **ailment**	(a) health	(b) disease	(c) temperature	(d) fever
10. **famous**	(a) silly	(b) sick	(c) well-known	(d) loyal
11. **internal**	(a) under	(b) above	(c) below	(d) inside
12. **finish**	(a) start	(b) begin	(c) rest	(d) complete
13. **hesitate**	(a) hurry	(b) haste	(c) pause	(d) speed
14. **joy**	(a) happiness	(b) sad	(c) anger	(d) perfection
15. **harass**	(a) bother	(b) kiss	(c) honor	(d) talk
16. **insane**	(a) smart	(b) crazy	(c) intelligent	(d) scholar
17. **final**	(a) excellent	(b) last	(c) fair	(d) poor
18. **laugh**	(a) serious	(b) crooked	(c) speechless	(d) chuckle
19. **main**	(a) side	(b) lateral	(c) chief	(d) view
20. **nap**	(a) rest	(b) jog	(c) fatigue	(d) ache

Exercise 4: Synonyms in Context

Circle the letter of the word or phrase that is similar, or almost similar, in meaning to the boldfaced word.

1. **accompany** means to
   - (a) to go with
   - (b) delay
   - (c) dare
   - (d) fight
2. earned **distinction**
   - (a) excellence
   - (b) marks
   - (c) pointers
   - (d) extinction
3. **accelerate** means to
   - (a) speed up
   - (b) slow
   - (c) crawl
   - (d) creep
4. **determine** the cost
   - (a) tell
   - (b) calculate
   - (c) ask
   - (d) note
5. **apparent** means
   - (a) invisible
   - (b) apart
   - (c) clear
   - (d) distort
6. in **dormancy**
   - (a) fastness
   - (b) swiftness
   - (c) consciousness
   - (d) inactivity
7. **appropriate** amount
   - (a) suitable
   - (b) unsuitable
   - (c) enormous
   - (d) low
8. **disloyal** employee
   - (a) faithful
   - (b) untrue
   - (c) fearless
   - (d) dependable
9. **affiliated** with
   - (a) joined
   - (b) located
   - (c) associated
   - (d) fail
10. **dislocate** means
    - (a) united
    - (b) disconnect
    - (c) locate
    - (d) join
11. **abduct** a child
    - (a) seize
    - (b) comfort
    - (c) protect
    - (d) care for
12. **dissatisfied** customer
    - (a) grateful
    - (b) regular
    - (c) dependable
    - (d) unhappy
13. **disillusion** means
    - (a) disappointment
    - (b) positive
    - (c) posterior
    - (d) encouragement
14. **abnormal** behavior
    - (a) usual
    - (b) strange
    - (c) normal
    - (d) friendly
15. a **discount** in the price
    - (a) reduction
    - (b) increase
    - (c) raise
    - (d) sale
16. **devastated** means
    - (a) honor
    - (b) obey
    - (c) destroyed
    - (d) vast
17. **absent-minded** professor
    - (a) forgetful
    - (b) tough
    - (c) easy
    - (d) lazy
18. to **distinguish** means to
    - (a) bring-together
    - (b) burden
    - (c) tell apart
    - (d) create
19. **donate** used clothes
    - (a) give
    - (b) accept
    - (c) keep
    - (d) take
20. a **derogatory** remark
    - (a) good
    - (b) negative
    - (c) compliment
    - (d) kind
21. **aggressive** behavior
    - (a) quiet
    - (b) pushy
    - (c) careless
    - (d) harmless
22. **dominate** the discussion
    - (a) control
    - (b) ignore
    - (c) interrupt
    - (d) conclude
23. to **disperse** means
    - (a) convince
    - (b) encourage
    - (c) to break up
    - (d) satisfy
24. an **anonymous** caller
    - (a) well-known
    - (b) dishonest
    - (c) friendly
    - (d) unidentified
25. **exploited** the laborers
    - (a) liked
    - (b) respected
    - (c) accepted
    - (d) take advantage of
26. to **exaggerate** means to
    - (a) ignore
    - (b) over-look
    - (c) over-state
    - (d) hasten
27. to **abbreviate** means to
    - (a) shorten
    - (b) increase
    - (c) deviate
    - (d) dissipate
28. **digress** means to
    - (a) stick to
    - (b) stray
    - (c) clear
    - (d) unknown
29. a **dynamic** speaker
    - (a) poor
    - (b) noisy
    - (c) disrespectful
    - (d) powerful
30. **charismatic** leader
    - (a) appealing
    - (b) selfish
    - (c) loyal
    - (d) caring
31. imprisoned the **dissident**
    - (a) friend
    - (b) relative
    - (c) rebel
    - (d) lawyer
32. **disappear** into the woods
    - (a) camp
    - (b) sleep
    - (c) hunt
    - (d) go away
33. **discreet** means
    - (a) careful
    - (b) constant
    - (c) honest
    - (d) habitual

Exercise 5: Words in Context

Fill in the blank with the correct word or another form of the word below.

abduct *9*	affiliated *7*	determine *3*	appropria...
discount *12*	accompany *1*	dislocate *8*	disillusio...
abnormal *11*	accelerate *2*	disloyal *6*	apparent *4*

1. If you have time, I would like you to _____ me to the doctor's office this afternoon.

2. Once he found a Japanese girlfriend, his progress in learning the language _____ .

3. The best way to _____ how much tip to leave in a restaurant is to double the tax.

4. It was _____ to everyone except his parents that he was using drugs.

5. Jeans are not _____ office attire.

6. Even though he was cheating on his wife, he did not see himself as _____ .

7. Our company is no way _____ with the other company down the block with a similar name.

8. His first and only attempt at bungee jumping caused him to _____ his back.

9. The town was horrified because the child had been _____ in broad daylight.

10. Although he emigrated with high hopes, within his first two weeks he was faced with _____ when he couldn't find work.

11. An _____ weight loss was his first symptom of the virus.

12. If you pay cash, there is a _____ of 5%.

Exercise 6: Words in Context

Fill in the blank with the correct word or another form of the word below.

charismatic *12*	donate *3*	abbreviate *8*	dynamic *10*
derogatory *4*	disappear *11*	devastated *5*	exaggerate *7*
discreet *1*	dominate *6*	aggressive *9*	distinguish *2*

1. She was _____ when she found out that she had failed the college entrance examination and all her friends had passed.

2. Because the symptoms are the same, it is hard to _____ between the flu and certain more serious illnesses.

3. If you _____ $100 or more to our radio station, you will receive a free tote bag.

4. Because he made _____ remarks about every proposal presented, he was not popular with his co-workers.

5. People who live in big cities are usually more _____ than those who live in small towns.

6. Although IBM initially _____ the computer market, they were soon overshadowed by a host of competitors.

7. Fishermen are known to _____ in recounting stories of their fishing exploits.

8. In formal writing, it is best not to _____ .

9. If we want to increase enrollment, we must hire more _____ teachers.

10. John F. Kennedy was one of the most _____ U.S. presidents.

...mething is not done in the next few years, the rain forests of the Amazon basin will soon _____

. Because Thomas was very _____ about his personal life, everyone was very surprised when they read in the paper that he was arrested for bigamy.

Exercise 7:   Antonyms

Match each word with its antonym.

_____ 1. betray   a. prosperous

_____ 2. deliberate   b. return

_____ 3. bankrupt   c. maintain

_____ 4. demonstrate   d. remain

_____ 5. burden   e. accidental

_____ 6. deprive   f. exonerate

_____ 7. deviate   g. aristocratic

_____ 8. brutal   h. malignant

_____ 9. detect   i. ease

_____ 10. blame   j. conceal

_____ 11. boredom   k. overlook

_____ 12. bourgeois   l. begin

_____ 13. benign   m. humane

_____ 14. brisk   n. unconscious

_____ 15. buoyant   o. discourage

_____ 16. cease   p. excitement

_____ 17. conscious   q. beginning

_____ 18. considerable   r. heavy

_____ 19. convincing   s. modest

_____ 20. conceited   t. trivial

_____ 21. conclusion   u. lethargic

_____ 22. compulsory   v. doubt

_____ 23. confidence   w. evasive

_____ 24. compliment   x. criticism

_____ 25. candid   y. voluntary

Exercise 8: Prefix

Match each prefix with its meaning.

_____ 1. pro-   a. before, against

_____ 2. re-   b. later, after

_____ 3. ante-   c. half

_____ 4. post-   d. again, back

_____ 5. semi-   e. favor, forward

Exercise 9: Spelling Practice

Circle the words that are spelled incorrectly. Then write the correct spelling of each word.

1. distant   concieve   count   carot   *carrot*   *conceive*
2. dicieve   dear   cheep   child   *cheap*   *deceive*
3. bulit   adress   child   kid   *built*   *address*
4. affeir   agrevate   book   pencil   *affair*   *aggrevate*
5. chair   begger   bisiness table   *business*   *beggar*

Exercise 1: Matching Meanings

Match each word with its definition or best meaning.

_F_	1. court	a.	guilty of a crime
_h_	2. judge	b.	a member of a jury
_K_	3. jail	c.	owns and rents real estate
_m_	4. defendant	d.	killing of one person by another
_a_	5. criminal	e.	study and investigation of crime and criminals
_d_	6. homicide	f.	a hall where trials are held
_b_	7. juror	g.	judges a dispute
_g_	8. litigation _L_	h.	passes judgment in a court of law
_o_	9. tenant	i.	an order to appear in court
_r_	10. rent	j.	betrayal of one's country
_q_	11. jailbreak	k.	a building where convicted people are confined
_c_	12. landlord	l.	a law suit
_i_	13. summons	m.	a person accused
_L_	14. bailiff _N_	n.	maintains order in courtroom
_l_	15. arbitrator _g_	o.	pays rent to occupy a building
_E_	16. criminology	p.	one who is often put in jail
	17. treason _j_	q.	breaking out of jail by force
_t_	18. cop	r.	payment for occupying a building
_s_	19. jailbird _p_	s.	to imprison
_q_	20. incarcerate _S_	t.	a policeman

Exercise 2: Synonyms Multiple Choice

Circle the letter of the word that is similar, or almost similar, in meaning to the boldfaced word.

1. **frugal**	(a) not wasteful	(b) smart	(c) old	(d) young
2. **gentle**	(a) soft	(b) tough	(c) hard	(d) hardy
3. **general**	(a) broad	(b) narrow	(c) constrict	(d) limited
4. **extraordinary**	(a) special	(b) stale	(c) useless	(d) void
5. **difficult**	(a) easy	(b) hard	(c) assist	(d) refuse
6. **habit**	(a) habitual	(b) practice	(c) honest	(d) holy
7. **consistent**	(a) inconsistent	(b) unsteady	(c) steady	(d) uneasy
8. **adversary**	(a) friend	(b) family	(c) enemy	(d) folly
9. **fashion**	(a) old	(b) unusual	(c) usual	(d) style
10. **elated**	(a) norm	(b) abnormal	(c) justice	(d) happy
11. **alias**	(a) title	(b) address	(c) alarm	(d) nickname
12. **compare**	(a) differ	(b) distant	(c) match	(d) dislike
13. **envy**	(a) guilt	(b) shame	(c) jealousy	(d) fear
14. **assertive**	(a) bossy	(b) outsmart	(c) outlay	(d) outlaw
15. **chastise**	(a) punish	(b) congratulate	(c) admire	(d) assist
16. **challenge**	(a) obey	(b) confront	(c) respect	(d) laugh
17. **expedite**	(a) slow	(b) speed up	(c) slower	(d) usual
18. **assist**	(a) neglect	(b) help	(c) avoid	(d) refuse
19. **ban**	(a) permit	(b) stay	(c) allow	(d) disallow
20. **constant**	(a) tolerate	(b) assist	(c) steady	(d) aloud

Exercise 3: Synonyms in Context

Circle the letter of the word or phrase that is similar, or almost similar, in meaning to the boldfaced word.

1. guilty of **manslaughter**	(a) killing	(b) theft	(c) rape	(d) burglary
2. **heterogeneous** means	(a) dissimilar	(b) agree	(c) disagree	(d) genius
3. **hazardous** materials	(a) dangerous	(b) safe	(c) chemicals	(d) expensive
4. a bad **habit**	(a) practice	(b) sleep	(c) time	(d) thing
5. **hamper** construction of	(a) hinder	(b) assist in	(c) study	(d) dislike
6. **decision** to remain	(a) conclusion	(b) anxious	(c) want	(d) afraid
7. **internal** means	(a) inside	(b) outside	(c) open-air	(d) frantic
8. **intervene** on my behalf	(a) save	(b) step in	(c) help	(d) represent
9. to **illustrate** means to	(a) conceal	(b) explain	(c) fell	(d) cancel
10. first **impression**	(a) attempt	(b) job	(c) feeling	(d) press
11. **inept** means	(a) honor	(b) award	(c) hero	(d) incompetent
12. during **intermission**	(a) movie	(b) performance	(c) play	(d) break
13. **impartial** means	(a) favorite	(b) fake	(c) fair	(d) part

14. **influence** his decision   (a) tell   (b) control   (c) guess   (d) forecast
15. **inhabitant** of an island   (a) occupant   (b) enemy   (c) friend   (d) governor
16. **intentional** remark   (a) deliberate   (b) petty   (c) harsh   (d) encouraging
17. **inferior** materials   (a) high-quality   (b) low-grade   (c) expensive   (d) cheap
18. **interpret** the passage   (a) dislike   (b) like   (c) understand   (d) read
19. to **investigate** means to   (a) inquire   (b) assist in   (c) partake   (d) observe
20. **illegible** handwriting   (a) clear   (b) good   (c) unreadable   (d) best
21. an **incredible** story   (a) sad   (b) true   (c) unbearable   (d) unbelievable
22. **initiate** a conversation   (a) end   (b) argue in   (c) participate in   (d) start
23. an **introvert** is   (a) withdrawn   (b) everybody   (c) nobody   (d) vivacious
24. **instigate** a riot   (a) cease   (b) stop   (c) control   (d) start
25. **intermittent** showers   (a) constant   (b) heavy   (c) plenty   (d) periodic
26. **intimidate** his enemy   (a) play with   (b) respect   (c) frighten   (d) fight
27. an **irate** student   (a) bright   (b) smart   (c) angry   (d) popular
28. first-aid **kit**   (a) pens   (b) package   (c) equipment   (d) story
29. **kidnap** the baby   (a) care for   (b) steal   (c) silence   (d) hit
30. **legible** handwriting   (a) dirty   (b) clear   (c) small   (d) large
31. **lien** on the property   (a) claim   (b) payment   (c) price   (d) purchase
32. **logical** conclusion   (a) stupid   (b) sensible   (c) wrong   (d) incorrect
33. to **locate** means to   (a) conceal   (b) find   (c) hide   (d) sell
34. **maintain** his average   (a) keep   (b) lower   (c) increase   (d) decrease
35. **maximum** sentence   (a) least   (b) greatest   (c) lowest   (d) correct
36. **minimum** sentence   (a) harsh   (b) lenient   (c) tough   (d) least

Exercise 4: Words in Context

Fill in the blank with the correct word or another form of the word below.

inept	inferior	impartial	hazardous
interpret	illustrate	hamper	influence
intermission	intervene	intentional	heterogenous

1. Unlike Japan, the population of the United States is _____

2. To _____ my point I will give several examples from recent history.

3. Don't let only the question of money _____ your decision to take the new job.

4. Walking in an open field during a thunderstorm can be _____.

5. Despite being _____ in all aspects of business, the boss's nephew was hired as the new office manager.

6. Please forgive me. If I offended you, it was certainly not _____.

7. Lack of a college degree _____ Catherine in her job search.

8. Because the movie is over three hours long, there will be an _____ after the first 90 minutes.

9. A lower price for an item often reflects _____ quality.

10. Although she usually remained neutral, the seriousness of the fight between the two brothers forced their mother to _____.

11. Although teachers claim to be _____, studies have shown that they pay more attention to boys than girls in the classroom.

12. Your handwriting is so bad I am having a difficult time trying to _____ it.

Exercise 5: Words in Context (cont'd)

Fill in the blank with the correct word or another form of the word below.

irate	incredible	logical	instigate
maximum	illegible	locate	intermittent
introvert	investigate	intimidate	legible

1. Ten detectives were assigned to _____ the case, but the missing child was never found.

2. When $50,000 was discovered missing, an investigation was _____ immediately.

3. After 100 years in the trunk, the handwriting on the letter was barely _____.

4. Most doctors' handwriting on prescriptions is _____.

5. The meteorologist predicted _____ showers throughout the day.

6. He is an eloquent speaker, but if you listen carefully you will see that he is not _____ .

7. Nowadays, if a letter arrives one day after it was mailed, people regard it as _____ .

8. Because Billy was six inches taller than his classmates, he was able to _____ them.

9. Bus stations always seem to be _LOCATE_ in the worst areas of big cities.

10. _INTROVOX_ should consider a career other than sales.

11. When the check he deposited two weeks before still hadn't cleared, the customer became _IRATE_ .

12. The _____ speed limit on most highways in the United States is 55 miles per hour.

Exercise 6: Synonyms - Antonyms

Select the synonym and antonym of each boldfaced word.

	syn.	*ant.*			
1. **offend**	_____	_____	(a) tender	(b) displease	(c) please
2. **often**	_____	_____	(a) thrifty	(b) frequently	(c) seldom

		syn.	*ant.*	(a)	(b)	(c)
3.	old	_____	_____	(a) antique	(b) young	(c) extensive
4.	onset	_____	_____	(a) beginning	(b) end	(c) remarkable
5.	opaque	_____	_____	(a) unclear	(b) easy	(c) clear
6.	oppose	_____	_____	(a) resist	(b) habitual	(c) agree
7.	ordinary	_____	_____	(a) consistent	(b) usual	(c) unusual
8.	pacify	_____	_____	(a) norm	(b) calm	(c) provoke
9.	particular	_____	_____	(a) special	(b) friend	(c) ordinary
10.	passive	_____	_____	(a) inactive	(b) old	(c) forceful
11.	pernicious	_____	_____	(a) damaging	(b) title	(c) harmless
12.	petite	_____	_____	(a) differ	(b) small	(c) big
13.	plausible	_____	_____	(a) slow	(b) believable	(c) unbelievable
14.	pleasant	_____	_____	(a) pleasing	(b) unpleasant	(c) guilt
15.	plentiful	_____	_____	(a) abundant	(b) scarce	(c) obey
16.	polite	_____	_____	(a) courteous	(b) rude	(c) permit
17.	potent	_____	_____	(a) strong	(b) tolerate	(c) weak
18.	possible	_____	_____	(a) smart	(b) likely	(c) impossible
19.	precious	_____	_____	(a) valuable	(b) inexpensive	(c) tough
20.	prejudice	_____	_____	(a) discrimination	(b) impartiality	(c) enough
21.	premature	_____	_____	(a) stole	(b) early	(c) late
22.	previous	_____	_____	(a) narrow	(b) earlier	(c) following
23.	profit	_____	_____	(a) gain	(b) hard	(c) loss
24.	proud	_____	_____	(a) boastful	(b) humble	(c) practice
25.	prudent	_____	_____	(a) careful	(b) careless	(c) unsteady
26.	prowess	_____	_____	(a) courage	(b) fear	(c) family
27.	punctual	_____	_____	(a) prompt	(b) late	(c) abnormal
28.	quarrelsome	_____	_____	(a) bad-tempered	(b) shame	(c) peaceful
29.	queer	_____	_____	(a) distant	(b) strange	(c) normal
30.	quell	_____	_____	(a) outsmart	(b) calm	(c) incite
31.	query	_____	_____	(a) question	(b) answer	(c) confront

	syn.	*ant.*

32. **question** _____ _____ (a) ask   (b) answer   (c) help

33. **quick** _____ _____ (a) fast   (b) assist   (c) slow

34. **quiet** _____ _____ (a) still   (b) noisy   (c) hurry

35. **radiant** _____ _____ (a) shining   (b) stay   (c) dull

36. **rage** _____ _____ (a) anger   (b) hard   (c) calm

37. **rapid** _____ _____ (a) quick   (b) old   (c) slow

38. **rational** _____ _____ (a) sensible   (b) foolish   (c) useless

39. **ravage** _____ _____ (a) damage   (b) restore   (c) stay

40. **ready** _____ _____ (a) prepared   (b) unprepared   (c) confront

41. **real** _____ _____ (a) assist   (b) true   (c) untrue

42. **rebuke** _____ _____ (a) rival   (b) scold   (c) praise

43. **recall** _____ _____ (a) justice   (b) remember   (c) forget

44. **recede** _____ _____ (a) withdraw   (b) alarm   (c) advance

45. **receive** _____ _____ (a) get   (b) match   (c) give

46. **reckless** _____ _____ (a) careless   (b) careful   (c) outlay

47. **recover** _____ _____ (a) get back   (b) lose   (c) admire

48. **refrain** _____ _____ (a) avoid   (b) respect   (c) indulge

49. **refuse** _____ _____ (a) reject   (b) slow   (c) accept

50. **refute** _____ _____ (a) disprove   (b) agree   (c) admire

51. **regular** _____ _____ (a) usual   (b) avoid   (c) irregular

52. **reinforce** _____ _____ (a) strengthen   (b) allow   (c) weaken

53. **release** _____ _____ (a) free   (b) hold   (c) consistent

54. **relevant** _____ _____ (a) suitable   (b) hardy   (c) unsuitable

55. **relish** _____ _____ (a) avoid   (b) enjoy   (c) dislike

56. **remain** _____ _____ (a) limited   (b) stay   (c) leave

57. **remember** _____ _____ (a) recall   (b) forget   (c) return

58. **remarkable** _____ _____ (a) special   (b) holy   (c) ordinary

59. **repair** _____ _____ (a) fix   (b) break   (c) uneasy

60. **responsible** _____ _____ (a) folly   (b) reliable   (c) unreliable

	syn.	*ant.*			
61. **retreat**	_____	_____	(a) style	(b) withdraw	(c) advance
62. **reveal**	_____	_____	(a) disclose	(b) nickname	(c) hide
63. **ridiculous**	_____	_____	(a) foolish	(b) dislike	(c) sensible
64. **rigorous**	_____	_____	(a) difficult	(b) mild	(c) fear
65. **rough**	_____	_____	(a) assist	(b) unsmooth	(c) gentle
66. **saturate**	_____	_____	(a) fill	(b) outlaw	(c) empty
67. **scatter**	_____	_____	(a) disperse	(b) gather	(c) laugh
68. **scrupulous**	_____	_____	(a) careful	(b) usual	(c) careless
69. **seal**	_____	_____	(a) close	(b) open	(c) refuse
70. **seldom**	_____	_____	(a) allow	(b) rarely	(c) often
71. **sensible**	_____	_____	(a) wise	(b) senseless	(c) aloud
72. **separate**	_____	_____	(a) isolate	(b) unite	(c) trauma
73. **serene**	_____	_____	(a) peaceful	(b) eradicate	(c) disturbed
74. **serious**	_____	_____	(a) important	(b) unimportant	(c) emotional
75. **shrewd**	_____	_____	(a) smart	(b) enmity	(c) dull-witted

Exercise 7: Antonyms

Match each word with its antonym.

_____ 1.	hamper	a.	biased
_____ 2.	inept	b.	believable
_____ 3.	impartial	c.	conclude
_____ 4.	interpret	d.	help
_____ 5.	illegible	e.	misinterpret
_____ 6.	incredible	f.	dexterous
_____ 7.	initiate	g.	establish
_____ 8.	instigate	h.	preserve
_____ 9.	intermittent	i.	gloom
_____ 10.	hot	j.	harmless
_____ 11	maximum	k.	legible
_____ 12.	eradicate	l.	check
_____ 13.	emotional	m.	boredom

_____ 14. enmity   n. extravagant

_____ 15. eliminate   o. minimum

_____ 16. excitement   p. constant

_____ 17. enough   q. cold

_____ 18. fun   r. internal

_____ 19. frugal   s. calm

_____ 20. fluctuate   t. apathy

_____ 21. erratic   u. goodwill

_____ 22. external   v. superior

_____ 23. fervor   w. consistent

_____ 24. fatal   x. persist

_____ 25. faulty   y. shortage

Exercise 8: Prefix

Match each prefix with its meaning.

_____ 1. peri-   a. among, between

_____ 2. dis-   b. apart, deprive of

_____ 3. inter-   c. around

_____ 4. uni-   d. excessive

_____ 5. over-   e. single, one

Exercise 9: Spelling Practice

Circle the words that are spelled incorrectly. Then write the correct spelling of each word.

1. pettite suprise young old   _pEtitE_   _SURPRISE_
2. shete sick healthy acuse   _shEEt_   _ACCUSE_
3. cycle atrak katch car   _AttRACt_   _catch_
4. norse marrage doctor son   _NOSE_   _mAiRAgE ?_
5. mony send sing peece   _moNEy_   _pEACE_

Exercise 1: Matching Meanings

Match each word with its definition or best meaning.

_____ 1. advocate
_____ 2. apprentice *n*
_____ 3. audit *F*
_____ 4. lecture
_____ 5. credit *a*
_____ 6. corpse
_____ 7. budget
_____ 8. bilingual
_____ 9. opponent
_____ 10. lunar *O*
_____ 11. solar
_____ 12. masculine
_____ 13. feminine
_____ 14. universe
_____ 15. sedative
_____ 16. nocturnal *g*
_____ 17. century
_____ 18. catalyst
_____ 19. diurnal *S*
_____ 20. comedian

a. praise or approval
b. an informative talk
c. amount of money needed for a specific purpose
d. a person against one; an adversary
e. having qualities of men or boys
f. examine and verify correctness of financial transactions
g. happening in the night
h. a person who tells jokes
i. that which brings about or hastens a result
j. pleads another cause or case
k. having qualities of women or girls
l. a dead body of a person
m. ability to speak two languages
n. a beginner acquiring a trade or skill
o. relating to the moon
p. relating to the sun
q. a period of 100 years
r. decreases irritation or nervousness
s. happening in the daytime
t. the world

Exercise 2: Synonyms Fill-in

Fill in the blanks to complete the word that is similar in meaning to the boldfaced word.

1. **naive**   in_ _ _ent
2. **nag**   an_ _y
3. **niche**   p_ _c_
4. **nurture**   _ _re
5. **nonchalant**   easy g_ _ _ _g
6. **negotiate**   _ _rga_n
7. **nod**   m_t_o_
8. **ominous**   thr_ _ _ten_ _g
9. **orientation**   in_ _ _du_ _ _ _n
10. **obsess**   pr_o_ _ _py
11. **obstacle**   _ _rr_ _r
12. **offend**   in_ _ _t

13. **occasionally** som _ _ _ _ es
14. **odor**   sc _ _ t
15. **omnipotent**   s _ _ rem _
16. **ordeal**   bu _ _ _ _ n
17. **outcome**   r _ _ _ _ lt
18. **owe**   _ ia _ le
19. **own**   p _ _ _ es _
20. **panacea**   rem _ _ _ y
21. **tangible**   _ _ ncr _ _ e
22. **tantrum**   out _ _ _ _ s _
23. **task**   c _ _ _ re
24. **temperamental** _ _ ody

Exercise 3: Synonyms Multiple Choice

Circle the letter of the word that is similar, or almost similar, in meaning to the boldfaced word.

1. **assume**	(a) reject	(b) accept	(c) retain	(d) retry
2. **dilapidate**	(a) reward	(b) decay	(c) strong	(d) rigid
3. **extrinsic**	(a) outside	(b) internal	(c) inside	(d) flee
4. **docile**	(a) passion	(b) obedient	(c) argue	(d) disobey
5. **brevity**	(a) conciseness	(b) elaborate	(c) lengthy	(d) long
6. **annual**	(a) yearly	(b) sporadic	(c) slow	(d) decade
7. **indicate**	(a) show	(b) hide	(c) conceal	(d) congest
8. **excited**	(a) indifferent	(b) gloomy	(c) distant	(d) thrilled
9. **animosity**	(a) friendship	(b) warmth	(c) hatred	(d) glory
10. **malice**	(a) affection	(b) love	(c) loyalty	(d) spite
11. **tranquil**	(a) noisy	(b) crowded	(c) peaceful	(d) plenty
12. **dispose**	(a) save	(b) get rid of	(c) retain	(d) revive
13. **exclude**	(a) keep out	(b) include	(c) inclusive	(d) exclusive
14. **inhuman**	(a) heartless	(b) kind	(c) human	(d) polite
15. **articulate**	(a) sloppy	(b) well-spoken	(c) disarray	(d) article
16. **multiple**	(a) many	(b) few	(c) must	(d) one
17. **dispute**	(a) agreement	(b) friendly	(c) fatal	(d) argue
18. **smile**	(a) frown	(b) feisty	(c) grin	(d) sad
19. **mediocre**	(a) great	(b) superior	(c) inferior	(d) excellent
20. **anticipate**	(a) expect	(b) reject	(c) seldom	(d) assist

Exercise 4: Synonyms in Context

Circle the letter of the word or phrase that is similar, or almost similar, in meaning to the boldfaced word.

1. country is in a **recession**	(a) slump	(b) progression	(c) war	(d) drought
2. **reduce** the amount	(a) lessen	(b) increase	(c) delete	(d) add
3. **resourceful** young man	(a) clever	(b) angry	(c) lazy	(d) talkative
4. **reputation** means	(a) fame	(b) dignity	(c) honor	(d) loneliness
5. **repeat** the lesson	(a) omit	(b) restate	(c) delete	(d) teach
6. obtain a **refund**	(a) down payment	(b) repayment	(c) discount	(d) fine
7. **register** for my courses	(a) delete	(b) select	(c) sign-up for	(d) drop
8. **respond** to my request	(a) reject	(b) deny	(c) confirm	(d) reply
9. **revise** the first draft	(a) add	(b) mail	(c) type	(d) improve

10. **regulate** the flow	(a) lower	(b) observe	(c) adjust	(d) stop
11. **remedial** courses	(a) developmental	(b) difficult	(c) easy	(d) long
12. **reserve** a seat	(a) keep	(b) take a	(c) discard	(d) overtook
13. **rely** on his parents	(a) help	(b) depend on	(c) disobey	(d) assist
14. **resume** working	(a) stop	(b) discontinue	(c) finish	(d) continue
15. **restrict** movement	(a) encourage	(b) rapid	(c) control	(d) slight
16. **removed** from school	(a) stay	(b) remain	(c) expelled	(d) failed
17. **reject** the proposal	(a) consider	(b) refuse	(c) study	(d) take
18. a **remote** village	(a) distant	(b) friendly	(c) war-like	(d) lonely
19. **revert** to her bad habits	(a) return	(b) reply	(c) ignore	(d) support
20. a **rigid** schedule	(a) fixed	(b) unstable	(c) difficult	(d) changing
21. **rural** area	(a) city	(b) suburban	(c) country	(d) urban
22. to **recommend** means to	(a) suggest	(b) hire	(c) fire	(d) discourage
23. **relapse** into a coma	(a) slip back	(b) recover	(c) go	(d) come out
24. **fast** asleep	(a) sound	(b) light	(c) wide	(d) little
25. to **drip** means to	(a) fall	(b) stay	(c) dry	(d) wet

Exercise 5: Words in Context

Fill in the blank with the correct word or another form of the word below.

rigid	**reputation**	**restrict**	**recession**	**revise**	**reduce**
replace	**refund**	**resourceful**	**respond**	**revert**	**register**

1. As the interest rates began to rise, the economy slipped into a _____ .

2. The best way to lower cholesterol is to _____ your consumption of animal products.

3. Only the most _____ can find a taxi in the rain.

4. Charlie's customers didn't mind waiting for their repairs as he had the _____ of being the best car mechanic in town.

5. If you file your tax return electronically, you will get your _____ in less than a month.

6. One hundred people had _____ for the conference, but only 50 showed up because of the snowstorm.

7. If you don't _____ to this notice in 30 days, your case will be canceled.

8. After listening to the weather forecast, they _____ their plans.

9. If a person faints, the first thing to do is to loosen all clothing that _____ breathing.

10. After losing 50 pounds on the diet, he _____ to his old eating habits and gained it all back.

11. The Browns sent their son to the military school because they thought the discipline of its _____ schedule would help him.

12. It is prudent to _____ the battery in a smoke detector once a year.

Exercise 6: Spelling Practice

Circle the words that are spelled incorrectly. Then write the correct spelling of each word.

1. far   abundon   first   abreviate   _____   _____

2. assist   set   seldome   abscent   _____   _____

3. close   acount   near   buglar   _____   _____

4. come   advisible ocur   gone   _____   _____

5. acros   beleive   tomorrow to   _____   _____

Exercise 1: Matching Meanings

Match each word with its definition or best meaning.

_____ 1. dictator

_____ 2. extrovert

_____ 3. diversity

_____ 4. buffet

_____ 5. blemish

_____ 6. carnivore

_____ 7. herbivorous

_____ 8. omnivorous

_____ 9. dilemma

_____ 10. extraterrestrial

_____ 11. hypersensitive

_____ 12. fugitive

_____ 13. novice

_____ 14. kin

_____ 15. installment

_____ 16. subsidy

_____ 17. phobia

_____ 18. claustrophobia

_____ 19. capitalism

_____ 20. communism

a. a flesh-eating mammal

b. a serious problem

c. feeding on plants or grass

d. abnormally sensitive

e. a beginner

f. abnormal fear of being in a small place

g. a relative; family

h. abnormal fear of something

i. difference or variety

j. eating animal or vegetable food

k. one who is expressive

l. a part of a debt

m. meal where guests serve themselves

n. run away from justice

o. has complete authority and power

p. outside the limits of the earth

q. a spot, stain or scar

r. a grant of money

s. system where businesses are privately controlled

t. system where economic activities are controlled by government

Exercise 2: Synonyms Multiple Choice

Circle the letter of the word that is similar, or almost similar, in meaning to the boldfaced word.

1. **velocity**	(a) speed	(b) city	(c) still	(d) upset
2. **verdict**	(a) answer	(b) question	(c) decision	(d) retreat
3. **yell**	(a) belittle	(b) quiet	(c) shout	(d) silent
4. **wander**	(a) adhere	(b) course	(c) stick	(d) stray
5. **lustrous**	(a) dark	(b) black	(c) unattractive	(d) shiny
6. **youth**	(a) youngster	(b) uncle	(c) old	(d) senile
7. **triumph**	(a) failure	(b) success	(c) try	(d) hard
8. **vacant**	(a) full	(b) empty	(c) rim	(d) control
9. **verify**	(a) neglect	(b) disobey	(c) support	(d) disloyal

10.	**sinister**	(a) angel	(b) saint	(c) heavenly	(d) evil
11.	**yield**	(a) return	(b) lose	(c) loss	(d) little
12.	**abandon**	(a) leave	(b) crowded	(c) care	(d) careless
13.	**quiver**	(a) strong	(b) tremble	(c) healthy	(d) rigid
14.	**qualm**	(a) certainty	(b) confide	(c) confess	(d) doubt
15.	**subsequent**	(a) retard	(b) regroup	(c) following	(d) retest
16.	**subjective**	(a) fair	(b) biased	(c) honest	(d) free
17.	**weird**	(a) strange	(b) well	(c) want	(d) waste
18.	**rehearse**	(a) sing	(b) play	(c) practice	(d) part
19.	**welcome**	(a) reject	(b) receive	(c) chase	(d) disown
20.	**salute**	(a) honor	(b) scold	(c) criticize	(d) fall

Exercise 3:   Synonyms in Context

Circle the letter of the word or phrase that is similar, or almost similar, in meaning to the boldfaced word.

1.	**tentative** plan	(a) sudden	(b) temporary	(c) urgent	(d) small
2.	**motivate** his students	(a) encourage	(b) discourage	(c) attack	(d) assist
3.	a **negative** remark	(a) discouraging	(b) honest	(c) dishonest	(d) bad
4.	feeling of **nausea**	(a) disgust	(b) anger	(c) happiness	(d) hate
5.	a **nutritious** meal	(a) complete	(b) enjoyable	(c) tasty	(d) nourishing
6.	**numerous** remarks	(a) few	(b) two	(c) many	(d) three
7.	feeling **nervous**	(a) restless	(b) prepared	(c) playful	(d) unconcerned
8.	**negotiate** a deal	(a) resist	(b) simple	(c) settle	(d) fasten
9.	possession of **narcotics**	(a) drugs	(b) missiles	(c) snacks	(d) beverages
10.	**oral** report	(a) written	(b) verbal	(c) usual	(d) simple
11.	**outrageous** incident	(a) excited	(b) fancy	(c) shocking	(d) saucy
12.	**optional** assignment	(a) voluntary	(b) compulsory	(c) important	(d) odd
13.	**odd** teacher	(a) good	(b) cheerful	(c) happy	(d) strange
14.	**occurred** at ten o'clock	(a) happened	(b) took	(c) lasted	(d) placed
15.	a **positive** attitude	(a) strange	(b) confident	(c) negative	(d) harmful
16.	a **pious** preacher	(a) happy	(b) inspire	(c) chubby	(d) religious
17.	dangerous **procedure**	(a) sequence of steps	(b) technique	(c) fever	(d) sinus
18.	careless **pedestrian**	(a) walker	(b) cyclist	(c) jogger	(d) runner
19.	**untidy** room	(a) clean	(b) messy	(c) organized	(d) small
20.	urgent **message**	(a) distress	(b) note	(c) communication	(d) letter
21.	**obscene** language	(a) disgusting	(b) clean	(c) clear	(d) easy
22.	**omit** details	(a) include	(b) leave out	(c) observe	(d) petty
23.	a strong **opponent**	(a) giant	(b) soldier	(c) enemy	(d) friend
24.	**persuade** him to go	(a) convince	(b) assist	(c) help	(d) please
25.	**obstruct** his view	(a) block	(b) clear	(c) fault	(d) assist
26.	a **passion** for sports	(a) love	(b) hatred	(c) eye	(d) ability

27. **observe** her behavior	(a) suspend	(b) note	(c) react	(d) avoid
28. **prolong** the suspense	(a) strengthen	(b) continue	(c) avoid	(d) notice
29. a **loud** uproar	(a) noisy	(b) noiseless	(c) quiet	(d) calm
30. **urban** area	(a) dirty	(b) clean	(c) city	(d) country
31. **ultimate** decision	(a) entry	(b) final	(c) urgent	(d) hasty
32. **undermine** their efforts	(a) weaken	(b) encourage	(c) strengthen	(d) applaud
33. **tolerate** his mannerisms	(a) hate	(b) dislike	(c) note	(d) put up with
34. **terminal** disease	(a) deadly	(b) not serious	(c) lengthy	(d) short
35. **stubborn** child	(a) excited	(b) angry	(c) sad	(d) obstinate
36. a **skeptic** is a	(a) doubtful person	(b) positive	(c) agreeable	(d) disloyal
37. a weekly **quiz**	(a) argument	(b) short examination	(c) gamble	(d) tour

Exercise 4: Words in Context

Fill in the blank with the correct word or another form of the word below.

nervous	pious	optional	outrageous
oral	numerous	odd	tentative
negotiate	nausea	motivate	negative

1. The couple set a _____ date of June, 1999 for their wedding.

2. No threats or bribes could _____ Henry to get a summer job; he preferred visiting his family in Jamaica.

3. _____ feedback caused Edith to abandon her idea of opening a vegetarian restaurant.

4. The _____ began as soon as she stepped aboard the boat and continued throughout the voyage.

5. Because of _____ complaints from customers, the automobile manufacturer completely redesigned the cooling system of the car.

6. Lisa consulted a therapist to try to control her _____ giggle.

7. That bicycle is not worth $400. Try to _____ a better price.

8. To get a doctorate degree both _____ and written examinations are required.

9. Half a million dollars is not an _____ price for a house in California.

10. The travel package included one week in Honolulu; trips to the other islands were _____ .

11. People from other countries find the American custom of treating pets like children very _____.

12. My grandmother was very _____ ; she went to church every morning throughout her life.

Exercise 5: Words in Context (Cont'd)

Fill in the blank with the correct word or another form of the word below.

obscene	skeptic	opponent	pedestrian
ultimate	procedure	persuade	obstruct
untidy	tolerate	message	omit

1. Please explain again the _____ for applying for a driver's license.

2. Because there are few traffic lights, being a _____ in Mexico City is taking your life in your hands.

3. Although her desk appeared _____, she was actually a very organized person.

4. At the sound of the tone, please leave a short _____ .

5. The school board declared the novel _____ and removed all copies from the shelves of the library.

6. When addressing the envelope, don't _____ the zip code.

7. The high school gym was packed for the game against Central High, their chief _____ in the district.

8. No matter how hard we tried, we could not _____ him to taste the pickled pigs' feet.

9. Twenty years ago there was a clear view of the river. Now the view is _____ by high rise apartment buildings.

10. I think the idea for your book is good; however, the _____ decision of whether it will be published lies with the editor.

11. People from rural areas find it difficult to _____ the noise level in big cities.

12. Even after reading several first hand accounts of abductions by space aliens, he remained a _____ .

Exercise 6: Synonyms - Antonyms

Select the synonym and antonym of each boldfaced word.

		syn.	*ant.*			
1.	**capacity**	_____	_____	(a) went	(b) capability	(c) inability
2.	**cite**	_____	_____	(a) want	(b) indicate	(c) plagiarize
3.	**coherent**	_____	_____	(a) consistent	(b) disjointed	(c) honest
4.	**compel**	_____	_____	(a) practice	(b) force	(c) coax
5.	**comparable**	_____	_____	(a) choose	(b) alike	(c) different
6.	**comfortable**	_____	_____	(a) relaxed	(b) penalized	(c) restless
7.	**competent**	_____	_____	(a) upset	(b) efficient	(c) inept
8.	**comply**	_____	_____	(a) retreat	(b) follow	(c) disobey
9.	**concede**	_____	_____	(a) admit	(b) silent	(c) deny
10.	**confirm**	_____	_____	(a) verify	(b) stray	(c) question

	syn.	*ant.*			
11. **consequence**	_____	_____	(a) result	(b) cause	(c) shine
12. **conservative**	_____	_____	(a) traditional	(b) senile	(c) liberal
13. **clandestine**	_____	_____	(a) secret	(b) hard	(c) overt
14. **collaborate**	_____	_____	(a) control	(b) cooperate	(c) conflict
15. **contingency**	_____	_____	(a) uncertainty	(b) play	(c) disloyal
16. **coincide**	_____	_____	(a) evil	(b) correspond	(c) disagree
17. **compose**	_____	_____	(a) create	(b) litter	(c) destroy
18. **contradict**	_____	_____	(a) dispute	(b) agree	(c) careless
19. **confront**	_____	_____	(a) challenge	(b) rigid	(c) avoid
20. **controversy**	_____	_____	(a) conflict	(b) doubt	(c) agreement
21. **callous**	_____	_____	(a) free	(b) insensitive	(c) sensitive
22. **capability**	_____	_____	(a) ability	(b) retest	(c) inability
23. **capture**	_____	_____	(a) arrest	(b) free	(c) waste
24. **care**	_____	_____	(a) captain	(b) protection	(c) neglect
25. **charming**	_____	_____	(a) disown	(b) pleasing	(c) obnoxious
26. **cheap**	_____	_____	(a) inexpensive	(b) own	(c) expensive
27. **clarify**	_____	_____	(a) explain	(b) fall	(c) confuse
28. **clean**	_____	_____	(a) pure	(b) inside	(c) dirty
29. **combine**	_____	_____	(a) hinder	(b) mix	(c) separate
30. **commotion**	_____	_____	(a) disturbance	(b) order	(c) judgment
31. **compassion**	_____	_____	(a) sympathy	(b) agree	(c) harshness
32. **complex**	_____	_____	(a) complicated	(b) simple	(c) safe
33. **confess**	_____	_____	(a) anxious	(b) admit	(c) deny
34. **conform**	_____	_____	(a) agree	(b) distort	(c) dissent
35. **convenient**	_____	_____	(a) want	(b) suitable	(c) unsuitable
36. **counterfeit**	_____	_____	(a) fake	(b) frantic	(c) real
37. **courteous**	_____	_____	(a) polite	(b) rude	(c) expensive
38. **deduct**	_____	_____	(a) subtract	(b) disagree	(c) add
39. **defy**	_____	_____	(a) conceal	(b) disobey	(c) obey

	syn.	*ant.*			
40. depart	_____	_____	(a) leave	(b) attempt	(c) arrive
41. demolish	_____	_____	(a) destroy	(b) move	(c) restore
42. deposit	_____	_____	(a) store	(b) tell	(c) withdraw
43. desist	_____	_____	(a) stop	(b) continue	(c) deliberate
44. destroy	_____	_____	(a) ruin	(b) analyze	(c) restore
45. detain	_____	_____	(a) delay	(b) dislike	(c) hurry
46. different	_____	_____	(a) unlike	(b) alike	(c) care
47. difficult	_____	_____	(a) hard	(b) sad	(c) easy
48. diminish	_____	_____	(a) decrease	(b) increase	(c) withdrawn
49. dilute	_____	_____	(a) weaken	(b) cease	(c) strengthen
50. discard	_____	_____	(a) reject	(b) keep	(c) constant
51. distinct	_____	_____	(a) clear	(b) indefinite	(c) claim
52. distress	_____	_____	(a) anguish	(b) comfort	(c) harsh
53. drastic	_____	_____	(a) severe	(b) least	(c) mild
54. dwindle	_____	_____	(a) lessen	(b) keep	(c) increase
55. dynamic	_____	_____	(a) mediate	(b) spirited	(c) dull
56. eager	_____	_____	(a) explain	(b) anxious	(c) unconcerned
57. ecstasy	_____	_____	(a) award	(b) joy	(c) sadness
58. eject	_____	_____	(a) expel	(b) fake	(c) include
59. elated	_____	_____	(a) overjoyed	(b) control	(c) unhappy
60. elder	_____	_____	(a) older	(b) younger	(c) enemy
61. eligible	_____	_____	(a) suitable	(b) petty	(c) ineligible
62. emit	_____	_____	(a) good	(b) discharge	(c) receive
63. encourage	_____	_____	(a) support	(b) true	(c) discourage
64. enhance	_____	_____	(a) improve	(b) stop	(c) impair
65. enlarge	_____	_____	(a) heavy	(b) increase	(c) reduce
66. entire	_____	_____	(a) correct	(b) complete	(c) part
67. enormous	_____	_____	(a) large	(b) loyal	(c) tiny

		syn.	*ant.*			
68.	erratic	_____	_____	(a) uncertain	(b) sell	(c) constant
69.	evacuate	_____	_____	(a) leave	(b) decrease	(c) arrive
70.	eternal	_____	_____	(a) forever	(b) large	(c) temporary
71.	evident	_____	_____	(a) hit	(b) clear	(c) vague
72.	excess	_____	_____	(a) extra	(b) popular	(c) lack
73.	exterior	_____	_____	(a) outside	(b) start	(c) interior
74.	explicit	_____	_____	(a) clear	(b) unclear	(c) amaze
75.	extravagant	_____	_____	(a) excessive	(b) observe	(c) meager

Exercise 7: Spelling Practice

Circle the words that are spelled incorrectly. Then write the correct spelling of each word.

1. fight   fist   nife   paket   _____   _____
2. toast   roast   prospur   bussy   _____   _____
3. dirt   dust   kurupt   fasen   _____   _____
4. eclips   esy   help   comfort   _____   _____
5. toe   boket   ear   cigaret   _____   _____

SEVENTH DAY

Exercise 1:   Matching Meanings

Match each word with its definition or best meaning.

_____ 1. kilometer	a. nine angles and nine sides
_____ 2. radius	b. to increase in number or amount
_____ 3. circumference	c. ten angles and ten sides
_____ 4. ton	d. a small part
_____ 5. square	e. seven angles and seven sides
_____ 6. multiply	f. three feet
_____ 7. triangle	g. eight angles and eight sides
_____ 8. quadrangle	h. has three sides and three angles
_____ 9. foot	i. a straight line from the center of a circle to the circumference
_____ 10. pentagon	j. six angles and six sides
_____ 11. hexagon	k. outer boundary of a circle
_____ 12. heptagon	l. has four equal sides
_____ 13. octagon	m. a unit of weight; 2.2046 pounds
_____ 14. nonagon	n. equals to 1,000 meters
_____ 15. decagon	o. 2,000 pounds
_____ 16. percentage	p. four sides and four angles
_____ 17. fraction	q. twelve inches
_____ 18. yard	r. five angles and five sides
_____ 19. kilogram	s. a rate or proportion per hundred
_____ 20. angle	t. the space between two lines diverging from a common point

Exercise 2:   Synonyms Fill-in

Fill in the blank(s) to complete the word that is similar in meaning to the boldfaced word.

1. **cab**	ta__i	6. **caress**	__ __ __dle
2. **calculate**	fig__ __e	7. **converse**	c__ __t
3. **camouflage**	d__sgui__ __	8. **calamity**	dis__ __ter
4. **candidate**	ap__ __ican__	9. **charisma**	ch__ __m
5. **capsize**	over__ __ __n	10. **comprehensive**	__ __ten__ive

11. **constitute**	com_ _ise	17. **caution**	ad_ _se
12. **contemplate**	_ _ditat_	18. **coerce**	fo_c_
13. **recipe**	form_ _a	19. **compensate**	_ _y
14. **curtail**	s_ _rten	20. **consecutive**	cont_ _u_us
15. **cheat**	_ _b	21. **purpose**	a_m
16. **chastise**	re_ _ke	22. **quantity**	amo_ _t

Exercise 3: Synonyms Multiple Choice

Circle the letter of the word that is similar, or almost similar, in meaning to the boldfaced word.

1. **intrinsic**	(a) inherent	(b) outside	(c) outlaw	(d) painful
2. **insinuate**	(a) suggest	(b) deny	(c) detain	(d) hear
3. **impromptu**	(a) unrehearsed	(b) prepared	(c) promise	(d) prompt
4. **manipulate**	(a) control	(b) many	(c) late	(d) plenty
5. **mammoth**	(a) gigantic	(b) tiny	(c) microscopic	(d) minute
6. **majestic**	(a) major	(b) dignified	(c) minor	(d) jest
7. **leisure**	(a) labor	(b) important	(c) later	(d) spare time
8. **latent**	(a) active	(b) alert	(c) hidden	(d) late
9. **lucid**	(a) loose	(b) difficult	(c) clear	(d) cloudy
10. **nocturnal**	(a) mighty	(b) nightly	(c) daily	(d) not
11. **lavish**	(a) little	(b) meager	(c) few	(d) extravagant
12. **loiter**	(a) leave	(b) idle	(c) depart	(d) later
13. **obvious**	(a) unseen	(b) uneasy	(c) understandable	(d) invisible
14. **objective**	(a) unprejudiced	(b) subjective	(c) bias	(d) favorite
15. **quota**	(a) quote	(b) proportion	(c) economic	(d) number
16. **obsolete**	(a) modern	(b) showy	(c) outdated	(d) current
17. **passive**	(a) alive	(b) energetic	(c) active	(d) inactive
18. **psychic**	(a) fortuneteller	(b) phony	(c) unreal	(d) scientific
19. **proverb**	(a) saying	(b) praise	(c) verb	(d) noun
20. **provoke**	(a) pacify	(b) irritate	(c) calm	(d) quiet

95

Exercise 4: Synonyms in Context

Circle the letter of the word that is similar, or almost similar, in meaning to the boldfaced word.

1. **principal** investigator — (a) assistant — (b) older — (c) chief — (d) elderly
2. to **protest** means to — (a) celebrate — (b) action — (c) complain — (d) incident
3. **pursued** the thief — (a) apprehend — (b) caught — (c) arrest — (d) chased
4. a **permanent** job — (a) difficult — (b) seasonal — (c) tedious — (d) lasting
5. a **prelude** is an — (a) opening — (b) closing — (c) entity — (d) operation
6. **prominent** politician — (a) well-known — (b) unpopular — (c) rude — (d) incompetent
7. to **procrastinate** means to — (a) delay — (b) hasten — (c) change — (d) hurry
8. **prosperous** businessman — (a) greedy — (b) successful — (c) dishonest — (d) famous
9. **punish** the child — (a) love — (b) notice — (c) scold — (d) care
10. **outstanding** performance — (a) excellent — (b) unsatisfactory — (c) disappointing — (d) poor
11. **unstable** mental condition — (a) stable — (b) acceptable — (c) uneasy — (d) unsteady
12. **traditional** life-style — (a) modern — (b) today's — (c) old-fashioned — (d) lavish
13. earth **tremor** — (a) latitude — (b) longitude — (c) vibration — (d) mechanic
14. a **tragic** accident — (a) non-serious — (b) devastating — (c) lonely — (d) harmless
15. **reliable** friend — (a) trustworthy — (b) able — (c) sincere — (d) wicked
16. a **remedy** for headache — (a) formula — (b) solution — (c) chemical — (d) cure
17. **reduce** my payment — (a) increase — (b) postpone — (c) decrease — (d) accept
18. **reluctant** to leave — (a) ready — (b) unwilling — (c) incapable — (d) apt
19. to **replicate** means to — (a) copy — (b) hide — (c) picture — (d) invent
20. union **representative** — (a) spokesperson — (b) thief — (c) enemy — (d) friend

Exercise 5: Words in Context

Fill in the blank with the correct word or another form of the word below.

prelude	reliable	prosperous	prominent
replicate	pursue	tragic	unstable
reluctant	principal	procrastinate	protest

1. What is the _____ reason you don't want to see this movie?

2. You can _____ all you want; the boss is not going to change the work schedule just for you.

3. The police had to _____ the robber for six blocks before they finally caught up with him.

4. The announcement of a 10 o'clock curfew was only the _____ of worse things to happen under the rule of the dictator.

5. Because he was a _____ name in the field of criminal law, he was able to charge fees of $200 per hour.

6. Because of her habit to _____ , Molly found herself always rushing to meet deadlines.

7. With the discovery of oil, the small country became _____ .

8. Because the economy was _____ , he chose to invest most of his money in gold coins.

9. The hit-and-run death of the mother and child was _____ .

10. Nowadays it is difficult to find _____ workers.

11. The bank was _____ to give Ms. Campbell the loan because the business she wanted to open seemed very risky.

12. The scientists were very excited by the experiment, but their excitement soon turned to frustration when they were unable to _____ the results in further tests.

Exercise 6: Spelling Practice

Circle the words that are spelled incorrectly. Then write the correct spelling of each word.

1. faitgue   fight   farm   scizzors   _____   _____

2. woman   terrifik   thing   flaim   _____   _____

3. advertice   advise   beggest   size   _____   _____

4. chiet   chief   floor   embrase   _____   _____

5. family   grammer   feer   fancy   _____   _____

Exercise 1: Matching Meanings

Match the word with its definition or best meaning.

_____ 1. thermostat

_____ 2. thermometer

_____ 3. barometer

_____ 4. chronometer

_____ 5. telescope

_____ 6. microscope

_____ 7. manometer

_____ 8. ambulance

_____ 9. lateral

_____ 10. speedometer

_____ 11. stethoscope

_____ 12. sphygmomanometer

_____ 13. cerebellum

_____ 14. therapeutic

_____ 15. intravenous

_____ 16. laryngitis

_____ 17. influenza

_____ 18. inflamed

_____ 19. inoculate

_____ 20. cerebrum

_____ 21. ulcer

_____ 22. ovary

_____ 23. stroke

_____ 24. stress

_____ 25. stomach

a. front part of the brain

b. back part of the brain

c. measures temperature

d. makes microorganisms look larger

e. indicates speed of a motor vehicle

f. measures atmospheric pressure

g. paralysis

h. measures time

i. mental or physical tension

j. regulates temperature

k. produces eggs

l. an open sore

m. makes distant objects appear nearer and larger

n. belly or abdomen

o. to inject serum or create immunity

p. sideways

q. vehicle for transporting the sick

r. measures the pressure of gases

s. temporary loss of voice

t. measures blood pressure

u. directly into a vein

v. feverish and swollen

w. used to listen to sounds in the body

x. curative

y. inflammation of respiratory tract caused by a virus

Exercise 2: Synonyms Fill-in

Fill in the blank(s) to complete the word that is similar in meaning to the boldfaced word.

1. **cohesive**	con _ _ _ted	13. **destination**	en_
2. **convey**	tra_ _ _it	14. **devise**	form_ _ _ _te
3. **constituent**	com_ _ _ent	15. **discriminate**	sep_ _ _ate
4. **content**	s_ _isfi_d	16. **diverge**	st_ _ _y
5. **criteria**	mea_ _re	17. **derelict**	_ um
6. **commitment**	pro_ _ _e	18. **designate**	app_ _ _ _ t
7. **component**	_ _gmen_ _	19. **devastate**	_ _ _ troy
8. **crisis**	emer_ _ _cy	20. **discipline**	pu _ _ _ _h
9. **draft**	sk_ _ch	21. **diplomacy**	t _ _ _t
10. **detract**	_ _ _trac_	22. **reciprocate**	ret _ _ _ n
11. **decipher**	_ _ter_ _et	23. **recur**	_ _ _ pea _
12. **derive**	g_ _n	24. **refuge**	sh _ _ _ er

Exercise 3: Synonyms Multiple Choice

Circle the letter of the word that is similar, or almost similar, in meaning to the boldfaced word.

1. **squander**	(a) save	(b) hoard	(c) keep	(d) misuse
2. **reject**	(a) accept	(b) take	(c) covet	(d) refuse
3. **penalty**	(a) sum	(b) reward	(c) honor	(d) fine
4. **militant**	(a) politician	(b) submissive	(c) aide	(d) activist
5. **subside**	(a) silent	(b) sink	(c) float	(d) loud
6. **invincible**	(a) unbeatable	(b) weak	(c) lazy	(d) feeble
7. **harmony**	(a) agreement	(b) discord	(c) detest	(d) harm
8. **criticize**	(a) judge	(b) praise	(c) plentiful	(d) cry
9. **copious**	(a) few	(b) faulty	(c) abundant	(d) little
10. **speculate**	(a) know	(b) certain	(c) sure	(d) guess
11. **cry**	(a) laugh	(b) sob	(c) excited	(d) joy
12. **perceptive**	(a) negligent	(b) ignorant	(c) observant	(d) sleepy
13. **innuendo**	(a) suggestion	(b) paper	(c) report	(d) assertion
14. **revoke**	(a) accept	(b) cancel	(c) keep	(d) restore
15. **possess**	(a) disown	(b) retreat	(c) own	(d) rest
16. **sustain**	(a) neglect	(b) support	(c) stagnant	(d) coy
17. **convince**	(a) discourage	(b) distant	(c) trust	(d) encourage
18. **assurance**	(a) doubt	(b) fault	(c) guarantee	(d) note
19. **concur**	(a) deny	(b) agree	(c) detest	(d) avoid
20. **proposal**	(a) paper	(b) story	(c) book	(d) offer

Exercise 4:   Synonyms in Context

Circle the letter of the word or phrase that is similar, or almost similar, in meaning to the boldfaced word.

1. a **trauma** is a ... (a) shock ... (b) fiction ... (c) myth ... (d) tale
2. **eradicate** the disease ... (a) eliminate ... (b) keep ... (c) control ... (d) treat
3. an **emotional** speech ... (a) fine ... (b) excitable ... (c) short ... (d) fiery
4. **enmity** means ... (a) jolly ... (b) fate ... (c) fear ... (d) hatred
5. to **appreciate** means to ... (a) like ... (b) limit ... (c) propose ... (d) propel
6. overcome with **excitement** ... (a) gloom ... (b) dismay ... (c) fervor ... (d) problems
7. **enough** food ... (a) little ... (b) sufficient ... (c) tasty ... (d) tasteless
8. drank **excessive** alcohol ... (a) too much ... (b) dangerous ... (c) expensive ... (d) too little
9. likes **fun** ... (a) play ... (b) jog ... (c) fighting ... (d) pleasure
10. a **frugal** man ... (a) harmful ... (b) stingy ... (c) harmless ... (d) dangerous
11. the price **fluctuates** ... (a) changes ... (b) stagnates ... (c) good ... (d) fair
12. **erratic** means ... (a) stable ... (b) foretell ... (c) irregular ... (d) unjust
13. **guilty** means ... (a) sad ... (b) innocent ... (c) criminal ... (d) charged
14. **external** means ... (a) outer ... (b) broad ... (c) narrow ... (d) restrict
15. **fervor** means ... (a) contain ... (b) boredom ... (c) dastard ... (d) enthusiasm
16. a **fatal** accident ... (a) harmless ... (b) serious ... (c) small ... (d) insignificant
17. to **generate** means to ... (a) sell ... (b) distribute ... (c) produce ... (d) show
18. **faulty** device ... (a) perfect ... (b) accurate ... (c) expensive ... (d) imperfect
19. expressed **gratitude** ... (a) appreciation ... (b) taste ... (c) distrust ... (d) disdain
20. **eminent** means ... (a) unpopular ... (b) famous ... (c) sane ... (d) sick
21. **homogenous** means ... (a) similar ... (b) dissimilar ... (c) genius ... (d) generous
22. **frolic** means ... (a) fun ... (b) fright ... (c) fear ... (d) fighting
23. **fury** means ... (a) shame ... (b) satisfaction ... (c) anger ... (d) tension
24. **frequent** interruption ... (a) intermittent ... (b) short ... (c) single ... (d) regular
25. **hostile** behavior ... (a) unfriendly ... (b) acceptable ... (c) tolerable ... (d) aggressive
26. **fictitious** means ... (a) real ... (b) imaginary ... (c) tangible ... (d) touchable
27. **superstition** is a ... (a) fear ... (b) attack ... (c) story ... (d) belief based on ignorance
28. **fulfilling** experience ... (a) disturbing ... (b) filling ... (c) pleasing ... (d) tiring
29. **facetious** means ... (a) serious ... (b) concerned ... (c) desperate ... (d) funny
30. a **frustrated** student ... (a) discouraged ... (b) dissatisfied ... (c) brilliant ... (d) talkative
31. looks **perplexed** ... (a) honest ... (b) puzzled ... (c) afraid ... (d) disturbed
32. **gait** means ... (a) tired ... (b) gate ... (c) speech ... (d) way of walking
33. a **generous** teacher ... (a) careless ... (b) selfish ... (c) unselfish ... (d) tough
34. **gamut** means ... (a) narrow ... (b) range ... (c) simple ... (d) complex
35. a **vivid** imagination ... (a) graphic ... (b) precise ... (c) simple ... (d) important

Exercise 5: Words in Context

Fill in the blank with the correct word or another form of the word below.

trauma	eradicate	frugal	guilty	appreciate
fluctuate	enmity	erratic	fervor	enough

1. The _____ between the two families lasted for 20 years even though no one could recall the original source of the discord.

2. After six months, she still hadn't recovered from the _____ of the earthquake.

3. I would _____ if you didn't talk during the movie.

4. With the discovery of the Salk vaccine, polio was _____.

5. They were such big eaters that a pound of spaghetti was barely _____ for the two of them.

6. Because she lived on a fixed pension, Diane was forced to be _____.

7. The price of gold has _____ very little in the past five years.

8. Because of his _____ driving patterns, the policeman stopped him and demanded that he take a sobriety test.

9. Although all the evidence pointed against him, the defendant insisted that he was not _____.

10. Her lack of _____ at the football game went unnoticed by her boyfriend.

Exercise 6: Words in Context (Cont'd)

Fill in the blank with the correct word or another form of the word below.

eminent	superstition	homogenous	hostile
fury	gratitude	frequent	fictitious
frolic	generate	fatal	faulty

1. Smoking causes many diseases, some of which are _____ .

2. Keeping your money in a savings account is safe, but will not _____ much interest.

3. The inspector traced the cause of the fire to _____ wiring.

4. When the policewoman brought the lost child home, words of _____ spilled forth from the mother's mouth.

5. Dr. Carter is one of the most _____ physicians in town.

6. The people of Korea are for the most part _____ .

7. The children loved to watch the lambs _____ in the meadow.

8. No one had witnessed a hurricane with as much _____ as this one; not one house was left unscathed.

9. Most airlines offer bonuses to _____ flyers.

10. A clean kitchen is a _____ environment for most cockroaches.

11. Although the book paralleled his life almost exactly, the author continued to claim that the story was _____ .

12. For reasons of _____ many buildings do not have a thirteenth floor.

Exercise 7: Antonyms

Match each word with its antonym.

_____ 1. accompany	a. unclear
_____ 2. distinction	b. active
_____ 3. accelerate	c. disassociated
_____ 4. apparent	d. increase
_____ 5. dormant	e. known
_____ 6. appropriate	f. abandon
_____ 7. disloyal	g. insignificance
_____ 8. affiliated	h. regular
_____ 9. abduct	i. expand
_____ 10. disillusion	j. delay
_____ 11. abnormal	k. passive
_____ 12. discount	l. unsuitable
_____ 13. donate	m. understate
_____ 14. derogatory	n. loyal
_____ 15. disperse	o. retain
_____ 16. anonymous	p. beguile
_____ 17. exaggerate	q. return
_____ 18. abbreviate	r. repulsive
_____ 19. digress	s. positive
_____ 20. dynamic	t. appear
_____ 21. charismatic	u. gather
_____ 22. disappear	v. careless
_____ 23. discreet	w. stay
_____ 24. recession	x. recovery
_____ 25. resourceful	y. inept

Exercise 8: Spelling Practice

Circle the words that are spelled incorrectly. Then write the correct spelling of each word.

1. sample   semple   seldum   unfair   _____   _____

2. soppose   selvefish   watch   ring   _____   _____

3. tell   sight   emidiate   introduse   _____   _____

4. test   sexi   vest   gest   _____   _____

5. sorey   walk   run   suport   _____   _____

102

Exercise 1:   Synonyms Fill-in

Fill in the blank(s) to complete the word that is similar in meaning to the boldfaced word.

1. **data**   fa_ _s
2. **decease**   d_e
3. **susceptible** he_ _ _ess
4. **dedicate**   de_ _te
5. **defeat**   over_ _ _e
6. **deficient**   _ _adeq_ _ _e
7. **delicious**   appe_ _ _ _ng
8. **demand**   com_ _ _d
9. **describe**   ex_ _ _in
10. **explain**   _ _ _rify
11. **exempt**   exc_ _ _ _e
12. **elicit**   ev_ _ _e
13. **rank**   po_ _ _t_ _ _n
14. **endeavor**   _tte_ _ _t
15. **recite**   re_ _ _at
16. **enhance**   str_ _ _gt_ _ _n
17. **escalate**   _ _crea_ _ _
18. **equate**   _qu_ _ _
19. **embezzle**   _tea_
20. **equip**   pro_ _ _de

Exercise 2:   Synonyms - Antonyms

Select the synonym and antonym of each boldfaced word.

		syn.	*ant.*			
1.	**erase**	___	___	(a) delete	(b) preserve	(c) greedy
2.	**establish**	___	___	(a) organize	(b) apprehend	(c) dissolve
3.	**fallible**	___	___	(a) difficult	(b) imperfect	(c) perfect
4.	**facilitate**	___	___	(a) delay	(b) assist	(c) hinder
5.	**futile**	___	___	(a) useless	(b) greedy	(c) effective
6.	**fabulous**	___	___	(a) fantastic	(b) terrible	(c) love
7.	**faith**	___	___	(a) belief	(b) stable	(c) doubt
8.	**fantasy**	___	___	(a) dream	(b) modern	(c) reality
9.	**fatigue**	___	___	(a) tiredness	(b) energy	(c) latitude
10.	**fault**	___	___	(a) mistake	(b) formula	(c) merit
11.	**festive**	___	___	(a) increase	(b) merry	(c) gloomy
12.	**flourish**	___	___	(a) prosper	(b) decline	(c) ready

	syn.	ant.			
13. **fluster**	_____	_____	(a) disturb	(b) copy	(c) compose
14. **foremost**	_____	_____	(a) principal	(b) minor	(c) older
15. **forever**	_____	_____	(a) always	(b) caught	(c) never
16. **forsake**	_____	_____	(a) action	(b) abandon	(c) retain
17. **grieve**	_____	_____	(a) mourn	(b) rejoice	(c) hasten
18. **grotesque**	_____	_____	(a) ugly	(b) normal	(c) acceptable
19. **graphic**	_____	_____	(a) colorful	(b) notice	(c) dull
20. **gang**	_____	_____	(a) group	(b) hide	(c) individual
21. **glimpse**	_____	_____	(a) glance	(b) postpone	(c) stare
22. **guest**	_____	_____	(a) willing	(b) visitor	(c) host
23. **halt**	_____	_____	(a) stop	(b) continue	(c) complain
24. **hilarious**	_____	_____	(a) comical	(b) chief	(c) serious
25. **immaculate**	_____	_____	(a) arrest	(b) faultless	(c) flawed
26. **implausible**	_____	_____	(a) tedious	(b) unbelievable	(c) credible
27. **implicit**	_____	_____	(a) definite	(b) uncertain	(c) plenty
28. **incentive**	_____	_____	(a) encouragement	(b) change	(c) discouragement
29. **incoherent**	_____	_____	(a) entity	(b) inconsistent	(c) clear
30. **incorporate**	_____	_____	(a) include	(b) scold	(c) exclude
31. **inquisitive**	_____	_____	(a) curious	(b) uninterested	(c) dishonest
32. **intricate**	_____	_____	(a) uneasy	(b) complex	(c) simple
33. **illuminate**	_____	_____	(a) brighten	(b) scold	(c) obscure
34. **impair**	_____	_____	(a) damage	(b) improve	(c) uneasy
35. **initiate**	_____	_____	(a) start	(b) common	(c) conclude
36. **intense**	_____	_____	(a) strong	(b) weak	(c) vibrate
37. **inevitable**	_____	_____	(a) sincere	(b) unavoidable	(c) avoidable
38. **innate**	_____	_____	(a) incapable	(b) inborn	(c) learned

	syn.	*ant.*

39. **isolate** _____ _____ (a) separate (b) include (c) decrease

40. **illicit** _____ _____ (a) forbidden (b) incapable (c) authorized

41. **imminent** _____ _____ (a) picture (b) approaching (c) distant

42. **intimate** _____ _____ (a) innermost (b) incident (c) distant

43. **identify** _____ _____ (a) recognize (b) mistake (c) chased

44. **idiot** _____ _____ (a) fool (b) genius (c) operation

45. **implore** _____ _____ (a) appeal (b) hurry (c) refuse

46. **include** _____ _____ (a) care (b) involve (c) exclude

47. **indiscriminate** _____ _____ (a) unsystematic (b) concern (c) orderly

48. **inherent** _____ _____ (a) inborn (b) foreign (c) famous

49. **inquisitive** _____ _____ (a) unsteady (b) curious (c) uninterested

50. **invite** _____ _____ (a) request (b) care (c) discourage

51. **irrevocable** _____ _____ (a) irreversible (b) lavish (c) reversible

52. **indelible** _____ _____ (a) harmless (b) unremovable (c) temporary

53. **inconspicuous** _____ _____ (a) low-profile (b) picture (c) noticeable

54. **inanimate** _____ _____ (a) lifeless (b) cure (c) active

55. **irrelevant** _____ _____ (a) unconnected (b) wicked (c) vital

56. **inform** _____ _____ (a) apt (b) tell (c) conceal

57. **involve** _____ _____ (a) include (b) cure (c) exclude

58. **irresistible** _____ _____ (a) compelling (b) accept (c) repulsive

59. **isolate** _____ _____ (a) separate (b) include (c) invent

60. **jealous** _____ _____ (a) envious (b) trusting (c) fight

61. **jeopardize** _____ _____ (a) manifest (b) risk (c) safeguard

62. **lucrative** _____ _____ (a) profitable (b) latent (c) unprofitable

63. **lenient** _____ _____ (a) loiter (b) lax (c) strict

64. **liberal** _____ _____ (a) tolerant (b) strict (c) quote

	syn.	*ant.*			
65. **labor**	_____	_____	(a) struggle	(b) obvious	(c) leisure
66. **lack**	_____	_____	(a) need	(b) have	(c) objective
67. **lapse**	_____	_____	(a) decline	(b) obsolete	(c) increase
68. **lure**	_____	_____	(a) major	(b) attract	(c) repulse
69. **learn**	_____	_____	(a) labor	(b) grasp	(c) forget
70. **linger**	_____	_____	(a) remain	(b) leave	(c) deny
71. **mandatory**	_____	_____	(a) compulsory	(b) optional	(c) difficult
72. **mobile**	_____	_____	(a) movable	(b) alert	(c) stationary
73. **manage**	_____	_____	(a) linger	(b) control	(c) follow
74. **manual**	_____	_____	(a) hand-operated	(b) opponent	(c) automatic
75. **maintain**	_____	_____	(a) support	(b) abandon	(c) bias

Exercise 3: Matching Meanings (Advanced Words)

Match each word with its definition or best meaning.

_____ 1. authenticate   a. indirect reference; indirect way

_____ 2. irrevocable   b. work well together; get along well

_____ 3. casual   c. hateful; evil; wicked

_____ 4. allude   d. not likely to cause damage or harm

_____ 5. disengage   e. a fraud or trick; deception

_____ 6. conspire   f. sociable; like the company of others

_____ 7. compatible   g. to verify as represented; reliable

_____ 8. gregarious   h. not planned; happening by chance

_____ 9. heinous   i. irresistible impulse to steal

_____ 10. hoax   j. set loose; detached

_____ 11. innocuous   k. to act together secretly

_____ 12. kleptomaniac   l. cannot be recalled

Exercise 4: Advanced Words in Context

Fill in the blank with the correct word or another form of the word below.

hoax	allude	conspire	authenticate
gregarious	casual	innocuous	heinous
irrevocable	kleptomaniac	disengage	compatible

1. Before he would buy the Picasso painting, Mr. Fredericks called in an expert to _____ it.

2. The decision to leave his country was _____ so he had to think long and hard.

3. Their first meeting was _____, but subsequent dates became more serious.

4. Although she never directly stated her net worth, Ms. Watkins _____ to her wealth many times during our conversation.

5. Be sure to _____ the clutch before you try to put the car in gear.

6. Benedict Arnold was convicted of treason for _____ with the enemy.

7. After a few years of marriage many couples find that they are not _____.

8. Unlike her older sister who was shy and unsociable, Judy was quite _____.

9. Child abuse is considered one of the most _____ crimes.

10. The radio announcer stated that Martians had landed, but when people began to call the station he was forced to tell his listeners that it was a _____.

11. Mega doses of vitamin C may help to prevent colds; at worst they are _____.

12. After her fourth arrest for shoplifting, a psychiatrist diagnosed her as being a _____.

Exercise 5: Matching Meanings (Advanced Words)

Match each word with its definition.

_____ 1. adamant
_____ 2. aristocrat
_____ 3. ambiguous
_____ 4. acrimonious
_____ 5. scurrilous
_____ 6. subservient
_____ 7. tenacious
_____ 8. trepidation
_____ 9. retaliate
_____ 10. redundant
_____ 11. incessant
_____ 12. impetuous

a. vague; not clear
b. not giving in; inflexible
c. using vulgar or indecent language
d. upper-class
e. stubborn; holding firmly
f. take revenge; fight back
g. without interruption; continuous
h. act with little thought
i. bitter especially in speech and manner
j. anxious; fearful; apprehensive
k. using more words than necessary
l. submissive; useful in an inferior capacity

Exercise 6: Advanced Words in Context

Fill in the blank with the correct word or another form of the word below.

incessant	scurrilous	trepidation	subservient
impetuous	adamant	retaliate	acrimonious
redundant	ambiguous	tenacious	aristocrat

1. She was _____ in not wanting to see the movie.

2. Although she was not from a royal family, many people considered Jacqueline Onasis to be a true _____.

3. The directions for assembling this bicycle are _____.

4. After a particularly _____ argument with his neighbor, Mr. Miller decided to build a fence between their yards.

5. The press made a _____ attack on the president.

6. Tired of being _____ to her employer, Jane quit her job as housekeeper.

7. Because habits are so _____, they are often hard to change.

8. Not being a strong swimmer, Bill stepped into the sea with _____.

9. The United States entered World War II to _____ against the bombing of Pearl Harbor.

10. Many people find the term "free gift" _____.

11. The new father was unable to cope with the baby's _____ crying.

12. Although she thought of herself as a free spirit, her friends considered her actions _____

TENTH DAY

Exercise 1:   Synonyms Multiple Choice

Circle the letter of the word that is similar, or almost similar, in meaning to the boldfaced word.

1. **trepidation**   (a) apprehension   (b) assumption   (c) guess   (d) dangerous
2. **tantalize**   (a) arrest   (b) tease   (c) tolerate   (d) surrender
3. **unique**   (a) common   (b) same   (c) different   (d) similar
4. **universal**   (a) worldwide   (b) restricted   (c) local   (d) commune
5. **stationary**   (a) mobile   (b) moving   (c) uneasy   (d) permanent
6. **stationery**   (a) materialize   (b) materials   (c) query   (d) space
7. **superb**   (a) terrible   (b) awful   (c) splendid   (d) miserable
8. **overwhelm**   (a) surrender   (b) over   (c) assist   (d) overpower
9. **originate**   (a) end   (b) begin   (c) final   (d) terminate
10. **obscure**   (a) unclear   (b) clear   (c) crystal   (d) cure
11. **quandary**   (a) puzzle   (b) laundry   (c) funny   (d) predict
12. **quadruple**   (a) fourfold   (b) forty   (c) square   (d) triangle
13. **perplexed**   (a) understand   (b) confused   (c) understate   (d) clear
14. **purposeful**   (a) wander   (b) stray   (c) deviate   (d) intentional
15. **transform**   (a) introvert   (b) covert   (c) convert   (d) form
16. **transparent**   (a) dull   (b) clear   (c) dirty   (d) opal
17. **spendthrift**   (a) stingy   (b) extravagant   (c) save   (d) hoard
18. **stingy**   (a) cheap   (b) generous   (c) give   (d) freely
19. **turmoil**   (a) normal   (b) disturbance   (c) peaceful   (d) quiet
20. **thrive**   (a) die   (b) waste   (c) live   (d) prosper

Exercise 2:   Synonyms - Antonyms

Select the synonym and antonym of each boldfaced word.

	syn.	*ant.*			
1. **fail**	_____	_____	(a) cancel	(b) underachieve	(c) succeed
2. **fake**	_____	_____	(a) represent	(b) false	(c) real
3. **false**	_____	_____	(a) break	(b) untrue	(c) real
4. **familiar**	_____	_____	(a) well-known	(b) press	(c) unknown
5. **famine**	_____	_____	(a) starvation	(b) part	(c) plenty
6. **fantastic**	_____	_____	(a) terrific	(b) awful	(c) cheap
7. **farewell**	_____	_____	(a) leaving	(b) ready	(c) arriving
8. **fascinate**	_____	_____	(a) help	(b) interest	(c) bore

	syn.	ant.	(a)	(b)	(c)
9. fasten			(a) fell	(b) attach	(c) untie
10. feasible			(a) possible	(b) impossible	(c) play
11. feeble			(a) neutral	(b) weak	(c) strong
12. ferocious			(a) fierce	(b) friend	(c) gentle
13. feud			(a) quarrel	(b) peace	(c) feisty
14. fiction			(a) fantasy	(b) tough	(c) truth
15. fidelity			(a) faithfulness	(b) disloyalty	(c) lowest
16. finish			(a) end	(b) increase	(c) beginning
17. fit			(a) suitable	(b) hide	(c) unfit
18. flaunt			(a) wrong	(b) display	(c) conceal
19. flaw			(a) price	(b) defect	(c) perfection
20. flippant			(a) rude	(b) small	(c) polite
21. foe			(a) enemy	(b) silence	(c) friend
22. fond			(a) loving	(b) disliking	(c) angry
23. forfeit			(a) lose	(b) plenty	(c) retain
24. forgive			(a) excuse	(b) blame	(c) frighten
25. formal			(a) control	(b) business-like	(c) informal
26. formidable			(a) difficult	(b) nobody	(c) easy
27. fortitude			(a) courage	(b) partake	(c) weakness
28. fragrant			(a) sweet-smelling	(b) foul	(c) joyful
29. frail			(a) weak	(b) hard	(c) strong
30. frank			(a) outspoken	(b) obscure	(c) deceitful
31. frantic			(a) friend	(b) excited	(c) calm
32. frigid			(a) cold	(b) guess	(c) warm
33. gather			(a) collect	(b) hero	(c) scatter
34. gigantic			(a) huge	(b) feeling	(c) tiny

	syn.	*ant.*

35. **glamorous** _____ _____   (a) attractive   (b) unattractive   (c) mediate

36. **gradual** _____ _____   (a) explain   (b) slow   (c) sudden

37. **gratitude** _____ _____   (a) thankfulness   (b) ungratefulness   (c) award

38. **hamper** _____ _____   (a) fake   (b) hinder   (c) help

39. **handsome** _____ _____   (a) attractive   (b) ugly   (c) fancy

40. **handy** _____ _____   (a) convenient   (b) lenient   (c) inconvenient

41. **haphazard** _____ _____   (a) lower   (b) random   (c) planned

42. **harm** _____ _____   (a) hurt   (b) find   (c) help

43. **harmonious** _____ _____   (a) agreeing   (b) conflicting   (c) reasonable

44. **harsh** _____ _____   (a) cruel   (b) kind   (c) payment

45. **havoc** _____ _____   (a) clear   (b) destruction   (c) restoration

46. **hide** _____ _____   (a) passage   (b) conceal   (c) explore

47. **hinder** _____ _____   (a) impede   (b) help   (c) respect

48. **hire** _____ _____   (a) employ   (b) smart   (c) fire

49. **homage** _____ _____   (a) control   (b) respect   (c) disrespect

50. **horrible** _____ _____   (a) enemy   (b) terrible   (c) splendid

51. **humble** _____ _____   (a) simple   (b) petty   (c) showy

52. **humiliate** _____ _____   (a) embarrass   (b) good   (c) honor

53. **hurt** _____ _____   (a) harm   (b) true   (c) help

54. **innocent** _____ _____   (a) blameless   (b) guilty   (c) save

55. **insane** _____ _____   (a) conceal   (b) crazy   (c) sane

56. **insignificant** _____ _____   (a) unimportant   (b) meaningful   (c) attempt

57. **insolent** _____ _____   (a) rude   (b) polite   (c) favorite

58. **inspire** _____ _____   (a) encourage   (b) tell   (c) discourage

59. **invalid** _____ _____   (a) ineffective   (b) valid   (c) deliberate

60. **irrelevant** _____ _____   (a) unrelated   (b) relevant   (c) dislike

	syn.	*ant.*			
61. **irritate**	_____	_____	(a) annoy	(b) analyze	(c) soothe
62. **ideal**	_____	_____	(a) perfect	(b) clear	(c) imperfect
63. **identical**	_____	_____	(a) alike	(b) sad	(c) different
64. **idle**	_____	_____	(a) frustrate	(b) inactive	(c) busy
65. **ignoble**	_____	_____	(a) disgraceful	(b) cease	(c) noble
66. **ignorant**	_____	_____	(a) foolish	(b) smart	(c) end
67. **ignore**	_____	_____	(a) avoid	(b) withdrawn	(c) mind
68. **illegal**	_____	_____	(a) unlawful	(b) bright	(c) legal
69. **illogical**	_____	_____	(a) dirty	(b) senseless	(c) logical
70. **immaculate**	_____	_____	(a) claim	(b) clean	(c) dirty
71. **immature**	_____	_____	(a) stupid	(b) underdeveloped	(c) mature
72. **immense**	_____	_____	(a) conceal	(b) enormous	(c) tiny
73. **immigrate**	_____	_____	(a) keep	(b) enter	(c) leave
74. **immoral**	_____	_____	(a) least	(b) wrong	(c) moral
75. **impair**	_____	_____	(a) weaken	(b) improve	(c) harsh

Exercise 3: Matching Meanings (Advanced Words)

Match each word with its definition or best meaning.

_____ 1.	annihilate	a.	disillusioned
_____ 2.	cognizant	b.	to go over a boundary; to trespass
_____ 3.	disenchanted	c.	to clear of accusation
_____ 4.	equivocal	d.	wipe out; to destroy completely
_____ 5.	fatuous	e.	easy-going; appearing casual
_____ 6.	transgress	f.	prevent; hold back
_____ 7.	ubiquitous	g.	incapable of error; faultless
_____ 8.	vindicate	h.	fully aware
_____ 9.	rapacious	i.	seeming to be everywhere

_____ 10. nonchalant   j. taking by force

_____ 11. inhibit   k. silly or foolish

_____ 12. infallible   l. vague; having two or more meanings

Exercise 4:   Advanced Words in Context

Fill in the blank with the correct word or another form of the word below.

| cognizant | infallible | equivocal | inhibit | fatuous | nonchalant |
| annihilate | rapacious | disenchanted | vindicate | ubiquitous | transgress |

1. Your attempt to _____ the roaches in this apartment is laudable, but in the end will prove futile.

2. Before you attempt skydiving you must be _____ of the potential dangers.

3. After seeing all the lying and stealing at the homeless shelter, she became _____ with her job as a volunteer there.

4. Although he spoke with great fervor, upon careful examination the argument he presented was _____.

5. The idea that men are more intelligent than women is _____.

6. The seeds of war were planted when the enemy tribe began to _____ the traditional borders.

7. TV's are as _____ in American homes now as radios were 50 years ago.

8. When the company was fined for not meeting pollution standards, the environmentalists felt _____.

9. Greed was the sole motive for the _____ plunder of the town by the soldiers.

10. Although he was extremely nervous, Brian was able to appear _____ during the job interview.

11. Morphine is given to terminal patients to _____ pain in their final hours.

12. Roman Catholics believe the Pope is _____ when pronouncing on moral issues.

Exercise 5:   Matching Meanings (Advanced Words)

Match each word with its definition or best meaning.

_____ 1. vivacious   a. full of scorn

_____ 2. supercilious   b. lively; full of spirit

_____ 3. reprimand   c. extremely careful and precise

_____ 4. nostalgia   d. an idea or thought

_____ 5. ingenious   e. enjoy pleasures of sensation

_____ 6. meticulous   f. insignificant

_____ 7. sensuous   g. clever; having great mental ability

_____ 8. aggrandize   h. to gain; to win over

_____ 9. concept   i. severely criticize; to rebuke

_____ 10. conciliate   j. perfect example

_____ 11. epitome   k. to increase; to make greater

_____ 12. frivolous   l. longing to return home; homesickness

Exercise 6: Advanced Words in Context

Fill in the blank with the correct word or another form of the word below.

frivolous	supercilious	conciliate	ingenious
nostalgia	epitome	vivacious	aggrandize
sensuous	concept	reprimand	meticulous

1. Most game shows on television want the contestants to be _____.

2. His _____ attitude toward his boss eventually caused him to be fired.

3. Steve was _____ for leaving the cash register unattended while he went to the restroom.

4. Although he suffered from recurring bouts of _____, he never had any desire to return to his hometown.

5. The company rewarded Mr. Johnson for his _____ solution to the problem.

6. Because he was less than _____ in balancing his checkbook, Fred frequently bounced checks.

7. Audrey loved the _____ feeling of sleeping on satin sheets.

8. The owner of the company _____ his wealth at the expense of his employees.

9. The _____ of a city without private cars is impossible for most people to understand.

10. All attempts to _____ the two brothers were in vain; they refused to speak to each other.

11. Because of his fine manners, he was known at the club as the _____ of politeness.

12. The gift was completely _____, but Stephanie treasured it nonetheless.

Exercise 1:   Matching Meanings

Match each word with its definition or best meaning.

_____ 1.   agronomy   a.   physical nature and history of the earth

_____ 2.   archaeology   b.   physical features of a place

_____ 3.   anthropology   c.   a study of weather

_____ 4.   astronomy   d.   the science of mental processes and behavior

_____ 5.   botany   e.   prepares drugs and medicines

_____ 6.   biology   f.   the science and economics of crop production

_____ 7.   economical   g.   science of human society

_____ 8.   ecology   h.   change of form

_____ 9.   geology   i.   deals with animal and animal life

_____ 10. geography   j.   something one likes to do in one's spare time

_____ 11. histology   k.   the study of past life and culture

_____ 12. meteorology   l.   relations between living organisms and their environment

_____ 13. metamorphosis   m. microscopic study of tissue structure

_____ 14. psychology   n.   the study of humans

_____ 15. history   o.   not wasting money

_____ 16. pharmacist   p.   recorded events of the past

_____ 17. zoology   q.   science of the universe

_____ 18. sociology   r.   study of plants and animals

_____ 19. hobby   s.   study of plants

_____ 20. hockey   t.   a game played on ice; players use a curved stick with a flat blade

Exercise 2: Synonyms Fill-in

Fill in the blank(s) to complete the word that is similar in meaning to the boldfaced word.

1. **exemplify**   s___ow
2. **endure**   und___ ___go
3. **errand**   ta___k
4. **erupt**   ex___ ___ ___de
5. **espionage**   sp___ ___ng
6. **formulate**   pre___ ___ ___e
7. **fluent**   well-ver___ ___d
8. **concoct**   cr___ ___te
9. **fraud**   tr___ ___ ___ery
10. **facade**   pre___ ___ ___se
11. **fade**   ___al___

12. **falter**   w___ ___er
13. **fame**   ren___ ___n
14. **sabotage**   unde ___ ___ ___ ne
15. **famish**   hun ___ ___ r
16. **favorite**   pref ___ ___ ___ ed
17. **fee**   ch ___ ___ge
18. **fetch**   ___ ___ ing
19. **restrain**   ___ ___ ntrol
20. **flame**   f ___ ___ e
21. **reside**   l ___ ___ e
22. **research**   inv ___ ___ ___ ___ gate

Exercise 3: Matching Meanings (Advanced Words)

Match each word with its definition or best meaning.

_____ 1. assiduous
_____ 2. boisterous
_____ 3. candid
_____ 4. decipher
_____ 5. exorbitant
_____ 6. magnanimous
_____ 7. obstinate
_____ 8. placid
_____ 9. rancor
_____ 10. tedious
_____ 11. debilitate
_____ 12. expedite

a. frank; straightforward
b. rising above pettiness; having or showing generosity
c. calm; untroubled
d. showing care and effort
e. feeling of bitterness or spitefulness
f. noisy; rough; violent
g. to weaken
h. find the meaning of
i. tiresome; weary
j. speed up
k. stubborn; not easily overcome
l. over-priced

Exercise 4:   Advanced Words in Context

Fill in the blank with the correct word or another form of the word below.

expedite	candid	tedious	decipher
rancor	assiduous	debilitate	exorbitant
boisterous	placid	obstinate	magnanimous

1. _____ study made Frank an expert in the bond market in six months.

2. The students became _____ when the teacher left the room to speak with a colleague.

3. Many foreigners find Americans too _____.

4. The letter was returned because the postman could not _____ the handwriting on the envelope.

5. Charles expected to pay higher prices while on vacation, but he thought $3 for a cup of coffee was _____.

6. Mrs. Richards gift of $100,000 to her alma mater was considered _____.

7. Mules have the reputation for being _____ animals.

8. The bright sunshine and the _____ water of the lake made it a perfect day to take pictures.

9. Although she claimed to have forgiven him, _____ filled her heart until her death.

10. The _____ hours he had to spend in the factory made him dread going to work.

11. Working two jobs and taking care of the house and children began to _____ her.

12. A stamped self-addressed envelope will _____ a response to your query.

Exercise 5:   Matching Meanings (Advanced Words)

Match each word with its definition or best meaning.

_____ 1. agitate   a. changeable; fickle

_____ 2. alleviate   b. disapprove of strongly

_____ 3. capricious   c. person living in a prison

_____ 4. controversy   d. example serving as a future rule

_____ 5. vicious   e. openly; manifest

_____ 6. condemn   f. nervous disorder

_____ 7. gaudy

_____ 8. inmate

_____ 9. neurosis

_____ 10. remorse

_____ 11. precedent

_____ 12. overt

g. to lessen; to relieve

h. cruel; corrupt

i. sorrowful repentance

j. opinions clash

k. lacking in good taste

l. disturb; rouse to action

Exercise 6: Advanced Words in Context

Fill in the blank with the correct word or another form of the word below.

overt	condemn	agitate	neurosis
controversy	remorse	gaudy	alleviate
inmate	vicious	precedent	capricious

1. After prices rose for the third time in six months, the citizens began to _____ for a revolution.

2. Aspirin will usually _____ most headaches.

3. Although women are said to be _____, they don't have a monopoly on this behavior.

4. The _____ over abortion has caused a division in the American public.

5. In the end, the _____ dog had to be shot.

6. The serial killer was _____ to life in prison.

7. Wearing too much jewelry can make one look _____.

8. He spent five years as an _____ in the state penitentiary.

9. Tony's _____ became so debilitating that he sought help from a psychologist.

10. Everyone in the courtroom was shocked by the murderer's lack of _____.

11. Henry refused to lend money to his friend because he didn't want to set a _____.

12. Although his hostility was not _____, everyone felt uncomfortable in his presence.

Exercise 1: Synonyms Multiple Choice

Circle the letter of the word that is similar, or almost similar, in meaning to the boldfaced word.

1. **overt**   (a) closed   (b) open   (c) half-way   (d) harmful
2. **oblong**   (a) elongated   (b) triangular   (c) abnormal   (d) absent
3. **satisfied**   (a) unhappy   (b) content   (c) resist   (d) sad
4. **terminate**   (a) begin   (b) initiate   (c) continue   (d) discontinue
5. **subversive**   (a) loyal   (b) lust   (c) dedicated   (d) traitor
6. **succinct**   (a) clean   (b) long   (c) concise   (d) terminal
7. **recruit**   (a) newcomer   (b) seasoned   (c) army   (d) friend
8. **condemn**   (a) criticize   (b) cautious   (c) friendly   (d) passion
9. **transpire**   (a) occur   (b) expectation   (c) give   (d) perspire
10. **reconciliation**   (a) harmony   (b) distrust   (c) mean   (d) miserable
11. **vanish**   (a) see   (b) disappear   (c) sight   (d) vain
12. **serene**   (a) cheerful   (b) chastise   (c) peaceful   (d) storm
13. **tangible**   (a) invisible   (b) powerful   (c) legible   (d) touchable
14. **retaliate**   (a) accept   (b) deny   (c) fight back   (d) sin
15. **spontaneous**   (a) unprepared   (b) planned   (c) prepared   (d) pretend
16. **vicinity**   (a) surroundings   (b) city   (c) town   (d) country
17. **subtle**   (a) indirect   (b) loud   (c) underline   (d) detect
18. **trait**   (a) brawl   (b) quality   (c) fighter   (d) traitor
19. **succumb**   (a) silent   (b) crumble   (c) surrender   (d) sick
20. **zeal**   (a) enthusiasm   (b) neglect   (c) pain   (d) sorrow

Exercise 2: Synonyms - Antonyms

Select the synonym and antonym of each boldfaced word.

	syn.	*ant.*			
1. **impatient**	_____	_____	(a) restless	(b) patient	(c) hamper
2. **imperfect**	_____	_____	(a) faulty	(b) perfect	(c) inept
3. **implement**	_____	_____	(a) carry out	(b) neglect	(c) impartial
4. **impolite**	_____	_____	(a) rude	(b) interpret	(c) polite
5. **import**	_____	_____	(a) bring in	(b) illegible	(c) export
6. **important**	_____	_____	(a) valuable	(b) incredible	(c) unimportant
7. **impractical**	_____	_____	(a) unworkable	(b) practical	(c) instigate
8. **improper**	_____	_____	(a) initiate	(b) incorrect	(c) proper
9. **improve**	_____	_____	(a) develop	(b) hot	(c) worsen
10. **impure**	_____	_____	(a) unclean	(b) clean	(c) intermittent

	syn.	*ant.*			
11. **inaccessible**			(a) unreachable	(b) accessible	(c) entrance
12. **inaccurate**			(a) eradicate	(b) incorrect	(c) accurate
13. **inactive**			(a) entity	(b) idle	(c) active
14. **inadequate**			(a) insufficient	(b) emotional	(c) enough
15. **inappropriate**			(a) unsuitable	(b) appropriate	(c) eliminate
16. **inclement**			(a) stormy	(b) excitement	(c) pleasant
17. **incompetent**			(a) unfit	(b) fun	(c) efficient
18. **incomplete**			(a) unfinished	(b) enough	(c) complete
19. **inconsiderate**			(a) thoughtless	(b) considerate	(c) frugal
20. **inconsistent**			(a) disagreeing	(b) consistent	(c) external
21. **indispensable**			(a) essential	(b) unnecessary	(c) fervor
22. **inedible**			(a) uneatable	(b) fatal	(c) edible
23. **inert**			(a) faulty	(b) inactive	(c) active
24. **inexpensive**			(a) cheap	(b) expensive	(c) conclude
25. **infamous**			(a) wicked	(b) good	(c) biased
26. **inflate**			(a) swell	(b) deflate	(c) conclude
27. **join**			(a) help	(b) connect	(c) separate
28. **jovial**			(a) misinterpret	(b) joyful	(c) sad
29. **jumble**			(a) dexterous	(b) mix	(c) organize
30. **junior**			(a) younger	(b) senior	(c) establish
31. **just**			(a) fair	(b) preserve	(c) unjust
32. **juvenile**			(a) young	(b) gloom	(c) old
33. **keen**			(a) sharp	(b) harmless	(c) dull
34. **keep**			(a) check	(b) hold	(c) discard
35. **kindle**			(a) boredom	(b) light	(c) extinguish
36. **languid**			(a) cold	(b) weak	(c) energetic

	syn.	*ant.*			
37. **large**			(a) big	(b) constant	(c) small
38. **last**			(a) end	(b) cold	(c) first
39. **lavish**			(a) plentiful	(b) stingy	(c) internal
40. **lax**			(a) calm	(b) careless	(c) rigid
41. **lazy**			(a) apathy	(b) inactive	(c) active
42. **leave**			(a) depart	(b) goodwill	(c) arrive
43. **legal**			(a) allowed	(b) illegal	(c) superior
44. **lenient**			(a) easy	(b) hard	(c) consistent
45. **liberal**			(a) persist	(b) generous	(c) conservative
46. **light**			(a) shortage	(b) weightless	(c) heavy
47. **limp**			(a) drooping	(b) pacify	(c) stiff
48. **literate**			(a) educated	(b) count	(c) illiterate
49. **load**			(a) pack	(b) unload	(c) shake
50. **luxury**			(a) prosperity	(b) take	(c) poverty
51. **magnify**			(a) enlarge	(b) decrease	(c) raise
52. **mad**			(a) praise	(b) crazy	(c) sane
53. **maternal**			(a) motherly	(b) move	(c) fatherly
54. **mature**			(a) developed	(b) cook	(c) immature
55. **melancholy**			(a) sad	(b) cheerful	(c) excited
56. **merge**			(a) combine	(b) gentle	(c) separate
57. **misfortune**			(a) general	(b) tragedy	(c) fortune
58. **misplace**			(a) lose	(b) habit	(c) find
59. **mobile**			(a) habit	(b) movable	(c) immobile
60. **moral**			(a) respectable	(b) immoral	(c) consistent
61. **more**			(a) fashion	(b) extra	(c) less
62. **mourn**			(a) elated	(b) grieve	(c) rejoice

	syn.	*ant.*			
63. **murmur**	_____	_____	(a) whisper	(b) envy	(c) shout
64. **naked**	_____	_____	(a) undressed	(b) covered	(c) alias
65. **neat**	_____	_____	(a) organized	(b) convey	(c) sloppy
66. **necessary**	_____	_____	(a) required	(b) envy	(c) unnecessary
67. **neglect**	_____	_____	(a) ignore	(b) compare	(c) care
68. **negligent**	_____	_____	(a) careless	(b) envy	(c) careful
69. **nervous**	_____	_____	(a) assertive	(b) restless	(c) calm
70. **neutral**	_____	_____	(a) chastise	(b) impartial	(c) involved
71. **normal**	_____	_____	(a) usual	(b) challenge	(c) abnormal
72. **noxious**	_____	_____	(a) harmful	(b) harmless	(c) expedite
73. **obey**	_____	_____	(a) assist	(b) listen to	(c) disobey
74. **oblivious**	_____	_____	(a) ban	(b) unaware	(c) aware
75. **obtain**	_____	_____	(a) acquire	(b) lose	(c) constant

Exercise 3: Matching Meanings (Advanced Words)

Match each word with its definition or best meaning.

_____	1. vociferous	a. a strange trait or mannerism
_____	2. unanimous	b. clearly evident; apparent
_____	3. reprehend	c. loud; noisy
_____	4. regression	d. to make less severe or painful
_____	5. quirk	e. sharing another person's feeling
_____	6. reticent	f. showing complete agreement
_____	7. ostensible	g. too showy
_____	8. oscillate	h. to find fault; to criticize
_____	9. mitigate	i. quiet; saying little
_____	10. fastidious	j. hard to please; quick to find fault
_____	11. flamboyant	k. going back
_____	12. empathy	l. swing to and fro

Exercise 4: Advanced Words in Context

Fill in the blank with the correct word or another form of the word below.

flamboyant	reprehend	mitigate	quirk
vociferous	empathy	reticent	unanimous
fastidious	ostensible	regression	oscillate

1. The students became _____ when they were served tuna casserole for the third time in two weeks.

2. The vote was _____ to elect Mr. Schweitzer as president of the co-op board of his building.

3. No matter how hard I try, my mother finds an opportunity to _____ me.

4. When a new baby arrives there is a often a tendency towards _____ by the older sibling.

5. Many people found Anne's husband's habit of drinking 20 glasses of water a day rather strange, but she excused it as just a _____.

6. Simon's parents thought their son _____ , but when he was with his peers he was quite garrulous.

7. In many countries the father is the _____ head of the family, but it is often the mother who makes the most important family decisions.

8. The earthquake caused the pendulum on the long silent clock to _____.

9. No amount of money will _____ the loss experienced when her child was killed by the drunken driver.

10. Although _____ in his dress, his apartment looked as if it hadn't been cleaned a year.

11. For a job interview it is advisable to dress in a conservative rather than a _____ manner.

12. Because of her gift of _____, Debbie was the first person her friends called when they had a problem.

Exercise 5: Matching Meanings (Advanced Words)

Match each word with its definition or best meaning.

_____ 1. hallucinate   a. incapable of being satisfied

_____ 2. hypocrite   b. unfortunate accident

_____ 3. interminable   c. endless; lasting; forever

_____ 4. insatiable   d. laughable; obvious absurdity

_____ 5. judicious   e. keen judgment or vision

_____ 6. mishap   f. to make less intense or painful

_____ 7. ludicrous

_____ 8. mitigate

_____ 9. ostentatious

_____ 10. perspicacious

_____ 11. surreptitious

_____ 12. empower

g. pretentious

h. to give power to

i. acting in a secret manner

j. having or showing sound judgment

k. to hear or see something that does not exist

l. on who pretends to be what he or she is not

Exercise 6:   Advanced Words in Context

Fill in the blank with the correct word or another form of the word below.

mishap	empower	hallucinate	perspicacious
hypocrite	judicious	surreptitious	mitigate
ostentatious	insatiable	ludicrous	interminable

1.   Severe sleep deprivation often causes people to _____.

2.   In his eyes owning a handgun and criticizing the media for its portrayal of violence in movies and on TV did not make him a _____ ; his critics thought otherwise.

3.   He said he would call back in an hour, but the wait seemed _____.

4.   No matter how much food she prepared, her teenager's appetite seemed _____.

5.   Getting a degree in business seemed _____ at the time, but later he regretted not following his dream of becoming a musician.

6.   If he had checked the brakes on his car, the _____ would never have happened.

7.   The idea that humans can continue treating the planet as they have without repercussions is _____.

8.   Because he was a first time offender, the judge chose to _____ his punishment.

9.   Their _____ displays of affection caused everyone to wonder if perhaps there was not something amiss in their relationship.

10.   The doctor made a _____ diagnosis based on her patient's symptoms.

11.   There is no need to be _____; this library is open to the public.

12.   In the event of the death of the president, the vice-president is _____ to succeed him.

THIRTEENTH DAY

Exercise 1: Matching Meanings

Match each word with its definition or best meaning.

_____ 1. amoeba   a. use pseudopodia to move about

_____ 2. fungi   b. onions

_____ 3. spirogyra   c. do not have true roots, stems and leaves; are parasites

_____ 4. mammal   d. carries and distributes sugars in plants

_____ 5. reptile   e. have a life cycle of more than two years

_____ 6. pseudopodia   f. has female mammary glands; warm blooded

_____ 7. micronutrients   g. an association of mutual advantage

_____ 8. macronutrients   h. a fish

_____ 9. bulbs   i. green algae

_____ 10. rhizomes   j. involves two nuclear divisions

_____ 11. symbiosis   k. cold blooded; bony skeleton

_____ 12. mistletoe   l. smallest particle of an element

_____ 13. xylem   m. by the day

_____ 14. phloem   n. a gas

_____ 15. perch   o. a creeping stem

_____ 16. annuals   p. process by which green plants make food

_____ 17. perennials   q. used to move about

_____ 18. transpire   r. plants that live only one year or season

_____ 19. per diem   s. required in tiny quantities

_____ 20. oxygen   t. required in large quantities

_____ 21. photosynthesis   u. formation of two new nuclei

_____ 22. meiosis   v. carries water and mineral salts in plants

_____ 23. mitosis   w. grows on branches and trunks of trees

_____ 24. molecule   x. to give off water vapor

_____ 25. weed   y. uncultivated plant

Exercise 2: Synonyms Fill-in

Fill in the blank(s) to complete the word that is similar in meaning to the boldfaced word.

1. **flatter**   com___ ___ ___ment
2. **foolproof**   ass___ ___ed
3. **forecast**   pre___ ___ ___ ___ion
4. **spank**   b___at
5. **founder**   dis___ ___ ___ ___ ___er
6. **guide**   di___ ___ct
7. **ghastly**   drea___ ___ul
8. **goal**   a___m
9. **gossip**   hea___ ___ay
10. **hardship**   dif___ ___c___lty

11. **hit**   st___ ___ke
12. **hurry**   ___ ___sh
13. **illustrious** fam___ ___ ___
14. **site**   loc___ ___ ___ ___n
15. **impact**   eff___ ___t
16. **sarcastic** moc___ ___ ___g
17. **indifferent** uncon___ ___ ___ ___ed
18. **solitude**   iso___ ___ ___ ___on
19. **infer**   con___ ___ ___de
20. **imposter**   pre___ ___ ___ ___er

Exercise 3: Matching Meanings (Advanced Words)

Match each word with its definition or best meaning.

_____ 1. gullible
_____ 2. genesis
_____ 3. hysterical
_____ 4. impeccable
_____ 5. lethargy
_____ 6. luscious
_____ 7. obnoxious
_____ 8. cumbersome
_____ 9. dubious
_____ 10. exonerate
_____ 11. elated
_____ 12. fictitious

a. faultless; without flaw
b. sweet and pleasant to taste
c. easily deceived
d. difficult to handle or deal with
e. declare blameless
f. unreal; imaginary
g. make lively and happy
h. beginning; origin
i. undecided; uncertainty
j. lack of energy
k. highly offensive; disagreeable
l. emotionally uncontrolled

Exercise 4: Advanced Words in Context

Fill in the blank with the correct word or another form of the word below.

dubious	gullible	elated	luscious
obnoxious	exonerate	genesis	fictitious
impeccable	cumbersome	hysterical	lethargy

1. Because she was so _____ , Amanda gave $25 to the stranger in the bus station who said she had lost her ticket.

2. The theory of relativity was the _____ of modern physics.

3. Mrs. Roberts became _____ when she found out she had won $10,000,000 in the lottery.

4. Although his opponents scrutinized his past, the candidate's record was _____.

5. _____ is often a sign of depression.

6. The smell of a freshly picked peach in the summertime is _____.

7. While he thought his practical jokes were funny, his classmates found him _____.

8. Carrying a purse, briefcase, and shopping bags made walking to work _____.

9. Most scientists regard the idea of cold fission as _____.

10. When the real murderer confessed, the prisoner was _____ and given compensation for the time he had spent in jail.

11. Susan was _____ when it was announced that she was valedictorian of her class.

12. Despite the author's claims to the contrary, most people believe his account of being abducted by aliens to be _____.

Exercise 5:   Matching Meanings (Advanced Words)

Match each word with its definition or best meaning.

_____ 1. luminous   a. secretly; concealed

_____ 2. capitulate   b. to waiver; to sway to and fro

_____ 3. condone   c. costly; great expense

_____ 4. covert   d. a contagious epidemic disease that is deadly

_____ 5. esoteric   e. lack of emotion, feeling or interest

_____ 6. vacillate   f. to forgive; overlook; disregard

_____ 7. unrest   g. banish or exclude

_____ 8. sumptuous   h. to give up or surrender

_____ 9. subjugate   i. intended for a small group

_____ 10. plague   j. glows in the dark

_____ 11. ostracize   k. to defeat or conquer

_____ 12. apathy   l. discontent; uneasiness

Exercise 6: Advanced Words in Context

Fill in the blank with the correct word or another form of the word below.

condone	apathy	vacillate	plague
luminous	esoteric	ostracize	sumptuous
unrest	subjugate	capitulate	covert

1. John bought an alarm clock with a _____ dial.

2. Because the discussion had gone on for two hours, Sidney decided to _____ rather than continue arguing.

3. The army's _____ operations in rural areas helped to overthrow the dictator.

4. Although the father understood the motives for his son's actions, he could not _____ them.

5. Despite the _____ nature of the lecture, a large crowd showed up.

6. Because Peter always _____ when pressed to make a decision, his wife usually made the choice for him.

7. A ten-o'clock curfew was imposed because of civilian _____.

8. After the _____ dinner, he had no choice but to take a nap.

9. Alice _____ her desire for a piece of chocolate cake by taking a walk.

10. The Black _____ of the 14th century wiped out a quarter of the population of present day Europe.

11. Because Billy was a tattletale, he was _____ by his classmates.

12. _____ set in after the death of her husband.

Exercise 1: Synonyms Multiple Choice

Circle the letter of the word that is similar, or almost similar, in meaning to the boldfaced word.

1. **yearn**   (a) testy   (b) satisfy   (c) sufficient   (d) crave
2. **zest**   (a) silence   (b) sinister   (c) simple   (d) passion
3. **yell**   (a) whisper   (b) murmur   (c) scream   (d) quiet
4. **seduce**   (a) tempt   (b) left   ((c) duty   (d) like
5. **vulgar**   (a) respectable (b) vulture   (c) obscene   (d) known
6. **vigilant**   (a) careless   (b) alert   (c) carefree   (d) sleepy
7. **vent**   (a) close   (b) shut   (c) opening   (d) valve
8. **whine**   (a) complain   (b) agree   (c) support   (d) team
9. **wrinkle**   (a) crease   (b) iron   (c) attractive   (d) hole
10. **synchronize** (a) illegal   (b) match   (c) resist   (d) marked
11. **surrender** (a) reject   (b) run   (c) speedy   (d) give up
12. **sullen**   (a) satisfied   (b) joyful   (c) depressing   (d) jubilant
13. **transient** (a) stable   (b) passing   (c) permanent   (d) stubborn
14. **trespass**   (a) intrude   (b) invite   (c) stay   (d) implore
15. **salient**   (a) noticeable (b) unimportant   (c) shocking   (d) sail
16. **vehement**   (a) passive   (b) blunt   (c) secure   (d) forceful
17. **vulnerable** (a) protected   (b) strong   (c) unprotected   (d) secure
18. **valiant**   (a) coward   (b) brave   (c) soldier   (d) general
19. **warp**   (a) deform   (b) normal   (c) confirm   (d) decisive
20. **whisper**   (a) shout   (b) murmur   (c) yell   (d) snore

Exercise 2: Synonyms - Antonyms

Select the synonym and antonym of each boldfaced word.

	syn.	ant.			
1. **moderate**			(a) average	(b) extreme	(c) myth
2. **morbid**			(a) control	(b) ghastly	(c) pleasant
3. **minute**			(a) tiny	(b) short	(c) enormous
4. **magnificent**			(a) splendid	(b) fear	(c) plain
5. **mandate**			(a) command	(b) request	(c) purpose
6. **miniature**			(a) small	(b) huge	(c) thrill
7. **miscellaneous**			(a) tasty	(b) mixed	(c) homogeneous
8. **mischievous**			(a) naughty	(b) exciting	(c) obedient
9. **mistreat**			(a) abuse	(b) protect	(c) propose
10. **mutual**			(a) common	(b) good	(c) unilateral
11. **negligent**			(a) careless	(b) careful	(c) irregular
12. **nuisance**			(a) annoyance	(b) criminal	(c) delight

syn.　　　ant.

13. **need**　＿＿＿＿　＿＿＿＿　(a) narrow　(b) want　(c) have

14. **nominal**　＿＿＿＿　＿＿＿＿　(a) small　(b) dastard　(c) large

15. **nullify**　＿＿＿＿　＿＿＿＿　(a) void　(b) enact　(c) small

16. **nebulous**　＿＿＿＿　＿＿＿＿　(a) unclear　(b) make　(c) clear

17. **nonchalant**　＿＿＿＿　＿＿＿＿　(a) easygoing　(b) tense　(c) expensive

18. **notify**　＿＿＿＿　＿＿＿＿　(a) inform　(b) withhold　(c) distrust

19. **objective**　＿＿＿＿　＿＿＿＿　(a) unbiased　(b) subjective　(c) same

20. **oblivious**　＿＿＿＿　＿＿＿＿　(a) genius　(b) unaware　(c) aware

21. **obligate**　＿＿＿＿　＿＿＿＿　(a) require　(b) fear　(c) release

22. **optimum**　＿＿＿＿　＿＿＿＿　(a) anger　(b) best　(c) worst

23. **optimistic**　＿＿＿＿　＿＿＿＿　(a) hopeful　(b) discouraging　(c) tolerable

24. **organize**　＿＿＿＿　＿＿＿＿　(a) tangible　(b) arrange　(c) disorganize

25. **pathetic**　＿＿＿＿　＿＿＿＿　(a) pitiful　(b) fright　(c) cheerful

26. **parallel**　＿＿＿＿　＿＿＿＿　(a) similar　(b) different　(c) please

27. **passive**　＿＿＿＿　＿＿＿＿　(a) desperate　(b) inactive　(c) active

28. **patron**　＿＿＿＿　＿＿＿＿　(a) customer　(b) brilliant　(c) owner

29. **pain**　＿＿＿＿　＿＿＿＿　(a) ache　(b) pleasure　(c) afraid

30. **patience**　＿＿＿＿　＿＿＿＿　(a) tolerance　(b) anxiety　(c) speech

31. **ponder**　＿＿＿＿　＿＿＿＿　(a) reflect　(b) forget　(c) liberal

32. **predominant**　＿＿＿＿　＿＿＿＿　(a) principal　(b) treat　(c) minor

33. **prerequisite**　＿＿＿＿　＿＿＿＿　(a) tale　(b) required　(c) non-essential

34. **prevalent**　＿＿＿＿　＿＿＿＿　(a) widespread　(b) fiery　(c) uncommon

35. **prompt**　＿＿＿＿　＿＿＿＿　(a) punctual　(b) late　(c) propel

36. **plausible**　＿＿＿＿　＿＿＿＿　(a) possible　(b) impossible　(c) hatred

37. **prudent**　＿＿＿＿　＿＿＿＿　(a) pleasure　(b) cautious　(c) careless

38. **proficient**　＿＿＿＿　＿＿＿＿　(a) capable　(b) dangerous　(c) inept

39. **panic**　＿＿＿＿　＿＿＿＿　(a) scare　(b) comfort　(c) fear

40. **paralyze**　＿＿＿＿　＿＿＿＿　(a) disable　(b) heal　(c) just

41. **pardon**　＿＿＿＿　＿＿＿＿　(a) charge　(b) forgive　(c) punish

42. **partial**　＿＿＿＿　＿＿＿＿　(a) incomplete　(b) restrict　(c) whole

43. **pensive**　＿＿＿＿　＿＿＿＿　(a) thoughtful　(b) uninterested　(c) show

	syn.	*ant.*			
44. **perturb**	_____	_____	(a) disturb	(b) calm	(c) imperfect
45. **postpone**	_____	_____	(a) disdain	(b) delay	(c) expedite
46. **positive**	_____	_____	(a) certain	(b) doubtful	(c) sick
47. **resign**	_____	_____	(a) quit	(b) remain	(c) fight
48. **rescue**	_____	_____	(a) tension	(b) save	(c) abandon
49. **retain**	_____	_____	(a) regular	(b) maintain	(c) discard
50. **revoke**	_____	_____	(a) cancel	(b) justice	(c) restore
51. **rupture**	_____	_____	(a) break	(b) mend	(c) aggressive
52. **respond**	_____	_____	(a) touchable	(b) reply	(c) question
53. **scandal**	_____	_____	(a) disgrace	(b) funny	(c) honor
54. **severe**	_____	_____	(a) serious	(b) talkative	(c) mild
55. **sane**	_____	_____	(a) sensible	(b) irrational	(c) disturbed
56. **satisfy**	_____	_____	(a) please	(b) tough	(c) displease
57. **stimulate**	_____	_____	(a) arouse	(b) stifle	(c) complex
58. **submit**	_____	_____	(a) present	(b) important	(c) withdraw
59. **solace**	_____	_____	(a) comfort	(b) distress	(c) dictator
60. **sporadic**	_____	_____	(a) irregular	(b) regular	(c) solace
61. **seduce**	_____	_____	(a) novice	(b) tempt	(c) repel
62. **select**	_____	_____	(a) kin	(b) choose	(c) reject
63. **sentimental**	_____	_____	(a) emotional	(b) subsidy	(c) unemotional
64. **significant**	_____	_____	(a) important	(b) trivial	(c) phobia
65. **steal**	_____	_____	(a) pilfer	(b) earn	(c) grant
66. **sterilized**	_____	_____	(a) abnormal	(b) disinfected	(c) contaminated
67. **substitute**	_____	_____	(a) replace	(b) regular	(c) cunning
68. **succulent**	_____	_____	(a) juicy	(b) dry	(c) intelligent
69. **surpass**	_____	_____	(a) exceed	(b) weep	(c) fail
70. **suspicious**	_____	_____	(a) distrustful	(b) transfer	(c) trusting
71. **render**	_____	_____	(a) give	(b) withdraw	(c) omit
72. **replenish**	_____	_____	(a) renew	(b) use	(c) misery
73. **request**	_____	_____	(a) ask	(b) respond	(c) invert

Exercise 3: Matching Meanings (Advanced Words)

Match each word with its definition or best meaning.

_____ 1. corroborate		a.	not respectable; having a bad reputation
_____ 2. dexterous		b.	to make more intense; to aggravate
_____ 3. disreputable		c.	to hint or suggest
_____ 4. dissent		d.	to give support; to conform
_____ 5. exacerbate		e.	noisy; disorder; confusion
_____ 6. fallacy		f.	that cannot be corrected; not curable
_____ 7. garrulous		g.	a record of daily happening
_____ 8. imply		h.	clever or skillful with hands or body
_____ 9. inculcate		i.	a false opinion or idea
_____ 10. pandemonium		j.	to differ in opinion or belief
_____ 11. incurable		k.	to impress upon by persistent urging
_____ 12. journal		l.	talking too much about unimportant things

Exercise 4: Advanced Words in Context

Fill in the blank with the correct word or another form of the word below.

fallacy	incurable	dexterous	imply
pandemonium	corroborate	garrulous	disreputable
journal	dissent	inculcate	exacerbate

1. The evidence _____ the witness's testimony.

2. One has to be somewhat _____ to master the art of origami.

3. Don't buy a used car from that man; he is _____.

4. A murmur of _____ arose from the populace when the president announced yet another tax increase.

5. Arguing with her will only _____ an already uncomfortable situation.

6. Since bulls are color blind, it is a _____ that they charge the matador because of the color of the cape.

7. A _____ nature is an asset to a salesperson.

8. Although he didn't directly say that he was unhappy, his frequent absences from home _____ a dissatisfaction with the marriage.

9. A love of literature can be _____ at an early age by parents reading to their children.

10. _____ broke out when they announced that the concert was sold out.

11. Many forms of cancer are _____.

12. Keeping a _____ is a good way to improve writing skills.

Exercise 5: Matching Meanings (Advanced Words)

Match each word with its definition or best meaning.

_____ 1. vehemence	a. shining through
_____ 2. tenuous	b. full of intense feeling; violent
_____ 3. urgent	c. too willing to serve or obey
_____ 4. superfluous	d. unclear; vague; indefinite
_____ 5. translucent	e. having little substance; weak
_____ 6. quagmire	f. overwhelm with a great amount
_____ 7. panorama	g. immediate action
_____ 8. obsequious	h. not attentive or observant; unintentional
_____ 9. malicious	i. spiteful; intentionally mischievous
_____ 10. nebulous	j. excessive; unnecessary
_____ 11. inadvertent	k. a wide view in all directions
_____ 12. inundate	l. in a difficult position

Exercise 6: Advanced Words in Context

Fill in the blank with the correct word or another form of the word below.

quagmire	vehemence	inundate	malicious
superfluous	nebulous	panorama	tenuous
inadvertent	urgent	obsequious	translucent

1. In spite of the _____ of his doctor's warnings, Oliver continued to smoke.

2. I can't agree with your _____ argument. I need more specific information.

3. The teacher received an _____ message in the middle of class to call home.

4. Taking mega doses of vitamins is thought to be _____ by many doctors.

5. Her skin was so white it almost appeared to be _____.

6. Having too many credit cards often leads to a _____ of debt from which it is difficult to escape.

7. The _____ in the Painted Desert is breathtaking.

8. His _____ behavior to the boss made him a figure of hatred to his fellow workers.

9. Her friend's _____ comment brought tears to her eyes.

10. The evidence is too _____ for me to make a decision.

11. Although the senator's remark was _____, it caused a major scandal in the newspapers the following day.

12. After winning the lottery, she was _____ with calls from friends and relatives.

Exercise 1:   Matching Meanings

Match each word with its definition or best meaning.

_____ 1.	artery	a.	inflammation of the liver
_____ 2.	arteriosclerosis	b.	high blood pressure
_____ 3.	hemoglobin	c.	higher than normal body temperature
_____ 4.	hepatitis	d.	an antibiotic
_____ 5.	pneumonia	e.	pumps blood; it contracts and expands
_____ 6.	leukemia	f.	a swelling
_____ 7.	cancer	g.	carries blood away from the heart
_____ 8.	lump	h.	calcium deficiency
_____ 9.	glucose	i.	red coloring matter of red blood corpuscles
_____ 10.	plasma	j.	excessive activity of thyroid gland
_____ 11.	pupil	k.	abnormally low blood sugar
_____ 12.	dermis	l.	infection associated with the lungs
_____ 13.	epidermis	m.	a malignant tumor
_____ 14.	anesthesia	n.	layer of skin below the epidermis
_____ 15.	acupuncture	o.	outermost layer of the skin
_____ 16.	kidney	p.	abnormal thickening of the walls of arteries
_____ 17.	liver	q.	a disease; excessive production of white blood cells
_____ 18.	heart	r.	opening in the center of the iris of the eye
_____ 19.	lung	s.	a sugar; found in fruits and the blood
_____ 20.	hypoglycemia	t.	loss of consciousness
_____ 21.	hyperthermia	u.	organ associated with excretion
_____ 22.	hypertension	v.	a respiratory organ
_____ 23.	hyperthyroidism	w.	secretes bile; detoxifies poisonous substances
_____ 24.	hypocalcemia	x.	fluid part of blood
_____ 25.	penicillin	y.	piercing parts of the body with needles to relieve pain

Exercise 2:   Synonyms Fill-in

Fill in the blank(s) to complete the word that is similar in meaning to the boldfaced word.

1. **idea**	th___ ___ ___ht		7. **implement**	st___ ___t
2. **imbecile**	f___ ___l		8. **symbolize**	rep___ ___ ___ent
3. **imitate**	c___ ___y		9. **interrogate**	qu___ ___t___on
4. **immerse**	sub___ ___ ___ge		10. **intuition**	___ ___stin___t
5. **impeach**	ch___ ___ge		11. **irreparable**	ru___ ___ ed
6. **impede**	___ind___r		12. **inspect**	ex___ ___ ___ne

13. **integrity**   __ __ nor   17. **job**   du __ __

14. **invalid**   dis __ __ __ ed   18. **journey**   t __ __ p

15. **jerk**   p __ l l   19. **judge**   med __ __ te

16. **jest**   _ ok _   20. **stereotype**   cat __ __ __ __ ize

Exercise 3: Matching Meanings (Advanced Words)

Match each word with its definition or best meaning.

_____ 1. gush   a. a sudden flow

_____ 2. gallant   b. continuous; never ending

_____ 3. infidelity   c. widely known in an unfavorable manner

_____ 4. innuendo   d. keep out or prevent

_____ 5. incessant   e. to surrender or give up

_____ 6. monotonous   f. brave and noble

_____ 7. notorious   g. to hypnotize or fascinate

_____ 8. mesmerize   h. substitute; taking the place of another person or thing

_____ 9. preclude   i. unfaithful or disloyal

_____ 10. retrospect   j. having no variety

__E___ 11. relinquish   k. thinking of the past

_____ 12. vicarious   l. a hint or sly remark

Exercise 4: Advanced Words in Context

Fill in the blank with the correct word or another form of the word below.

vicarious	monotonous	gush	preclude
gallant	relinquish	mesmerize	innuendo
incessant	retrospect	infidelity	notorious

1. The townspeople cheered when the first _____ of oil spouted from the ground.

2. Opening a door for a woman was considered _____ 20 years ago; now many women consider it sexist.

3. The judge granted the divorce on grounds of _____ by the husband.

4. Although there was never any proof, the _____ of an extramarital affair caused the candidate to lose the election.

5. Her _____ chatter made her an unwelcome guest at the party.

6. People hate elevator music because it is so _____

7. Seattle is _____ for its rainy weather.

8. The prosecutor _____ the jury with his exacting account of the crime.

9. The slightness of evidence in the case _____ a conviction.

10. In _____, Jenny saw that marrying at such a young age had been a mistake.

11. The kidnapper said he would _____ the hostage upon the receipt of $100,000.

12. Because his job in the bank was so boring, Paul read detective novels for _____ thrills.

Exercise 5: Matching Meanings (Advanced Words)

Match each word with its definition or best meaning.

_____ 1. arsonist	a. something added to complete a whole
_____ 2. compliment	b. an odd person
_____ 3. charismatic	c. involving confidence or trust
_____ 4. complement	d. done or provided without charge; free
_____ 5. eloquent	e. popular; arousing; leadership quality
_____ 6. extricate	f. express clearly and persuasively
_____ 7. eccentric	g. delicate; easily broken
_____ 8. fragile	h. to express courtesy or respect
_____ 9. fiduciary	i. conspicuously bad; outrageous; notorious
_____ 10. flagrant	j. to come together; to assemble
_____ 11. gratuitous	k. to set free from a difficulty
_____ 12. gather	l. malicious burning of property by someone

Exercise 6: Advanced Words in Context

Fill in the blank with the correct word or another form of the word below.

fragile	gather	arsonist	eloquent
gratuitous	eccentric	fiduciary	charismatic
extricate	compliment	flagrant	complement

1. At first the fire department thought the fire was an accident; later they discovered it was set by an _____.

2. Upon seeing her stunning dress, he could not help but _____ her.

3. Janet's _____ personality made her an instant hit at any party.

4. Could you tell me which wine would best _____ Mexican food?

5. After an _____ plea by their pastor, the parishioners gave generously to help the victims of the earthquake.

6. Despite his best effort, Chang was not able to _____ himself from the web of lies which he had woven.

7. Mr. Wagman was known as an _____ because in spite of having a fleet of limousines at his disposal, he chose to travel about town by bicycle.

8. Please handle this box with care as the contents are very _____.

9. A banker must be scrupulous in the exercise of his _____ responsibilities.

10. Sam was arrested for driving at 70 miles per hour, a _____ violation of the local speed limit of 55.

11. Although never asked, Vincent was always ready to offer _____ advice.

12. Although they lived spread out all over the country, every year the family _____ together for a reunion.

Exercise 1: Synonyms Multiple Choice

Circle the letter of the word that is similar, or almost similar, in meaning to the boldfaced word.

1. **weep**	(a) sing	(b) sob	(c) laugh	(d) mock
2. **withdraw**	(a) jeer	(b) retreat	(c) reside	(d) resign
3. **transfer**	(a) take	(b) move	(c) covet	(d) settle
4. **temporary**	(a) short-lived	(b) permanent	(c) stable	(d) stylish
5. **quit**	(a) start	(b) begin	(c) slow	(d) discontinue
6. **omit**	(a) include	(b) instill	(c) exclude	(d) inside
7. **misery**	(a) happiness	(b) jeer	(c) sorrow	(d) jest
8. **lethal**	(a) safe	(b) secure	(c) warm	(d) fatal
9. **invert**	(a) capsize	(b) bottom	(c) top	(d) slanted
10. **hasty**	(a) swift	(b) silent	(c) slow	(d) sluggish
11. **decision**	(a) verdict	(b) delay	(c) speech	(d) report
12. **easy**	(a) difficult	(b) simple	(c) hard	(d) tough
13. **collaborate**	(a) sly	(b) cooperate	(c) cunning	(d) sharp
14. **astonished**	(a) disappoint	(b) detest	(c) amazed	(d) deplore
15. **brawl**	(a) match	(b) game	(c) season	(d) fight
16. **chaos**	(a) order	(b) organize	(c) confusion	(d) file
17. **complicate**	(a) confuse	(b) easy	(c) distant	(d) far
18. **abandon**	(a) obey	(b) forsake	(c) accept	(d) assist
19. **convert**	(a) change	(b) unchange	(c) uneasy	(d) inert
20. **enemy**	(a) friend	(b) friendship	(c) pal	(d) foe

Exercise 2: Synonyms - Antonyms

Select the synonym and antonym of each boldfaced word.

	syn.	ant.			
1. **spacious**	_____	_____	(a) excitement	(b) roomy	(c) confining
2. **strenuous**	_____	_____	(a) spacious	(b) hard	(c) easy
3. **sturdy**	_____	_____	(a) strong	(b) weak	(c) fun
4. **successful**	_____	_____	(a) prosperous	(b) failing	(c) fluctuate
5. **suitable**	_____	_____	(a) fitting	(b) unsuitable	(c) erratic
6. **summarize**	_____	_____	(a) condense	(b) external	(c) expand
7. **surplus**	_____	_____	(a) guilty	(b) excess	(c) lack
8. **suspend**	_____	_____	(a) postpone	(b) fatal	(c) resume
9. **thorough**	_____	_____	(a) complete	(b) incomplete	(c) faulty
10. **tolerate**	_____	_____	(a) eminent	(b) permit	(c) prohibit

	syn.	ant.			
11. timid			(a) shy	(b) frolic	(c) bold
12. tremendous			(a) vast	(b) small	(c) fury
13. trouble			(a) disturb	(b) calm	(c) frequent
14. tumult			(a) uproar	(b) hostile	(c) quiet
15. turbulent			(a) fictitious	(b) violent	(c) peaceful
16. unable			(a) gait	(b) incapable	(c) able
17. uncertain			(a) unsure	(b) sure	(c) perplexed
18. under			(a) below	(b) above	(c) generous
19. underrate			(a) vivid	(b) belittle	(c) overrate
20. unfair			(a) unjust	(b) gamut	(c) fair
21. unfit			(a) unsuitable	(b) suitable	(c) fine
22. unreal			(a) imaginary	(b) shock	(c) real
23. unskilled			(a) inexperienced	(b) jolly	(c) skilled
24. vacant			(a) empty	(b) gloom	(c) occupied
25. vague			(a) unclear	(b) little	(c) clear
26. weak			(a) feeble	(b) play	(c) strong
27. deficit			(a) shortage	(b) harmful	(c) abundance
28. degenerate			(a) deteriorate	(b) improve	(c) stable
29. deplete			(a) sad	(b) drain	(c) replace
30. detrimental			(a) outer	(b) harmful	(c) beneficial
31. diligent			(a) sell	(b) hard-working	(c) lazy
32. deceive			(a) betray	(b) contain	(c) enlighten
33. defy			(a) oppose	(b) harmless	(c) support
34. denounce			(a) condemn	(b) praise	(c) sell
35. detain			(a) delay	(b) perfect	(c) release
36. deter			(a) discourage	(b) encourage	(c) appreciation
37. deteriorate			(a) similar	(b) decay	(c) improve
38. deplore			(a) condemn	(b) approve	(c) unpopular
39. detest			(a) hate	(b) fun	(c) love
40. despondent			(a) discouraged	(b) shame	(c) cheerful
41. detrimental			(a) intermittent	(b) harmful	(c) beneficial

	syn.	*ant.*			
42. **dexterous**			(a) real	(b) skillful	(c) inept
43. **discreet**			(a) careful	(b) fear	(c) careless
44. **despair**			(a) hopelessness	(b) disturbing	(c) hope
45. **disparity**			(a) dissimilarity	(b) similarity	(c) serious
46. **dissipate**			(a) disperse	(b) gather	(c) honest
47. **deprive**			(a) rob	(b) bestow	(c) honest
48. **disgrace**			(a) careless	(b) shame	(c) honor
49. **disturb**			(a) narrow	(b) irritate	(c) calm
50. **debate**			(a) graphic	(b) argument	(c) agreement
51. **deduct**			(a) discount	(b) fiction	(c) add
52. **delicate**			(a) weak	(b) keep	(c) healthy
53. **deliver**			(a) hand over	(b) retain	(c) excitable
54. **donor**			(a) fate	(b) supporter	(c) recipient
55. **drastic**			(a) limit	(b) extreme	(c) moderate
56. **egocentric**			(a) self-centered	(b) dismay	(c) selfless
57. **entertain**			(a) amuse	(b) bore	(c) plenty
58. **emerge**			(a) appear	(b) disappear	(c) job
59. **endorse**			(a) sponsor	(b) denounce	(c) stingy
60. **encounter**			(a) foretell	(b) face	(c) avoid
61. **endow**			(a) bestow	(b) innocent	(c) deprive
62. **esteem**			(a) respect	(b) scorn	(c) broader
63. **extensive**			(a) broad	(b) narrow	(c) boredom
64. **elaborate**			(a) detailed	(b) disastrous	(c) simple
65. **embarrass**			(a) disgrace	(b) honor	(c) distribute
66. **exhaust**			(a) taste	(b) deplete	(c) conserve
67. **explicit**			(a) definite	(b) famous	(c) ambiguous
68. **expel**			(a) dismiss	(b) fright	(c) welcome
69. **excel**			(a) surpass	(b) fail	(c) short
70. **estrange**			(a) separate	(b) reconcile	(c) acceptable
71. **exhilarate**			(a) enliven	(b) puzzle	(c) discourage
72. **escalate**			(a) gait	(b) increase	(c) decrease
73. **earn**			(a) obtain	(b) spend	(c) selfish

	syn.	*ant.*			
74. **emphasize**	_____ _____		(a) stress	(b) downplay	(c) range
75. **employ**	_____ _____		(a) precise	(b) hire	(c) dismiss

Exercise 3: Matching Meanings (Advanced Words)

Match each word with its definition or best meaning.

_____ 1. voracious

_____ 2. viable

_____ 3. transform

_____ 4. unscrupulous

_____ 5. uncanny

_____ 6. ratify

_____ 7. synthesize

_____ 8. scrutinize

_____ 9. quandary

_____ 10. replete

_____ 11. preposterous

_____ 12. plagiarize

a. weird; strange; mysterious

b. greedy in eating or some desire

c. to combine or bring together in a whole

d. state of uncertainty; dilemma

e. to take an idea and pass off as one's own

f. foolish; laughable

g. able to live or survive

h. well-filled; plentifully supplied

i. to change

j. without principles; not honorable

k. to confirm or approve

l. examine or look at closely and carefully

Exercise 4: Advanced Words in Context

Fill in the blank with the correct word or another form of the word below.

scrutinize	unscrupulous	plagiarize	viable	preposterous	voracious
replete	synthesize	transform	quandary	ratify	uncanny

1. Her _____ appetite for knowledge was astounding.

2. Becoming a vegetarian is not a _____ solution for most people with high cholesterol.

3. The gymnasium was _____ into a winter wonderland for the high school prom.

4. Throughout the town he was known as being _____ so no one wanted to do business with him.

5. Her _____ knowledge of customer preferences made her one of the top salespeople in the company.

6. As soon as the bill is _____ by Congress, it will become law.

7. Many drugs formerly obtained from plants are now _____ in a laboratory.

8. It is always a good idea to _____ a contract before signing.

9. Being presented with two excellent job offers put her in a _____.

10. The hotel bathroom was _____ with every item imaginable for a luxurious bath.

11. The idea that there could be life on other planets is no longer _____.

12. When it was discovered that he had _____ his doctoral dissertation, his degree was revoked.

Exercise 5: Matching Meanings (Advanced Words)

Match each word with its definition or best meaning.

_____ 1. acute	a.	easily seen or noticed
_____ 2. adroit	b.	to lessen the value or price
_____ 3. bigot	c.	a baffling person or situation
_____ 4. bias	d.	frivolously amusing
_____ 5. conspicuous	e.	intolerant of a race that is not his or her own
_____ 6. condescend	f.	showing great intensity of feeling
_____ 7. depreciate	g.	extremely joyful
_____ 8. dissuade	h.	cleverly skillful; resourceful
_____ 9. enigmatic	i.	beneath one's dignity
_____ 10. exuberant	j.	to advise against
_____ 11. facetious	k.	sharp; severe
_____ 12. fervent	l.	prejudice; predisposed point of view

Exercise 6: Advanced Words in Context

Fill in the blank with the correct word or another form of the word below.

fervent	dissuade	conspicuous	bigot	facetious	depreciate
enigmatic	adroit	exuberant	bias	acute	

1. Animals have a more _____ sense of smell than humans.

2. When it came to fixing cars no one was more _____ than my brother.

3. The _____ of the neighborhood united when Mr. Sullivan wanted to sell his house to foreign investors.

4. Many young children have a _____ against green vegetables.

5. Although he claimed to be an expert, his lack of knowledge was _____ whenever he was asked a question.

6. Mobile homes are not considered to be a good buy because their value generally _____ over the years.

7. Despite their pleas, her parents were unable to _____ her from marrying her unemployed boyfriend.

8. The Mona Lisa is famous for her _____ smile.

9. The children were _____ when they heard school had been canceled because of snow.

10. Although said with a straight face, everyone knew Tim's comment was meant to be _____.

11. _____ golfers will play even in the rain.

Exercise 1: Matching Meanings

Match each word with its definition or best meaning.

_m_	1. cardiologist	a.	a cancerous growth
	2. dermatologist	b.	specializes in the nervous system and its diseases
_k_	3. podiatrist	c.	prediction of the course of a disease
_r_	4. opthamologist	d.	infects plants and animals
_y_	5. gynecologist	e.	initiates or speeds up certain chemical reactions
	6. urologist	f.	weariness
_o_	7. neurologist	g.	a one-celled microorganism
_v_	8. orthopedics	h.	protected against a certain disease
	9. bacteria	i.	reduction in the number of red blood corpuscles
	10. virus	j.	removal of body tissue for examination
	11. cardiovascular	k.	specializes in the care of the feet
	12. cholesterol	l.	increased body temperature
	13. prognosis	m.	studies the heart and its functions
	14. enzyme	n.	specializes in the skin and its diseases
	15. fatigue	o.	specializes in the urinary system and its diseases
	16. allergy	p.	performs specific functions; has specialized tissues
	17. cell	q.	relating to the heart and blood vessels
	18. serum	r.	studies the anatomy, function and diseases of the eyes
	19. insulin	s.	structural unit of plant and animal life
	20. immune	t.	a clear yellowish fluid of the blood
_l_	21. fever	u.	hypersensitive to certain substances or conditions
	22. carcinoma	v.	correction or prevention of deformities of the skeleton
	23. anemia	w.	associated with atherosclerosis
	24. biopsy	x.	assists the body to use carbohydrates
	25. organ	y.	specializes in diseases of the female reproductive system

Exercise 2: Synonyms Fill-in

Fill in the blank(s) to complete the word that is similar in meaning to the boldfaced word.

1. **knock**   h__t
2. **lead**   __ui__e
3. **motive**   pur__ __ __e
4. **liable**   acc__ __ __ __able
6. **magnitude**   gre__ __ __ess
7. **vertical**   er__ __t
8. **mania**   fix__ __ __on
9. **menace**   thr__ __t

5. **label**   m___ ___k   10. **morale**   sp __ __ __ t

11. **massage**   str __ __ e   15. **meander**   __ wis__

12. **matrimony** we __ __ __ ng   16. **merchandise** go __ __ s

13. **malady**   si __ __ ness   17. **mistake**   er __ or

14. **massacre** slau __ __ __ e __   18. **modify**   ch __ __ ge

Exercise 3: Synonyms - Antonyms

Select the synonym and antonym of each boldfaced word.

		syn.	*ant.*			
1.	**prefer**	____	____	(a) favor	(b) dislike	(c) inert
2.	**prevent**	____	____	(a) obstruct	(b) allow	(c) assist
3.	**prohibit**	____	____	(a) prevent	(b) allow	(c) fight
4.	**purchase**	____	____	(a) buy	(b) fill	(c) sell
5.	**puzzle**	____	____	(a) deplore	(b) perplex	(c) enlighten
6.	**quite**	____	____	(a) short	(b) truly	(c) perhaps
7.	**resist**	____	____	(a) tough	(b) oppose	(c) comply
8.	**render**	____	____	(a) give	(b) sluggish	(c) refuse
9.	**rational**	____	____	(a) logical	(b) unreasonable	(c) slanted
10	**refute**	____	____	(a) disprove	(b) fatal	(c) support
11.	**rebuke**	____	____	(a) jest	(b) scold	(c) praise
12.	**resilient**	____	____	(a) flexible	(b) stiff	(c) inside
13.	**repugnant**	____	____	(a) disgusting	(b) stylish	(c) attractive
14.	**resist**	____	____	(a) settle	(b) oppose	(c) succumb
15.	**reply**	____	____	(a) answer	(b) ask	(c) resign
16.	**regret**	____	____	(a) uneasy	(b) sorrow	(c) satisfaction
17.	**recognize**	____	____	(a) identify	(b) forget	(c) pal
18.	**recollect**	____	____	(a) accept	(b) remember	(c) forget
19.	**recommend**	____	____	(a) suggest	(b) distant	(c) discourage
20.	**record**	____	____	(a) register	(b) delete	(c) confusion
21.	**rectify**	____	____	(a) correct	(b) season	(c) damage
22.	**relax**	____	____	(a) amazed	(b) rest	(c) work
23.	**relentless**	____	____	(a) persistent	(b) intermittent	(c) cunning
24.	**require**	____	____	(a) hard	(b) need	(c) have

146

	syn.	ant.			
25. **sufficient**	_____	_____	(a) speech	(b) enough	(c) deficient
26. **superficial**	_____	_____	(a) shallow	(b) slow	(c) thorough
27. **supplement**	_____	_____	(a) addition	(b) reduce	(c) top
28. **taste**	_____	_____	(a) experience	(b) warm	(c) dislike
29. **talent**	_____	_____	(a) sorrow	(b) ability	(c) weakness
30. **tear**	_____	_____	(a) rip	(b) exchange	(c) mend
31. **tell**	_____	_____	(a) notify	(b) slow	(c) conceal
32. **tense**	_____	_____	(a) anxious	(b) calm	(c) stable
33. **threaten**	_____	_____	(a) intimidate	(b) comfort	(c) covert
34. **turbulent**	_____	_____	(a) stormy	(b) reside	(c) quiet
35. **ultimate**	_____	_____	(a) final	(b) initial	(c) laugh
36. **unforgettable**	_____	_____	(a) lasting	(b) unchanged	(c) forgettable
37. **uproar**	_____	_____	(a) chaos	(b) order	(c) forsake
38. **usual**	_____	_____	(a) common	(b) easy	(c) atypical
39. **unique**	_____	_____	(a) organize	(b) different	(c) common
40. **uncomfortable**	_____	_____	(a) uneasy	(b) game	(c) relaxed
41. **unconscious**	_____	_____	(a) detest	(b) unaware	(c) deliberate
42. **undercover**	_____	_____	(a) private	(b) cooperate	(c) public
43. **understand**	_____	_____	(a) simple	(b) grasp	(c) misinterpret
44. **urge**	_____	_____	(a) delay	(b) encourage	(c) discourage
45. **unrest**	_____	_____	(a) dissension	(b) silent	(c) harmony
46. **unstable**	_____	_____	(a) erratic	(b) stable	(c) secure
47. **unanimous**	_____	_____	(a) unified	(b) dissenting	(c) jeer
48. **void**	_____	_____	(a) instill	(b) empty	(c) full
49. **vile**	_____	_____	(a) begin	(b) impure	(c) pure
50. **vindictive**	_____	_____	(a) permanent	(b) spiteful	(c) forgiving
51. **valid**	_____	_____	(a) genuine	(b) move	(c) false
52. **validate**	_____	_____	(a) authorize	(b) refute	(c) retreat
53. **versatile**	_____	_____	(a) flexible	(b) sob	(c) limited
54. **vigorous**	_____	_____	(a) energetic	(b) frail	(c) change
55. **vital**	_____	_____	(a) important	(b) unimportant	(c) confuse
56. **vacation**	_____	_____	(a) order	(b) holiday	(c) work

	syn.	ant.			
57. **virtue**	_____	_____	(a) match	(b) goodness	(c) wickedness
58. **various**	_____	_____	(a) many	(b) difficult	(c) few
59. **vary**	_____	_____	(a) change	(b) disappoint	(c) maintain
60. **vast**	_____	_____	(a) immense	(b) sly	(c) limited
61. **vengeance**	_____	_____	(a) retaliation	(b) difficult	(c) forgiveness
62. **verbal**	_____	_____	(a) spoken	(b) written	(c) verdict
63. **veto**	_____	_____	(a) reject	(b) swift	(c) approve
64. **visible**	_____	_____	(a) capsize	(b) noticeable	(c) invisible
65. **variety**	_____	_____	(a) assortment	(b) happiness	(c) similarity
66. **warn**	_____	_____	(a) caution	(b) start	(c) praise
67. **wash**	_____	_____	(a) clean	(b) soil	(c) jeer

Exercise 4: Matching Meanings (Advanced Words)

Match each word with its definition or best meaning.

_____ 1. belligerent   a. obvious; conspicuous *h*

_____ 2. benevolent   b. self-satisfied

_____ 3. bereft   c. engage in sexual intercourse with many persons *9*

_____ 4. blatant   d. mixture of petals and spices used as a fragrance *11*

_____ 5. cantankerous   e. ready to fight or quarrel *1*

_____ 6. clandestine   f. ill-tempered; quarrelsome *5*

_____ 7. complacent   g. lasting forever

_____ 8. capacitate   h. self-important

_____ 9. promiscuous   i. done secretly *6*

_____ 10. perpetual   j. to do good; kindly *2*

_____ 11. potpourri   k. to prepare, fit *8*

_____ 12. pompous   l. to deprive of *3*

Exercise 5: Advanced Words in Context

... ect word or another form of the word below.

	cantankerous	perpetual	promiscuous
...acent	bereft	belligerent	clandestine
...ourri	blatant	capacitate	benevolent

1. His _____ attitude made him unpopular with the other boys at school.

2. Robert could never pass a beggar without giving something; he was known as the most _____ man in the neighborhood.

3. When in love, many people are _____ of their senses.

4. Even though the teacher's error was _____ , none of the students dared to point it out.

5. Because he was so _____, most of us avoided Uncle Jim at family gatherings.

6. Since their parents disapproved of their relationship, all meetings between the lovers had to be _____.

7. She stopped being so _____ about her studies after she failed the midterm examination.

8. Increasing the memory on your computer will _____ it to run faster.

9. Neighbors gossiped that the new tenant was _____ because she had male visitors all hours of the day and night.

10. Buffalo, New York is known for its _____ snows in the wintertime.

11. The aroma of _____ filled the living room.

12. His overly correct English made everyone regard him as _____.

Exercise 6: Matching Meanings (Advanced Words)

Match each word with its definition or best meaning.

_____ 1. ambivalent
_h_ 2. antihistamine
_i_ 3. aesthetic
_a_ 4. arbitrary
_____ 5. proponent
_____ 6. profound
_____ 7. poignant
_____ 8. pacify
_____ 9. impeach
_F_ 10. intoxicate
_____ 11. insidious
_____ 12. inexorable

a. left to one's judgment or choice
b. deeply felt
c. to calm
d. to discredit a person's reputation
e. more dangerous than seems evident
f. drunk
g. cannot be influenced
h. a synthetic drug
i. doubtful; having conflicting feeling
j. emotionally touching or moving
k. one who makes a proposal
l. exquisite taste

Exercise 7:   Advanced Words in Context

Fill in the blank with the correct word or another form of the word below.

profound	inexorable	arbitrary	impeach
antihistamine	pacify	insidious	proponent
intoxicate	aesthetic	poignant	ambivalent

1. Cynthia was _____ about her feelings toward Frank, so when he proposed she had to turn him down.

2. People with hay fever must take an _____ in the spring and summer.

3. Susan always asks Bill for decorating advice because he has _____ taste.

4. It was an _____ decision to cancel the meeting.

5. Don't wear your fur coat to Sally's party because she is a _____ of animal rights.

6. When her grandmother died, Helen felt a _____ sense of loss.

7. I was enjoying the movie I rented last night until my smoke alarm went off at the most _____ moment.

8. Nothing would _____ the child when he found out that his favorite blanket was lost.

9. Many people thought Richard Nixon should be _____ for his part in the Watergate scandal.

10. Someone added vodka to the punch and soon all the guests were _____ .

11. His drinking became so _____ that he was unable to stop on his own.

12. Right or wrong, he was _____ in his opinions.

149

REFERENCES

1. Ann Raimes, *Grammar Troublespots: An Editing Guide for Students*, 2nd edition (New York: St. Martin's Press, Inc., 1992).

2. Ann Raimes, *How English Works: A Grammar Handbook with Readings*, (New York: St. Martin's Press, Inc., 1990).

3. R. Kent Smith and Janet M. Goldstein, *English Brushup* (Marlton: Townsend Press, Inc., 1993).

4. A. Robert Young and Ann O. Strauch, *Nitty Gritty Grammar* (New York: St. Martin's Press, Inc., 1994).

5. Carolyn H. Fitzpatrick and Marybeth B. Ruscica, *The Complete Sentence Workout Book*, 2nd edition (Lexington: D.C. Heath and Company, 1988).

6. Louis Crane, *Phonics is Fun*, Book 3 (Cleveland: Modern Curriculum Press, 1985).

7. *Webster's New World Dictionary*, 3rd college edition (New York: Simon & Schuster, Inc., 1988).

8. Harriet Wittels and Joan Greisman, *The Clear and Simple Thesaurus Dictionary* (New York: Grosset & Dunlap, Inc., 1971).

ANSWER KEY

FIRST DAY

Exercise 1   (1) e   (2) d   (3) c   (4) a   (5) b

Exercise 2   (1) a   (2) e   (3) b   (4) d   (5) c

Exercise 3   (1) a   (2) e   (3) c   (4) d   (5) b

Exercise 4

(1) lap	(2) hat	(3) run	(4) swim	(5) all	(6) ham	(7) lock
(8) rock	(9) it	(10) age	(11) an	(12) on	(13) man	(14) band
(15) fat	(16) moth	(17) fume	(18) hair	(19) kin	(20) law	(21) ink
(22) lap	(23) rip	(24) lose	(25) rob	(26) rest	(27) play	(28) may
(29) ass	(30) get	(31) for	(32) when	(33) low	(34) ill	(35) pipe
(36) rag	(37) ray	(38) sail	(39) ant	(40) farm	(41) grow	(42) mow
(43) sow	(44) land	(45) rage	(46) gent	(47) ill	(48) lot	

Exercise 5

(1) bout, tab, boat (2) ridge, bridge, dear (3) rate, clear, bet (4) ate, ace, car (5) mount, ton, rap
(6) mate, leg, team (7) ripple, lip, rice (8) shed, tin, sting (9) boar, tear, tab (10) rage, age, nag
(11) stain, as, sit (12) arm, ram, harm (13) stable, lean, quest (14) ant, mantle, list (15) part, tent, meat
(16) reap, date, dirt (17) rum, sold, sum (18) use, bus, sea (19) terse, sent, nest (20) cover, toe, cot

Exercise 6

(1) option, dot, pot (2) stern, nation, stone (3) stress, sit, rest (4) hospital, able, pit (5) tent, tint, term
(6) sob, sit, sour (7) ant, gate, tag (8) flu, fan, fence (9) train, strain, stain (10) main, man, maid
(11) boy, ant, toy (12) thrift, dent, spit (13) them, seam, mat (14) ration, flag, lag (15) tablet, men, stable
(16) red, tie, ring (17) point, pin, tap (18) contempt, tempt, notice (19) wind, led, lend (20) rate, rob, rote

Exercise 7

(1) lap, pal, lad (2) pious, cop, soup (3) liver, ride, live (4) hen, spoil, come (5) sand, land, soul
(6) ate, bat, tea (7) dice, tear, read (8) date, come, coat (9) be, wild, bed (10) ton, sin, as
(11) rid, or, rod (12) tail, let, lad (13) in, fall, fell (14) still, stand, ant (15) rate, ate, late
(16) lion, except, ton (17) ant, bore, taint (18) red, tie, ring (19) as, sew, sea (20) ink, kin, in

Exercise 8

(1) claim, aim, lead (2) for, fort, to (3) fraud, red, dear (4) able, measure, sure (5) bell, linger, lit
(6) flag, lag, gleam (7) feat, eat, at (8) dent, neat, dice (9) lid, coil, ill (10) agree, able, grease
(11) pimp, pierce, blimp (12) can, tank, us (13) dip, mat, plot (14) men, merit, pen (15) cat, hat, toast
(16) bin, mob, come (17) fin, ten, fed (18) dent, rude, mint (19) rich, sir, his (20) cut, cute, ace

Exercise 9

(1) norm, roam, lamb (2) bash, head, shed (3) age, dame, mad (4) angle, nag, lead (5) ark, red, are
(6) crease, read, ease (7) cap, city, pat (8) sure, sun, run (9) team, men, late (10) yes, say, easy
(11) light, ten, let (12) leg, gain, lean (13) farm, arm, far (14) vent, ten, coin (15) hub, by, buy
(16) for, ward, war (17) rate, tear, ill (18) tear, feat, are (19) crow, row, now (20) lance, bale, lean

SECOND DAY

Exercise 1   (1) d   (2) e   (3) a   (4) c   (5) b

Exercise 2   (1) c   (2) d   (3) a   (4) e   (5) b

Exercise 3   (1) d   (2) c   (3) e   (4) b   (5) a

Exercise 4   (1) T   (2) F   (3) T

Exercise 5   (1) athlete   (2) General Price (3) river   (4) Kaieteur Falls (5) wheel

Exercise 6 (1) T   (2) T

Exercise 7 (1) F   (2) T

Exercise 8
1. I, me, mine, my, you, yours, your, he, his, him, her, hers, it, its, we, they, our, theirs
2. who, whom, which, whose, that, whomever, whichever
3. anybody, nobody, everybody, somebody, someone, everyone, anyone, nothing, everything, anything, several, all
4. those, these, this, that
5. what, which, who, whom
6. himself, herself, itself, myself, themselves, yourselves, ourselves

Exercise 9 (1) F (2) T (3) T (4) T (5) F (6) T (7) T

Exercise 10 (1) T (2) T (3) T (4) T (5) F

Exercise 11 (1) in, on, of, off, to, for, by, at, under, above, up, upon, with, across, around, without, before, between, below, behind, except, during, outside

Exercise 12 (1) F   (2) T (3) T

Exercise 13 (1) T   (2) F (3) F (4) T (5) T (6) T   (7) T

Exercise 14 (1) yet, or, so, nor, but, for   (2) where, when, while, whether, wherever, whenever, if, since,
            after, until, although, because   (3) therefore, however, furthermore, otherwise, consequently, thus

Exercise 15

(1) F	(2) F	(3) T	(4) T	(5 T	(6) T	(7) F
(8) T	(9) T	(10) F	(11) T	(12) F	(13) F	(14) T
(15) F	(16) T	(17) T				

Exercise 16 (1) d   (2) e   (3) a   (4) b   (5) c

Exercise 17 (1) c   (2) e   (3) a   (4) b   (5) d

Exercise 18 (1) include, illustrate (2) journey, magnet (3) neighbor, possess (4) repair, reduce (5) qualify, pursue

Exercise 19

(1) rate	(2) vibrate	(3) tolerance	(4) endure	(5) sufferer	(6) likely	(7) spend
(8) abound	(9) stance	(10) irritating	(11) procession	(12) punish	(13) relate	(14) steal
(15) compassion	(16) toxic	(17) oath	(18) own	(19) prepare	(20) trick	(21) subject
(22) noxious	(23) dangerous	(24) prize				

Exercise 20

(1) a, c	(2) a, c	(3) a, c	(4) a, c	(5) b, c	(6) b, c	(7) a, b
(8) a, b	(9) b, a	(10) a, c	(11) b, c	(12) b, c	(13) a, c	(14) a, b
(15) a, b	(16) a, c	(17) b, c	(18) b, c	(19) a, c	(20) a, c	(21) a, c
(22) a, b	(23) a, b	(24) b, c	(25) b, c	(26) a, c	(27) a, b	(28) a, c
(29) b, c	(30) b, c	(31) a, b	(32) a, b	(33) a, c	(34) a, c	(35) b, c
(36) a, c	(37) a, c	(38) a, b	(39) b, c	(40) b, c	(41) a, c	(42) a, c
(43) b, c	(44) a, c	(45) a, c	(46) b, c	(47) b, c	(48) a, c	(49) a, b
(50) a, b	(51) a, c	(52) b, c	(53) b, c	(54) a, c	(55) a, b	(56) b, c
(57) b, c	(58) a, c	(59) a, b	(60) a, c	(61) a, b	(62) a, c	(63) a, c
(64) b, c	(65) a, b	(66) a, c	(67) a, c	(68) a, c	(69) a, c	(70) b, c
(71) b, c	(72) b, c	(73) b, c	(74) a, c	(75) a, b		

Exercise 21

(1) a (2) a (3) d (4) b (5) a (6) a (7) b (8) d (9) a (10) c (11) b (12) a (13) b
(14) c (15) d (16) d (17) a (18) b (19) c (20) d (21) a (22) b (23) c (24) a (25) b (26) c
(27) a (28) d (29) b (30) c (31) a (32) a

Exercise 22
(1) betray   (2) deliberating (3) bankrupt   (4) demonstrate (5) burden   (6) depriving (7) deviated
(8) brutal   (9) detect   (10) blamed   (11) desperate (12) boredom

Exercise 23
(1) bourgeois (2) benign   (3) brisk   (4) buoyant   (5) categorize (6) ceased
(7) conscious (8) considerable (9) candid   (10) compliments (11) compulsory(12) catastrophe

THIRD DAY

Exercise 1
 (1) g (2) n   (3) f   (4) b   (5) j   (6) a   (7) d   (8) i   (9) c   (10) o   (11) t   (12) e   (13) p
(14) m(15) q (16) h (17) s (18) k (19) l (20) r

Exercise 2
 (1) option   (2) familiarize (3) escort   (4) entry   (5) examine (6) foreign (7) learn
 (8) clever   (9) accomplish(10) border   (11) skim   (12) package (13) brief   (14) pay
(15) categorize (16) trust   (17) stocky   (18) task   (19) treasure (20) convert (21) foretell
(22) assume   (23) cursing   (24) chase

Exercise 3
 (1) d (2) d   (3) b   (4) a   (5) b   (6) a   (7) a   (8) a   (9) b   (10) c   (11) d   (12) d   (13) c
(14) a(15) a (16) b (17) b (18) d (19) c (20) a

Exercise 4
 (1) a (2) a   (3) a   (4) b   (5) c   (6) d   (7) a   (8) b   (9) c   (10) b   (11) a   (12) d   (13) a
(14) b(15) a (16) c (17) a (18) c (19) a (20) b (21) b (22) a (23) c (24) d (25) d (26) c
(27) a(28) b (29) d (30) a (31) c (32) d
(33) a

Exercise 5
(1) accompany (2) accelerated (3) determine (4) apparent (5) appropriate (6) disloyal
(7) affiliated (8) dislocate (9) abducted (10) disillusionment (11) abnormal (12) discount

Exercise 6
(1) devastated (2) distinguish (3) donate   (4) derogatory (5) aggressive (6) dominated
(7) exaggerate (8) abbreviate (9) dynamic   (10) charismatic (11) disappear (12) discreet

Exercise 7
 (1) c (2) e (3) a (4) j (5) i (6) b (7) d (8) m (9) j (10) f (11) p (12) g (13) h
(14) u(15) r (16) l (17) n (18) t (19) o (20) s (21) q (22) y (23) v (24) x (25) w

Exercise 8   (1) e   (2) d   (3) a   (4) b   (5) c

Exercise 9
(1) conceive, carrot (2) deceive, cheap (3) bullet, address (4) affair, aggravate (5) beggar, business

FOURTH DAY

Exercise 1
 (1) f (2) h   (3) k   (4) m   (5) a   (6) d   (7) b   (8) l   (9) o   (10) r   (11) q   (12) c   (13) i
(14) n(15) g (16) e (17) j (18) t (19) p (20) s

Exercise 2
 (1) a (2) a   (3) a   (4) a   (5) b   (6) b   (7) c   (8) c   (9) d   (10) d   (11) d   (12) c   (13) c
(14) a(15) a (16) b (17) b (18) b (19) d (20) c
Exercise 3
 (1) a (2) a   (3) a   (4) a   (5) a   (6) a   (7) a   (8) b   (9) b   (10) c   (11) d   (12) d   (13) c
(14) b(15) a (16) a (17) b (18) c (19) a (20) c (21) d (22) d (23) a (24) d (25) d (26) c
(27) c(28) c (29) b (30) b (31) a (32) b (33) b (34) a (35) b (36) d

Exercise 4

(1) heterogenous (2) illustrate (3) influence (4) hazardous (5) inept (6) intentional
(7) hampered (8) intermission (9) inferior (10) intervene (11) impartial (12) interpret

Exercise 5

(1) investigate (2) instigated (3) legible (4) illegible (5) intermittent (6) logical
(7) incredible (8) intimidate (9) located (10) introverts (11) irate (12) maximum

Exercise 6

(1) b, c	(2) b, c	(3) a, b	(4) a, b	(5) a, c	(6) a, c	(7) b, c
(8) b, c	(9) a, c	(10) a, c	(11) a, c	(12) b, c	(13) b, c	(14) a, b
(15) a, b	(16) a, b	(17) a, c	(18) b, c	(19) a, b	(20) a, b	(21) b, c
(22) b, c	(23) a, c	(24) a, b	(25) a, b	(26) a, b	(27) a, b	(28) a, c
(29) b, c	(30) b, c	(31) a, b	(32) a, b	(33) a, c	(34) a, b	(35) a, c
(36) a, c	(37) a, c	(38) a, c	(39) a, b	(40) a, b	(41) b, c	(42) b, c
(43) b, c	(44) a, c	(45) a, c	(46) a, b	(47) a, b	(48) a, c	(49) a, c
(50) a, b	(51) a, c	(52) a, c	(53) a, b	(54) a, c	(55) b, c	(56) b, c
(57) a, b	(58) a, c	(59) a, b	(60) b, c	(61) b, c	(62) a, c	(63) a, c
(64) a, b	(65) b, c	(66) a, c	(67) a, b	(68) a, c	(69) a, b	(70) b, c
(71) a, b	(72) a, b	(73) a, c	(74) a, b	(75) a, c		

Exercise 7

(1) d (2) f (3) a (4) e (5) k (6) b (7) c (8) l (9) p (10) q (11) o (12) g (13) s
(14) u (15) h (16) i (17) y (18) m (19) n (20) x (21) w (22) r (23) t (24) j (25) v

Exercise 8 (1) c (2) b (3) a (4) e (5) d

Exercise 9 (1) petite, surprise (2) sheet, accuse (3) attract, catch (4) nurse, marriage (5) money, peace

FIFTH DAY

Exercise 1

(1) j (2) n (3) f (4) b (5) a (6) l (7) c (8) m (9) d (10) o (11) p (12) e (13) k
(14) t (15) r (16) g (17) q (18) i (19) s (20) h

Exercise 2

(1) innocent (2) annoy (3) place (4) care (5) easy-going (6) bargain (7) motion
(8) threatening (9) introduction (10) preoccupy (11) barrier (12) insult (13) sometimes (14) scent
(15) supreme (16) burden (17) result (18) liable (19) possess (20) remedy (21) concrete
(22) outburst (23) chore (24) moody

Exercise 3

(1) b (2) b (3) a (4) b (5) a (6) a (7) a (8) d (9) c (10) d (11) c (12) b (13) a
(14) a (15) b (16) a (17) d (18) c (19) c (20) a

Exercise 4

(1) a (2) a (3) a (4) a (5) b (6) b (7) c (8) d (9) d (10) c (11) a (12) a (13) b
(14) d (15) c (16) c (17) b (18) a (19) a (20) a (21) c (22) a (23) a (24) a (25) a

Exercise 5

(1) recession (2) reduce (3) resourceful (4) reputation (5) refund (6) registered
(7) respond (8) revised (9) restrict (10) reverted (11) rigid (12) replace

Exercise 6

(1) abandon, abbreviate (2) seldom, absent (3) account, burglar (4) advisable, occur (5) across, believe

SIXTH DAY

Exercise 1

(1) o (2) k (3) i (4) m (5) q (6) a (7) c (8) j (9) b (10) p (11) d (12) n (13) e
(14) g (15) l (16) r (17) h (18) f (19) s (20) t

Exercise 2
(1) a (2) c (3) c (4) d (5) d (6) a (7) b (8) b (9) c (10) d (11) a (12) a (13) b
(14) d (15) c (16) b (17) a (18) c (19) b (20) a

Exercise 3
(1) b (2) a (3) a (4) a (5) d (6) c (7) a (8) c (9) a (10) b (11) c (12) a (13) d
(14) a (15) b (16) d (17) a (18) a (19) b (20) c (21) a (22) b (23) c (24) a (25) a (26) a
(27) b (28) b (29) a (30) c (31) b (32) a (33) d (34) a (35) d (36) a (37) b

Exercise 4
(1) tentative (2) motivate (3) negative (4) nausea (5) numerous (6) nervous
(7) negotiate (8) oral (9) outrageous (10) optional (11) odd (12) pious

Exercise 5
(1) procedure (2) pedestrian (3) untidy (4) message (5) obscene (6) omit
(7) opponent (8) persuade (9) obstructed (10) ultimate (11) tolerate (12) skeptic

Exercise 6
(1) b, c (2) b, c (3) a, b (4) b, c (5) b, c (6) a, c (7) b, c
(8) b, c (9) a, c (10) a, c (11) a, b (12) a, c (13) a, c (14) b, c
(15) a, b (16) b, c (17) a, c (18) a, b (19) a, c (20) a, c (21) b, c
(22) a, c (23) a, b (24) b, c (25) b, c (26) a, c (27) a, c (28) a, c
(29) b, c (30) a, b (31) a, c (32) a, b (33) b, c (34) a, c (35) b, c
(36) a, c (37) a, b (38) a, c (39) b, c (40) a, c (41) a, c (42) a, c
(43) a, b (44) a, c (45) a, c (46) a, b (47) a, c (48) a, b (49) a, c
(50) a, b (51) a, b (52) a, b (53) a, c (54) a, c (55) b, c (56) b, c
(57) b, c (58) a, c (59) a, c (60) a, b (61) a, c (62) b, c (63) a, c
(64) a, c (65) b, c (66) b, c (67) a, c (68) a, c (69) a, c (70) a, m
(71) b, c (72) a, c (73) a, c (74) a, b (75) a,c

Exercise 7
(1) knife, pocket (2) prosper, busy (3) corrupt, fasten (4) eclipse, easy (5) bucket, cigarette

SEVENTH DAY

Exercise 1
(1) n (2) i (3) k (4) o (5) l (6) b (7) h (8) p (9) q (10) r (11) j (12) e (13) g
(14) a (15) c (16) s (17) d (18) f (19) m (20) t

Exercise 2
(1) taxi (2) figure (3) disguise (4) applicant (5) overturn (6) fondle (7) chat
(8) disaster (9) charm (10) extensive (11) comprise (12) meditate (13) formula (14) shorten
(15) rob (16) rebuke (17) advise (18) force (19) pay (20) continuous (21) aim
(22) amount

Exercise 3
(1) a (2) a (3) a (4) a (5) a (6) b (7) d (8) c (9) c (10) b (11) d (12) b (13) c
(14) a (15) b (16) c (17) d (18) a (19) a (20) b

Exercise 4
(1) c (2) c (3) d (4) d (5) a (6) a (7) a (8) b (9) c (10) a (11) d (12) c (13) c
(14) b (15) a (16) d (17) c (18) b (19) a (20) a

Exercise 5
(1) principal (2) protest (3) pursue (4) prelude (5) prominent (6) procrastinate
(7) prosperous (8) unstable (9) tragic (10) reliable (11) reluctant (12) replicate

Exercise 6
(1) fatigue, scissors (2) terrific, flame (3) advertise, biggest (4) cheat, embrace (5) grammar, fear

EIGHT DAY

Exercise 1
(1) j (2) c (3) f (4) h (5) m (6) d (7) r (8) q (9) p (10) e (11) w (12) t (13) b
(14) x (15) u (16) s (17) y (18) v (19) o (20) a (21) l (22) k (23) g (24) i (25) n

Exercise 2
(1) connected   (2) transmit   (3) component   (4) satisfied   (5) measure   (6) promise
(7) segment   (8) emergency (9) sketch   (10) distract   (11) interpret   (12) gain
(13) end   (14) formulate (15) separate   (16) stray   (17) bum   (18) appoint
(19) destroy   (20) punish   (21) tact   (22) return   (23) repeat   (24) shelter

Exercise 3
(1) d (2) d (3) d (4) d (5) b (6) a (7) a (8) a (9) c (10) d (11) b (12) c (13) a
(14) b (15) c (16) b (17) d (18) c (19) b (20) d

Exercise 4
(1) a   (2) a   (3) b   (4) d   (5) a   (6) c   (7) b
(8) a   (9) d   (10) b   (11) a   (12) c   (13) d   (14) a
(15) d   (16) b   (17) c   (18) d   (19) a   (20) b   (21) a
(22) a   (23) c   (24) d   (25) a   (26) b   (27) d   (28) c
(29) d   (30) a   (31) b   (32) d   (33) c   (34) b   (35) a

Exercise 5
(1) enmity   (2) trauma   (3) appreciate   (4) eradicated   (5) enough   (6) frugal
(7) fluctuated (8) erratic   (9) guilty   (10) fervor

Exercise 6
(1) fatal   (2) generate   (3) faulty   (4) gratitude   (5) eminent   (6) homogenous
(7) frolic   (8) fury   (9) frequent   (10) hostile   (11) fictitious (12) superstition

Exercise 7
(1) f   (2) g   (3) j   (4) a   (5) b   (6) l   (7) n
(8) c   (9) q   (10) p   (11) h   (12) d   (13) o   (14) s
(15) u   (16) e   (17) m   (18) i   (19) w   (20) k   (21) r
(22) t   (23) v   (24) x   (25) y

Exercise 8
(1) simple, seldom   (2) suppose, selfish   (3) immediate, introduce   (4) sexy, guest   (5) sorry, support

NINTH DAY

Exercise 1
(1) facts   (2) die   (3) helpless   (4) devote   (5) overcome   (6) inadequate
(7) appetizing (8) command   (9) explain   (10) clarify   (11) excluded   (12) evoke
(13) position   (14) attempt   (15) repeat   (16) strengthen (17) increase   (18) equal
(19) steal   (20) provide

Exercise 2
(1) a, b   (2) a, c   (3) b, c   (4) b, c   (5) a, c   (6) a, b   (7) a, c
(8) a, c   (9) a, b   (10) a, c   (11) b, c   (12) a, b   (13) a, c   (14) a, b
(15) a, c   (16) b, c   (17) a, b   (18) a, b   (19) a, c   (20) a, c   (21) a, c
(22) b, c   (23) a, b   (24) a, c   (25) b, c   (26) b, c   (27) a, b   (28) a, c
(29) b, c   (30) a, c   (31) a, b   (32) b, c   (33) a, c   (34) a, b   (35) a, c
(36) a, b   (37) a, c   (38) b, c   (39) a, b   (40) a, c   (41) b, c   (42) a, c
(43) a, b   (44) a, b   (45) a, c   (46) b, c   (47) a, c   (48) a, b   (49) b, c
(50) a, c   (51) a, c   (52) b, c   (53) a, c   (54) a, c   (55) a, c   (56) b, c
(57) a, c   (58) a, c   (59) a, b   (60) a, b   (61) b, c   (62) a, c   (63) b, c
(64) a, b   (65) a, c   (66) a, b   (67) a, c   (68) b, c   (69) b, c   (70) a, b
(71) a, b   (72) a, c   (73) b, c   (74) a, c   (75) a, b

Exercise 3
(1) g   (2) l   (3) h   (4) a   (5) j   (6) k   (7) b   (8) f   (9) c
(10) e   (11) d   (12) i

Exercise 4
(1) authenticate (2) irrevocable (3) casual   (4) alluded   (5) disengage   (6) conspiring
(7) compatible   (8) gregarious   (9) heinous (10) hoax   (11) innocuous (12) kleptomaniac

Exercise 5
(1) b   (2) d   (3) a   (4) i   (5) c   (6) l   (7) e   (8) j   (9) f
(10) k   (11) g   (12) h

Exercise 6
(1) adamant   (2) aristocrat   (3) ambiguous   (4) acrimonious (5) scurrilous (6) subservient
(7) tenacious (8) trepidation (9) retaliate   (10) redundant   (11) incessant (12) impetuous

TENTH DAY

Exercise 1
(1) a   (2) b   (3) c   (4) a   (5) d   (6) b   (7) c
(8) d   (9) b   (10) a   (11) a   (12) a   (13) b   (14) d   (15) c   (16) b
(17) b   (18) a   (19) b   (20) d

Exercise 2
(1) b, c   (2) b, c   (3) b, c   (4) a, c   (5) a, c   (6) a, b   (7) a, c
(8) b, c   (9) b, c   (10) a, b (11) b, c (12) a, c (13) a, b (14) a, c
(15) a, b (16) a, c (17) a, c (18) b, c (19) b, c (20) a, c (21) a, c
(22) a, b (23) a, c (24) a, b (25) b, c (26) a, c (27) a, c (28) a, b
(29) a, c (30) a, c (31) b, c (32) a, c (33) a, c (34) a, c (35) a, b
(36) b, c (37) a, b (38) b, c (39) a, b (40) a, c (41) b, c (42) a, c
(43) a, b (44) a, b (45) b, c (46) b, c (47) a, b (48) a, c (49) b, c
(50) b, c (51) a, c (52) a, c (53) a, c (54) a, b (55) b, c (56) a, b
(57) a, b (58) a, c (59) a, b (60) a, b (61) a, c (62) a, c (63) a, c
(64) b, c (65) a, c (66) a, b (67) a, c (68) a, c (69) b, c (70) b, c
(71) b, c (72) b, c (73) b, c (74) b, c (75) a, b

Exercise 3
(1) d   (2) h   (3) a   (4) l   (5) k   (6) b   (7) i
(8) c   (9) j   (10) e   (11) f   (12) g

Exercise 4
(1) annihilate (2) cognizant (3) disenchanted (4) equivocal   (5) fatuous   (6) transgress
(7) ubiquitous (8) vindicated (9) rapacious   (10) nonchalant (11) inhibit (12) infallible

Exercise 5
(1) b   (2) a   (3) i   (4) l   (5) g   (6) c   (7) e
(8) k   (9) d   (10) h   (11) j   (12) f

Exercise 6
(1) vivacious (2) supercilious (3) reprimanded (4) nostalgia   (5) ingenious (6) meticulous
(7) sensuous   (8) aggrandized   (9) concept   (10) conciliate (11) epitome   (12) frivolous

ELEVENTH DAY

Exercise 1
(1) f	(2) k	(3) n	(4) q	(5) s	(6) r	(7) o
(8) l	(9) a	(10) b	(11) m	(12) c	(13) h	(14) d
(15) p	(16) e	(17) i	(18) g	(19) j	(20) t	

Exercise 2
(1) show	(2) undergo	(3) task	(4) explode	(5) spying	(6) prepare	(7) well-versed
(8) create	(9) trickery	(10) pretense	(11) pale	(12) waver	(13) renown	(14) undermine
(15) hunger	(16) preferred	(17) charge	(18) bring	(19) control	(20) fire	(21) live
(22) investigate						

Exercise 3
(1) d	(2) f	(3) a	(4) h	(5) l	(6) b	(7) k
(8) c	(9) e	(10) i	(11) g	(12) j		

Exercise 4
(1) assiduous	(2) boisterous	(3) candid	(4) decipher	(5) exorbitant	(6) magnanimous
(7) obstinate	(8) placid	(9) rancor	(10) tedious	(11) debilitate	(12) expedite

Exercise 5
(1) l	(2) g	(3) a	(4) j	(5) h	(6) b	(7) k
(8) c	(9) f	(10) i	(11) d	(12) e		

Exercise 6
(1) agitate	(2) alleviate	(3) capricious	(4) controversy	(5) vicious	(6) condemned
(7) gaudy	(8) inmate	(9) neurosis	(10) remorse	(11) precedent	(12) overt

TWELFTH DAY

Exercise 1
(1) b	(2) a	(3) b	(4) d	(5) d	(6) c	(7) a
(8) a	(9) a	(10) a	(11) b	(12) c	(13) d	(14) c
(15) a	(16) a	(17) a	(18) b	(19) c	(20) a	

Exercise 2
(1) a, b	(2) a, b	(3) a, b	(4) a, c	(5) a, c	(6) a, c	(7) a, b
(8) b, c	(9) a, c	(10) a, b	(11) a, b	(12) b, c	(13) b, c	(14) a, c
(15) a, b	(16) a, c	(17) a, c	(18) a, c	(19) a, b	(20) a, b	(21) a, b
(22) a, c	(23) b, c	(24) a, b	(25) a, b	(26) a, b	(27) b, c	(28) b, c
(29) b, c	(30) a, b	(31) a, c	(32) a, c	(33) a, c	(34) b, c	(35) b, c
(36) b, c	(37) a, c	(38) a, c	(39) a, b	(40) b, c	(41) b, c	(42) a, c
(43) a, b	(44) a, b	(45) b, c	(46) b, c	(47) a, c	(48) a, c	(49) a, b
(50) a, c	(51) a, b	(52) b, c	(53) a, c	(54) a, c	(55) a, b	(56) a, c
(57) b, c	(58) a, c	(59) b, c	(60) a, b	(61) b, c	(62) b, c	(63) a, c
(64) a, b	(65) a, c	(66) a, c	(67) a, c	(68) a, c	(69) b, c	(70) b, c
(71) a, c	(72) a, b	(73) b, c	(74) b, c	(75) a, b		

Exercise 3
(1) c	(2) f	(3) h	(4) k	(5) a	(6) i	(7) b	(8) l	(9) d
(10) j	(11) g	(12) e						

Exercise 4
(1) vociferous	(2) unanimous	(3) reprehend	(4) regression	(5) quirk	(6) reticent
(7) ostensible	(8) oscillate	(9) mitigate	(10) fastidious	(11) flamboyant	(12) empathy

Exercise 5
(1) k	(2) l	(3) c	(4) a	(5) j	(6) b	(7) d	(8) f	(9) g
(10) e	(11) i	(12) h						

Exercise 6
(1) hallucinate (2) hypocrite (3) interminable (4) insatiable (5) judicious (6) mishap
(7) ludicrous (8) mitigate (9) ostentatious (10) perspicacious (11) surreptitious (12) empowered

THIRTEENTH DAY

Exercise 1

(1) a	(2) c	(3) i	(4) f	(5) k	(6) q	(7) s
(8) t	(9) b	(10) o	(11) g	(12) w	(13) v	(14) d
(15) h	(16) r	(17) e	(18) x	(19) m	(20) n	(21) p
(22) j	(23) u	(24) l	(25) y			

Exercise 2
(1) compliment (2) assured (3) prediction (4) beat (5) discoverer (6) direct (7) dreadful
(8) aim (9) hearsay (10) difficulty (11) strike (12) rush (13) famous (14) location (15) effect
(16) mocking (17) unconcerned (18) isolation (19) conclude (20) pretender

Exercise 3

(1) c	(2) h	(3) l	(4) a	(5) j	(6) b	(7) k
(8) d	(9) i	(10) e	(11) g	(12) f		

Exercise 4
(1) gullible (2) genesis (3) hysterical (4) impeccable (5) lethargy (6) luscious
(7) obnoxious (8) cumbersome (9) dubious (10) exonerated (11) elated (12) fictitious

Exercise 5

(1) j	(2) h	(3) f	(4) a	(5) i	(6) b	(7) l	(8) c	(9) k
(10) d	(11) g	(12) e					

Exercise 6
(1) luminous (2) capitulate (3) covert (4) condone (5) esoteric (6) vacillated
(7) unrest (8) sumptuous (9) subjugated (10) plague (11) ostracized (12) apathy

FOURTEENTH DAY

Exercise 1

(1) d	(2) d	(3) c	(4) a	(5) c	(6) b	(7) c
(8) a	(9) a	(10) b	(11) d	(12) c	(13) b	(14) a
(15) a	(16) d	(17) c	(18) b	(19) a	(20) b	

Exercise 2

(1) a, b	(2) b, c	(3) a, c	(4) a, c	(5) a, b	(6) a, b	(7) b, c
(8) a, c	(9) a, b	(10) a, c	(11) a, b	(12) a, c	(13) b, c	(14) a, c
(15) a, b	(16) a, c	(17) a, b	(18) a, b	(19) a, b	(20) b, c	(21) a, c
(22) b, c	(23) a, b	(24) b, c	(25) a, c	(26) a, b	(27) b, c	(28) a, c
(29) a, b	(30) a, b	(31) a, b	(32) a, c	(33) b, c	(34) a, c	(35) a, b
(36) a, b	(37) b, c	(38) a, c	(39) a, b	(40) a, b	(41) b, c	(42) a, c
(43) a, b	(44) a, b	(45) b, c	(46) a, b	(47) a, b	(48) b, c	(49) b, c
(50) a, c	(51) a, b	(52) b, c	(53) a, c	(54) a, c	(55) a, b	(56) a, c
(57) a, b	(58) a, c	(59) a, b	(60) a, b	(61) b, c	(62) b, c	(63) a, c
(64) a, b	(65) a, b	(66) b, c	(67) a, b	(68) a, b	(69) a,c	(70) a, c
(71) a, b	(72) a, b	(73) a, b				

Exercise 3

(1) d	(2) h	(3) a	(4) j	(5) b	(6) i	(7) l
(8) c	(9) k	(10) e	(11) f	(12) g		

Exercise 4
(1) corroborates (2) dexterous (3) disreputable (4) dissent (5) exacerbate (6) fallacy
(7) garrulous (8) implied (9) inculcated (10) pandemonium (11) incurable (12) journal

160

Exercise 5
(1) b   (2) e   (3) g   (4) j   (5) a   (6) l   (7) k
(8) c   (9) i   (10) d   (11) h   (12) f

Exercise 6
(1) vehemence (2) tenuous   (3) urgent   (4) superfluous (5) translucent (6) quagmire
(7) panorama   (8) obsequious (9) malicious (10) nebulous   (11) inadvertent (12) inundated

FIFTEENTH DAY

Exercise 1
(1) g   (2) p   (3) i   (4) a   (5) l   (6) q   (7) m
(8) f   (9) s   (10) x   (11) r   (12) n   (13) o   (14) t
(15) y   (16) u   (17) w   (18) e   (19) v   (20) k   (21) c
(22) b   (23) j   (24) h   (25) d

Exercise 2
(1) thought (2) fool   (3) copy   (4) submerge (5) charge   (6) hinder   (7) start
(8) represent (9) question (10) instinct (11) ruined (12) examine (13) honor (14) disabled
(15) pull   (16) joke   (17) duty   (18) trip   (19) mediate   (20) categorize

Exercise 3
(1) a   (2) f   (3) i   (4) l   (5) b   (6) j   (7) c
(8) g   (9) d   (10) k   (11) e   (12) h

Exercise 4
(1) gush   (2) gallant   (3) infidelity (4) innuendo (5) incessant (6) monotonous
(7) notorious (8) mesmerized (9) precluded (10) retrospect (11) relinquish (12) vicarious

Exercise 5
(1) l   (2) h   (3) e   (4) a   (5) f   (6) k   (7) b
(8) g   (9) c   (10) i   (11) d   (12) j

Exercise 6
(1) arsonist (2) compliment (3) charismatic (4) complement (5) eloquent (6) extricate
(7) eccentric (8) fragile   (9) fiduciary (10) flagrant   (11) gratuitous (12) gathered

SIXTEENTH DAY

Exercise 1
(1) b   (2) b   (3) b   (4) a   (5) d   (6) c   (7) c
(8) d   (9) a   (10) a   (11) a   (12) b   (13) b   (14) c
(15) d   (16) c   (17) a   (18) b   (19) a   (20) d

Exercise 2
(1) b, c   (2) b, c   (3) a, b   (4) a, b   (5) a, b   (6) a, c   (7) b, c
(8) a, c   (9) a, b   (10) b, c   (11) a, c   (12) a, b   (13) a, b   (14) a, c
(15) b, c   (16) b, c   (17) a, b   (18) a, c   19) b, c   (20) a, c   (21) a, b
(22) a, c   (23) a, c   (24) a, c   (25) a, c   (26) a, c   (27) a, c   (28) a, b
(29) b, c   (30) b, c   (31) b, c   (32) a, c   (33) a, c   (34) a, b   (35) a, c
(36) a, b   (37) b, c   (38) a, b   (39) a, c   (40) a, c   (41) b, c   (42) b, c
(43) a, c   (44) a, c   (45) a, b   (46) a, b   (47) a, b   (48) b, c   (49) b, c
(50) b, c   (51) a, c   (52) a, c   (53) a, b   (54) b, c   (55) b, c   (56) a, c
(57) a, b   (58) a, b   (59) a, b   (60) b, c   (61) a, c   (62) a, b   (63) a, b
(64) a, c   (65) a, b   (66) b, c   (67) a, c   (68) a, c   (69) a, b   (70) a, b
(71) a, c   (72) b, c   (73) a, b   (74) a, b   (75) b, c

Exercise 3
(1) b   (2) g   (3) i   (4) j   (5) a   (6) k   (7) c
(8) l   (9) d   (10) h   (11) f   (12) e

Exercise 4
(1) voracious   (2) viable   (3) transformed   (4) unscrupulous   (5) uncanny   (6) ratified
(7) synthesized   (8) scrutinize   (9) quandary   (10) replete   (11) preposterous   (12) plagiarized

Exercise 5
(1) k   (2) h   (3) e   (4) l   (5) a   (6) i   (7) b
(8) j   (9) c   (10) g   (11) d   (12) f

Exercise 6
(1) acute   (2) adroit   (3) bigots   (4) bias   (5) conspicuous   (6) depreciates
(7) dissuade   (8) enigmatic   (9) exuberant   (10) facetious   (11) fervent

SEVENTEENTH DAY

Exercise 1
(1) m   (2) n   (3) k   (4) r   (5) y   (6) o   (7) b
(8) v   (9) g   (10) d   (11) q   (12) w   (13) c   (14) e
(15) f   (16) u   (17) s   (18) t   (19) x   (20) h   (21) l
(22) a   (23) i   (24) j   (25) p

Exercise 2
(1) hit   (2) guide   (3) purpose   (4) accountable   (5) mark   (6) greatness   (7) erect
(8) fixation   (9) threat   (10) spirit   (11) stroke   (12) wedding   (13) sickness   (14) slaughter
(15) twist   (16) goods   (17) error   (18) change

Exercise 3
(1) a, b   (2) a, b   (3) a, b   (4) a, c   (5) b, c   (6) b, c   (7) b, c
(8) a, c   (9) a, b   (10) a, c   (11) b, c   (12) a, b   (13) a, c   (14) b, c
(15) a, b   (16) b, c   (17) a, b   (18) b, c   (19) a, c   (20) a, b   (21) a, c
(22) b, c   (23) a, b   (24) b, c   (25) b, c   (26) a, c   (27) a, b   (28) a, c
(29) b, c   (30) a, c   (31) a, c   (32) a, b   (33) a, b   (34) a, c   (35) a, b
(36) a, c   (37) a, b   (38) a, c   (39) b, c   (40) a, c   (41) b, c   (42) a, c
(43) b, c   (44) b, c   (45) a, c   (46) a, b   (47) a, b   (48) b, c   (49) b, c
(50) b, c   (51) a, c   (52) a, b   (53) a, c   (54) a, b   (55) a, b   (56) b, c
(57) b, c   (58) a, c   (59) a, c   (60) a, c   (61) a, c   (62) a, b   (63) a, c
(64) b, c   (65) a, c   (66) a, c   (67) a, b

Exercise 4
(1) e   (2) j   (3) l   (4) a   (5) f   (6) i   (7) b
(8) k   (9) c   (10) g   (11) d   (12) h

Exercise 5
(1) belligerent   (2) benevolent   (3) bereft   (4) blatant   (5) cantankerous   (6) clandestine
(7) complacent   (8) capacitate   (9) promiscuous   (10) perpetual   (11) potpourri   (12) pompous

Exercise 6
(1) i   (2) h   (3) l   (4) a   (5) k   (6) b   (7) j
(8) c   (9) d   (10) f   (11) e   (12) g

Exercise 7
(1) ambivalent   (2) antihistamine   (3) aesthetic   (4) arbitrary   (5) proponent   (6) profound
(7) poignant   (8) pacify   (9) impeached   (10) intoxicated   (11) insidious   (12) inexorable